SEASONALLY INSPIRED CUISINE FROM SOUTHERN CALIFORNIA

MARKET
RESTAURANT + BAR
COOKBOOK

BY CARL SCHROEDER

with Maria Desiderata Montana, Coauthor and Photographer

Globe
Pequot

GUILFORD, CONNECTICUT

To my wife Brandi,
my children Jake, Eric, and Ava,
and of course my parents,
for being my motivation.

Globe Pequot

An imprint of Rowman & Littlefield
Distributed by NATIONAL BOOK NETWORK
Copyright © 2016 by Carl Schroeder

Photography © 2016 by Maria Desiderata Montana
Photos © Vincent Knakal on pages iv, vi (bottom), 2 (right), 4, 21, 210, and 292
Photos © Joseph Wong on pages v, vi (top), viii, and 293
Text design: Nancy Freeborn

British Library Cataloguing in Publication Information Available

Library of Congress Cataloging-in-Publication Data

Schroeder, Carl (Chef), author.
  Market Restaurant + Bar cookbook : seasonally inspired cuisine from Southern California / by Carl Schroeder ; with Maria Desiderata Montana, Coauthor and Photographer.
      pages cm
  Includes index.
  ISBN 978-1-4930-0632-8 (hardback : alk. paper) - ISBN 978-1-4930-1974-8 (ebook)
1. Cooking, American-California style. 2. Seasonal cooking-California, Southern.
3. Market Restaurant + Bar. I. Montana, Maria Desiderata, author, illustrator. II. Title.
  TX715.2.C34S365 2015
  641.59794-dc23
                                                                                    2015031051

TABLE OF CONTENTS

FALL

WINTER

SPRING

SUMMER

ACKNOWLEDGMENTS

I would like to thank notable San Diego author, writer, and photographer Maria Desiderata Montana for all her dedicated work to make this book a reality. I told Maria time and time again that no other writer could have taken on the job of writing my cookbook. In addition, I found Maria's cooking and photography skills truly exceptional. I'd like to thank my editor, Amy Lyons, for her guidance, knowledge, and support. And a special thank you to my wife Brandi and my children Jake, Eric, and Ava, for making me proud and for the sacrifices they made in support of my passion.

I would like to express my deepest gratitude to my coworkers who helped and supported me with this cookbook: James Foran (Pastry Chef), Gabrielle Clift (General Manager of Market Restaurant), Nicolas Martinez (Executive Sous Chef), Tyler Nollenberger (Sous Chef), Steve Slimak (Kitchen Expediter) Ted Smith (Chef at Banker's Hill Bar & Restaurant), and all my cooks and staff.

A special thanks to Steve Pagano for his insight and advice throughout the years. And also thanks to close friend Terryl Gavre for assisting in the early days of Market's development.

To my investors, who without their belief in me, I would never have been able to pursue my dream of owning a restaurant.

And finally, I'd like to make one special acknowledgement to John Thompson (Chef de Cuisine of Market Restaurant). John was instrumental in the early stages of the opening of Market. When no one thought we had a chance to succeed, John was a positive driving force, pushing for an innovative food culture that has stood the test of time. It goes without saying that Market restaurant would not be what it is today without John.

John Thompson (left), Steve Slimak (below)

FOREWORD

Carl Schroeder is like a brother to me, and we have established a very close bond over the years. I originally met the inspiring young cook at my first restaurant, Lark Creek Inn in San Francisco, in 1996. If I asked him to report to work at 7:00 a.m., he'd be there at 6:00 a.m. He had a strong work ethic, loved the business, and respected my philosophical views of "farm-to-table" cuisine. I immediately hired him as my sous chef, and he worked with me for ten years.

As a child, I was always around farms and growers. My summer months were spent on my grandma's farm in Windsor, Ontario, eating beefsteak tomatoes straight from the garden, fried chicken, and fresh baked pie. I retained this philosophy of farm-to-table eating, making it a top priority in my life as a chef, and Carl would be right there with me at the farmers' markets and cheese producers. He was there to witness local fisherman dropping off salmon and sturgeon at our back door. Carl was a big proponent of my seasonally inspired cuisine.

I hired Carl as my opening chef at Arterra in San Diego in 2002, where he quickly gained national recognition. Carl taught the farm-to-table philosophy to his cooks, who looked up to him because he provided good solid training and was able to thoroughly talk them through the intricacies of putting a dish together. He taught his cooks to taste and care about the food, while remaining dedicated. He brought passion and commitment to his food as well as a unique style and detail that gained respect from diners. He has a certain style and way of doing things. It comes naturally to Carl. He has the foresight to understand the correct things to build the business. He leads by example.

Carl talked about owning his own restaurant someday and was interested in becoming an entrepreneur in addition to being a great chef. He opened Market Restaurant + Bar in 2006 with great success and a very loyal following. I would say that his ethics, passion, and beliefs in organic and natural foods, as well as his dedication in working with the local farmer are identical to mine.

From Carl's table to yours, these easily adaptable recipes will surely tempt you to try every unique dish in his new cookbook!

Sincerely,

Chef Bradley Ogden
Owner/Founder of Bradley Ogden Hospitality
Award-winning cookbook author

INTRODUCTION

I want this book to represent San Diego as a burgeoning food destination. There's so much great cuisine here, and so many people are beginning to look at San Diego for the amazing products we have. We are a coastal city, so we have access to an abundance of seafood. This is an exciting time to be a chef in this amazing city. I'm a native. I know the lay of the land. I know the farmers and the fisherman. I want to represent what we're about and what Market is about in hard copy. It's a life of work all in one book.

I offer food that is inventive, food that you couldn't necessarily make at home without a large amount of knowledge. I have taken my many years of experience combined with schooling and working at great restaurants and paired it with my creativity. For example, I have been in that ocean where our fish come from. I understand those fish. The yellowtail that comes into my restaurant is from a local fisherman. They are relatives of the same fish that I've been spearing and fishing since I was old enough to walk. I know how to butcher them. And it's not just the seafood; I also know the farmers, what they produce and what time of year they produce it.

I believe that you could study one cuisine your entire life and not ever really and truly master it. You could be the master of one thing in a cuisine, but it's very hard to be a master of every aspect of that cuisine. I feel as though I haven't mastered any type of cuisine. There's always a new level to reach. There is always room for improvement.

Today, some people who want to be chefs have no idea what it involves, and when they get into the kitchen they can't believe the work it entails. They think being a chef will be glamorous. My theory has always been to make sure my food and service are solid. I prefer for the experience to be about the meal my customers have eaten and the service their server has given them.

Over the years, I've cultivated a relationship with my customers through my time spent in the kitchen, watching over the food and making sure that what my guests are paying for is on point and what I want it to be. If I am not in the kitchen making sure it's done the way I want it and things go bad, then I have a problem. In this profession you are only as good as every plate of food you produce.

The things that make Market the most unique are the consistency, the freshness, the creativity, and the dedicated staff. We offer seasonally inspired cuisine. And now we bring those recipes to you. I believe that there is nothing too difficult for the home cook in my recipes. At Market, we take great ingredients and turn them into great dishes.

—Carl Schroeder

FALL

When the leaves start to turn color, you can't help but notice all the little
changes in the air, including the smell and even the varying shadows of light in
the sky. It's what you know and what you come to expect with the changing of
the seasons, a kind of autumn calmness here in San Diego. As the excitement
of summer slowly comes to an end, the simplicity of fall produce brings us
to a starting point for a new beginning. It's all about squash roasting in the
oven and the sweet smell of farmers' market apples. In this chapter, try your
hand at my Roasted Kabocha Soup and Brandy Braised Fuji Apples or Porcini
Mushroom Agnolotti with Butternut Squash Sauce.

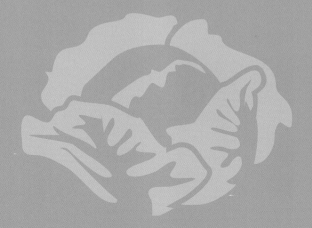

Manzana Picante

SERVES 2

2 sprigs fresh basil
2 green apple wedges
2 ounces sweet and sour
2 ounces Hangar One Chipotle Vodka
1½ ounces Hangar One Vodka
2 pieces thinly shaved green apple

In a martini shaker, muddle basil, apples, and sweet and sour with ice. Add the vodkas and strain into 2 prechilled martini glasses. Garnish with thinly shaved pieces of green apple.

Ginger Pear

SERVES 2

3 ounces Grey Goose Pear
2 ounces Domaine De Canton Ginger Liqueur
2 ounces fresh lemon juice
2 egg whites
2 ounces high-grade maple syrup
Orange peel and zest, for garnish

Combine all ingredients in a martini shaker. Shake and double strain over ice into a coupe glass. (Double straining means to strain through a fine-mesh sieve into the glass. This is what will give the nice frothiness to the egg white.) Garnish with orange peel and zest.

Broccoli Soup and Duck Egg Benedict Hollandaise

Cheddar Biscuits, Country Ham, and Lemon Sour Cream

SERVES 6 / MAKES 8-10 BISCUITS

With the addition of fresh spinach and a dollop of lemon sour cream, this fresh and creamy broccoli soup is more than just a soup. Paired with a Duck Egg Benedict, this makes for an easy meal and a nice choice for an early morning brunch or a late afternoon lunch.

Suggested wine pairing: Chardonnay

For the broccoli soup

1 pound broccoli
3 tablespoons butter
1 Spanish onion, peeled and chopped
1 leek (white part only), chopped
6 cloves garlic, chopped
½ cup peeled and chopped potato
1 teaspoon salt, more to taste
5 cups vegetable stock (page 288)
1 bay leaf
½ cup fresh baby spinach
1 cup heavy cream
Pepper, to taste

For the cheddar biscuits

2 cups all-purpose flour
1 teaspoon salt
1 tablespoon baking powder
¼ cup butter (room temperature)
¾ cup whole milk
1 cup shredded cheddar cheese
Light olive oil, for brushing biscuits

For the hollandaise sauce

4 egg yolks
1 tablespoon lemon juice
½ cup melted unsalted butter
Pinch of cayenne
Pinch of salt

For the lemon sour cream

½ cup sour cream
½ teaspoon lemon juice
¼ teaspoon salt
½ teaspoon lemon zest

For the Eggs Benedict

12 thin slices of your favorite ham, warmed
6 duck (or chicken) eggs, cooked sunny side up

For the garnish

3 scallions, finely chopped
2 jalapeño peppers, seeds removed and sliced into
    rounds

FOR THE BROCCOLI SOUP

Remove the broccoli florets. Peel off the exterior fibrous broccoli stems. Reserve 18 broccoli florets for garnish. Roughly chop any remaining florets.

Melt butter in a medium pot over low heat. Add onions, leek, garlic, potatoes, and salt; cook over medium heat until onions are translucent, about 20 minutes.

Add stock and bay leaf and bring to a boil. Add all the broccoli stems and any broccoli florets not reserved for garnish; cook on a full boil for 5 minutes.

Add spinach and cream, stir to incorporate, and remove from heat. Remove bay leaf and add salt and pepper.

In small batches add soup to a blender and process until smooth. Just before serving, return soup to its original saucepot, warm over low heat, and immersion blend.

Blanch the 18 broccoli florets (for garnish) in a pot of boiling water for 30 seconds. Remove florets and place in a bowl of ice water. Remove florets to a plate lined with a paper towels.

FOR THE CHEDDAR BISCUITS

Preheat oven to 450°F.

In a large mixing bowl, combine dry ingredients.

Chop butter into the mixture until flour is crumbly. Slowly add the milk, while stirring with fork, until the mix forms a soft dough.

Add cheese, and knead into dough with your fingers. Take the ball of dough out of the bowl and flatten into a ½-inch-thick sheet on a cutting board.

Using a 3½-inch ring mold, cut circles out of the biscuit dough. Bake biscuits until slightly brown on the top, 8–10 minutes. Remove from oven and brush with olive oil.

FOR THE HOLLANDAISE SAUCE

In a large mixing bowl, whisk the egg yolks and lemon juice until mixture is thickened and doubled in volume.

Place the bowl over a saucepan containing a small amount of simmering water (or use a double boiler). The water should not touch the bottom of the bowl. Continue to whisk rapidly (don't let the eggs get too hot or they will scramble).

Slowly drizzle in the melted butter and continue to whisk until sauce is thickened and doubled in volume.

Remove from heat and whisk in cayenne and salt. Cover and set aside.

FOR THE LEMON SOUR CREAM

Add all ingredients to a small mixing bowl and whisk until creamy.

AT SERVICE

Ladle the soup into bowls. Garnish with the broccoli florets, a dollop of lemon sour cream, and a sprinkle of scallions. Place the soup bowls onto rectangular plates. Place biscuits on the opposite ends of the plates and top each with a slice of ham, one egg, a drizzle of hollandaise sauce, and sliced jalapeños.

Chef's Tip: *This soup is also great served cold.*

Organic Cauliflower Soup and Curried Dungeness Crab

Spice-Roasted Pepitas, Organic Swiss Chard, and Lemon Essence

SERVES 6

Organic cauliflower is plentiful in the fall, and this rich soup is quick and easy to prepare. Larger chunks of crab pair well with the creaminess of the soup, the crunchiness of the pepitas, and the earthiness of the swiss chard. All of the textures make this one of my favorite fall soups.

Suggested wine pairing: Sauvignon Blanc

For the soup

2 tablespoons butter
2 tablespoons light olive oil
4 leeks (white part only), chopped
3 cups thinly sliced Spanish onion
2 cups roughly chopped organic cauliflower
1 fennel bulb, coarsely chopped
5 garlic cloves, peeled and roughly chopped
1 tablespoon salt, plus more to taste
8 cups vegetable stock (page 288)
2 bay leaves
1 sprig thyme
2 cups heavy cream
Pepper, to taste

For the toasted pepitas

½ cup pepitas (shelled pumpkin seeds)
1 egg white, whisked
½ teaspoon paprika
¼ teaspoon cayenne
¼ teaspoon salt

For the crab and lemon butter

½ cup softened butter, divided
1 tablespoon curried spice blend (page 284)
1 cup lump crabmeat, large leg pieces
1 teaspoon lemon juice

For the swiss chard

1 bunch swiss chard (any color)
2 tablespoons light olive oil
2 teaspoons finely chopped garlic
½ teaspoon salt

FOR THE SOUP

Melt butter and olive oil in a large saucepot over medium-low heat.

Add leeks, onions, cauliflower, fennel, garlic, and salt. Cover and cook on medium-low heat for about 15 minutes, checking and stirring every 5 minutes until all the vegetables are very soft.

Add stock, bay leaves, and thyme. Bring to a boil, then reduce heat to medium low and simmer soup, covered, for 35 minutes.

Let soup cool slightly, then, in small batches, add to a blender and process until smooth.

Place soup back in its original saucepot and stir in cream and salt and pepper. Just before serving, warm over low heat and immersion blend.

FOR THE TOASTED PEPITAS

Preheat oven to 325°F.

In a small mixing bowl, combine the pepitas with just enough egg white to distribute and moisten all the seeds. Add paprika, cayenne, and salt and incorporate.

Spread pepita mixture loosely and evenly onto a baking sheet lined with parchment paper and toast in oven until one shade darker, about 10 minutes.

FOR THE CRAB AND LEMON BUTTER

Melt 2 tablespoons of butter in a small sauté pan over low heat. Add curried spice blend and incorporate.

Gently fold in the crabmeat. When crabmeat is warmed, remove pan from heat and set aside.

Melt the remaining 2 tablespoons of butter in a small saucepot and stir in lemon juice.

FOR THE SWISS CHARD

Strip leaves from stalks of swiss chard and roughly chop.

In a large sauté pan over medium heat, add olive oil and garlic and cook until just fragrant.

Add chard and salt. Lightly toss and cook until wilted.

AT SERVICE

Ladle the soup into bowls and garnish with swiss chard, crabmeat, and a drizzle of lemon butter. Finish with a sprinkle of pepitas.

Chef's Tip: *I like to use Dungeness crab because it's indigenous to the west coast.*

Roasted Kabocha Squash Soup and Brandy Braised Fuji Apples

Cinnamon Spiced Froth, Charred Rapini, Sage Butter

SERVES 6

When the leaves start to turn color, this recipe is reflective of all the fruits and vegetables that come to mind. Roasted squash and braised apples from our local farms paired with hints of cinnamon and brandy remind me of the many flavors of Thanksgiving. This autumn soup unquestionably makes a statement on my menu at Market restaurant.

Suggested wine pairing: Riesling

For the squash

1 kabocha squash
3 tablespoons butter, softened
Salt and pepper, to taste

For the soup

2 tablespoons light olive oil
2 tablespoons butter, softened
1 Spanish onion, thinly sliced
1 leek, thinly sliced
6 cloves garlic, chopped
1 apple, peeled, seeded, and chopped
2 sticks cinnamon
3 star anise
¼ teaspoon cayenne pepper
1 tablespoon salt
6 cups vegetable stock (page 288)
1 sprig thyme
1 bay leaf
1 cup heavy cream

For the froth

1 cup nonfat milk
½ teaspoon ground cinnamon
2 teaspoons granulated sugar

For the apples

1 tablespoon butter
1 tablespoon light olive oil
2 Fuji apples, peeled, seeded, and sliced into
    ¼-inch pieces
¼ cup brandy

For the charred rapini

1 large bunch rapini
1 tablespoon light olive oil
Salt and pepper, to taste

For the sage butter

4 tablespoons butter
12 fresh sage leaves

For the garnish

2 tablespoons finely chopped chives

FOR THE SQUASH

Preheat oven to 375°F.

Cut the squash in half and remove the seeds from the inside cavity. Place it upright on a baking sheet. Using a brush, rub the inside cavity of the squash with butter, and season with salt and pepper. Cook until the flesh is soft, about 45 minutes. Remove the squash and cool to room temperature.

FOR THE SOUP

Heat oil and butter in a large saucepot over medium heat. Add onion, leek, garlic, apples, cinnamon, star anise, cayenne pepper, and salt.

Cover saucepot, and stirring occasionally, cook until the onions are translucent.

Pour in stock, thyme, and bay leaf and bring mixture to high heat.

With a spoon, scoop squash out of its skin and add to the saucepot

Bring soup to a boil, then reduce to medium-low heat and cook for about 20 minutes.

Remove soup from heat and, using a slotted spoon, remove thyme, bay leaf, cinnamon sticks, and star anise. Add cream, and incorporate.

In small batches, place soup in a blender and puree until smooth. Set aside.

Just before serving, return soup to its original saucepot, warm over low heat, and immersion blend.

FOR THE FROTH

Combine all ingredients in a small saucepot over low heat, stirring until just warm. Remove from heat and immersion blend until frothy.

FOR THE APPLES

Combine butter, oil, and apples in a large sauté pan over medium-high heat. Cook for 1 minute.

Add brandy, and incorporate. Simmer over low heat, braising apples until they are almost dry. Remove from heat.

FOR THE CHARRED RAPINI

Cut an inch off the bottom stalks of the rapini and discard. Cut the rapini into 1-inch pieces.

Heat olive oil in a large skillet over high heat. Add rapini and cook until caramelized on one side, about 30 seconds. Flip rapini over and caramelize the other side for an additional 30 seconds.

Reduce heat to low and cook rapini until tender, 1–2 minutes. Season with salt and pepper.

FOR THE SAGE BUTTER

Melt butter in a small saucepot over medium heat. Add sage, cover saucepot, and turn off heat. Allow the flavors to infuse for 5 minutes. Remove sage with a slotted spoon.

AT SERVICE

Ladle the soup into bowls. Garnish with apples and rapini, and drizzle with sage butter. Top with a dollop of the cinnamon froth and a sprinkle of chives.

Chef's Tip: *Substitute Delicata, Buttercup, or Red Kuri squash*

Curried Carrot Soup and Gingered Chicken Meatballs

Whipped Coconut Milk, Coriander, and Cumin Spiced Croutons

SERVES 6 / MAKES APPROXIMATELY 20 MEATBALLS

When the weather starts to get cold in the fall and winter, everything heads to the ground, and we go into the amazing root vegetable season. Rather than just create a one-dimensional carrot-ginger soup like I started doing early in my career, I've taken this traditional fall and winter soup to the next level. This recipe is a spin on a classic.

Suggested wine pairing: Viognier

For the soup

2 large carrots, roughly chopped
1 large Spanish onion, peeled and roughly chopped
2 scallions, roughly chopped
1 (½-inch) ginger cube, peeled and roughly chopped
1 leek, roughly chopped
1 Roma tomato, roughly chopped
1 pasilla pepper, seeded and finally chopped
4 cloves garlic, roughly chopped
1 handful cilantro, stems only
2 tablespoons light olive oil
½ tablespoon salt
1 cinnamon stick
1 cardamom pod
1 star anise
1 (13.5-ounce) can coconut milk
4 cups vegetable stock (page 288)
2 tablespoons soy sauce
¼ tablespoon sriracha sauce
¼ tablespoon curry powder
1 tablespoon cumin/coriander spice blend
   (page 283)
1 bay leaf

For the chicken meatballs

2 tablespoons light olive oil, divided
1 Spanish onion, finely minced
6 cloves garlic, finely minced
1 (1-inch) ginger cube, finely minced
1½ pounds ground chicken
¼ cup panko bread crumbs
3 tablespoons hoisin sauce
1 teaspoon salt

For the croutons

¼ baguette, cut into ½–inch cubes or desired size
½ cup light olive oil
Cumin/coriander spice blend, to taste (page 283)

For the whipped coconut milk

1 (13.5-ounce) can coconut milk
2 tablespoons granulated sugar
1 tablespoon tapioca starch

For the garnish

¼ cup roughly chopped cilantro
¼ cup roughly chopped scallions

FOR THE SOUP

Preheat oven to 400°F.

In a large mixing bowl, combine carrots, onion, scallions, ginger, leek, tomato, pepper, garlic, and cilantro.

Add olive oil and salt, and toss to incorporate.

Add cinnamon, cardamom, and star anise.

Place mixture onto a baking sheet and roast for 30 minutes, occasionally tossing during the cooking process.

Remove mixture from oven and add to a large saucepot with coconut milk, stock, soy sauce, sriracha, curry powder, cumin/coriander, and bay leaf. Stir to incorporate.

Bring soup to a boil, then lower heat to medium high. Stirring occasionally, simmer soup for about 15 minutes.

Remove soup from heat. Remove cinnamon stick, star anise, and bay leaf.

In small batches, place the soup in a blender and puree until smooth.

Just before serving, return soup to its original saucepot, warm over low heat, and immersion blend.

FOR THE CHICKEN MEATBALLS

Preheat oven to 375°F.

Heat 1 tablespoon of olive oil in a small sauté pan over medium heat. Add onion, garlic, and ginger, and cook until translucent, about 5 minutes.

Pour the mixture into a large mixing bowl and add chicken, bread crumbs, hoisin sauce, and salt. Combine with your hands and roll into 1-inch meatballs.

Add 1 tablespoon of olive oil to a baking dish. Place meatballs inside the baking dish and cook for 15 minutes.

FOR THE CROUTONS

Preheat oven to 325°F.

Add bread cubes to a large mixing bowl. Drizzle with olive oil, and toss evenly until incorporated.

Place bread cubes loosely onto a large baking sheet lined with parchment paper. Bake until golden brown and crunchy all the way through, approximately 15 minutes.

Remove bread cubes from oven and immediately sprinkle with cumin/coriander. Cool to room temperature.

FOR THE WHIPPED COCONUT MILK

Combine all ingredients in a large mixing bowl and whisk until mixture is frothy and slightly thickened.

FOR THE GARNISH

Combine all ingredients in a small bowl.

AT SERVICE

Ladle the soup into bowls. Place 2 or 3 meatballs in the center of each and swirl the whipped coconut milk around the meatballs. Garnish with the cilantro/scallion mixture and croutons.

Chef's Tip: *To peel ginger, use the side of a spoon. The skin will scrape away easily.*

Petite Kale and Swiss Chard Greek Salad

Baby Beets, Goat's Milk Feta, Marinated Peppers, and Castelvetrano Olives

SERVES 6

If you love salad but get bored with the same old version, I urge you to try this one. Its bright and refreshing flavors bring the taste of the Mediterranean to your table. Vitamin-packed super greens and beets are enhanced further by the flavors of the marinated peppers and Castelvetrano olives. The creaminess of the goat's milk cheese brings it all together.

Suggested wine pairing: Albariño

For the salad

8 cups super green mix or organic mixed greens
House vinaigrette, for drizzling (page 285)
Salt and pepper, to taste
1½ cups sliced Castelvetrano olives
½ red onion, peeled and sliced
1½ cups crumbled feta cheese

For the beets

30 baby beets, assorted colors
8 cups water
¾ cup granulated sugar
1 tablespoon salt
House vinaigrette, for drizzling (page 285)

For the roasted peppers

3 red bell peppers
Light olive oil, for coating peppers
Salt and pepper, to taste

For the rosemary garlic toast

6 slices of your favorite loaf of bread, thinly sliced, more if desired
Light olive oil, for drizzling
Salt and pepper, to taste
Finely chopped fresh rosemary, for sprinkling
3 cloves garlic, peeled, for rubbing on toast

FOR THE SALAD

Combine greens in a large mixing bowl with enough vinaigrette to evenly coat the leaves. Season with salt and pepper and lightly toss.

FOR THE BEETS

Wash the beets under cold running water. Cut off the tops, leaving the skin on and leaving an inch from the stalk (this ensures that the beets retain their nutrients and bright color). Leave the bottom part of the beet attached.

Add water, sugar, and salt to a large saucepot and stir to incorporate.

Add beets to the water and bring to a boil, then reduce heat to medium low. Simmer the beets until fork tender, about 20 minutes.

Remove beets with a slotted spoon to a baking sheet and cool to room temperature. Slice beets in half and refrigerate.

FOR THE ROASTED PEPPERS

Preheat oven to 450°F.

Coat peppers with olive oil, salt, and pepper and place on a baking sheet. Roast peppers in

the oven until they are completely wrinkled and charred, turning them twice during the roasting process, 10–15 minutes.

Place peppers in a bowl, cover with plastic wrap, and let rest for 5 minutes, then peel and remove stems and seeds.

Cut peppers into ½-inch pieces and combine with beets in a mixing bowl with some of the vinaigrette.

FOR THE ROSEMARY GARLIC TOAST

Preheat oven to 325°F.

Lay out 6 bread slices on a baking sheet lined with parchment paper. Brush lightly with olive oil and sprinkle with salt, pepper, and rosemary.

Bake until crispy and golden brown, about 20 minutes.

Remove bread from oven and gently rub each side of toast with garlic.

AT SERVICE

Distribute the lettuce evenly onto 6 plates. Place the beets and peppers on and around the lettuce. Garnish with the olives, onions, and feta cheese. Top each plate with 1 slice of rosemary garlic toast.

Chef's Tip: *For this salad, I like to use goat's milk feta cheese and sourdough wheat bread for the rosemary garlic toast.*

Fuyu Persimmon Salad with Braised Bacon and Bûcheron Goat Cheese

Butter Lettuce, Curry Vinaigrette, Toasted Almonds

SERVES 6

I like butter leaf lettuce because it's a nice neutral green, but this salad can be easily executed with any lettuce. The bacon is a nice play of smoky and salty off the acidity of the curry vinaigrette and sweetness of the persimmons.

Suggested wine pairing: French Sauvignon Blanc

For the salad

1 head butter lettuce, cut into 6 quarter pieces with core intact
1 head red or yellow Belgian endive, cut into long strips lengthwise
6 fuyu persimmons, peeled and cut into small wedges
1 cup Bûcheron goat cheese (substitute any goat or feta cheese)
¼ cup chives, cut into 1-inch pieces (optional)

For the curry vinaigrette

3 tablespoons light olive oil
2 teaspoons finely minced garlic
2 teaspoons finely minced ginger
2 tablespoons finely minced green onion
2 teaspoons minced lemongrass
1 teaspoon yellow curry powder
1 teaspoon paprika
Small pinch of turmeric
¼ teaspoon salt
¼ cup orange juice
¼ cup apple cider vinegar
¼ cup peeled and diced apple
1½ teaspoons honey
¼ cup light olive oil

For the bacon

¼ cup light olive oil
18 strips thick-cut bacon, cut in half (substitute standard bacon if necessary)

For the candied almonds

1 cup sliced, raw almonds
1 egg white, whisked
1 tablespoon granulated sugar
Pinch of salt
Pinch of black pepper

FOR THE CURRY VINAIGRETTE

Heat olive oil in a small saucepot over medium heat. Add garlic, ginger, onion, and lemongrass, and cook until fragrant and a little soft, about 2 minutes.

Reduce heat to low. Add curry powder, paprika, turmeric, and salt, and cook until fragrant, about 30 seconds (being careful not to burn).

Add orange juice, vinegar, apple, and honey. Simmer for 10 minutes over medium-low heat.

Strain through a fine-mesh sieve lined with a double layer of cheesecloth (don't force the liquid, just allow it to strain through on its own for about 20 minutes, then give it a couple light presses with the back of a spoon or ladle).

Add liquid to a blender over low speed, and slowly drizzle in olive oil.

Chill in refrigerator.

FOR THE BACON

Preheat oven to 325°F.

Heat olive oil in a large ovenproof sauté pan over medium heat. Add bacon and cook for 15 seconds per side (bacon should be sizzling).

Remove pan from heat and cover with tin foil.

Place pan in the oven and cook the bacon for 30 minutes.

FOR THE CANDIED ALMONDS

Preheat oven to 300°F.

Combine almonds and egg white in a small mixing bowl and thoroughly combine. Add sugar, salt, and pepper and stir to mix.

Arrange almonds on a baking sheet coated with nonstick cooking spray, and roast for 10 minutes.

Remove almonds from oven, flip over with a spatula, place back in oven, and cook for an additional 5 minutes. Remove from oven and cool to room temperature.

AT SERVICE

Place lettuce wedges onto plates and drizzle with curry vinaigrette. Add persimmons and 3 bacon strips to each plate. Garnish with goat cheese, chives, and candied almonds.

Chef's Tip: *When selecting persimmons, choose fruit with deep orange color that are firm but yield slightly to pressure. Persimmons should never be rock hard.*

Pink Lady Apple and Red Flame Grape Waldorf Salad

*Romaine Hearts, Goat's Milk Feta, Fennel-Dusted Croutons,
Citrus-Anise Vinaigrette*

SERVES 6

My cooks were in the kitchen one day making a family salad for our employees. One of the cooks had apple scraps left over and decided it might be fun to create a unique spin on a "Waldorf." We added it to our dinner menu, and it's been a hit ever since.

Suggested wine pairing: Semillon

For the salad

¼ cup finely chopped fresh mint
¼ cup finely chopped fresh cilantro
36 red grapes, halved
3 Fuji apples, cored and sliced
2 heads romaine hearts, cut into 8 quarters
1 cup crumbled feta cheese

For the citrus-anise vinaigrette

¼ cup light olive oil
1 teaspoon chopped jalapeño
1 teaspoon chopped ginger
1 teaspoon chopped shallots
¼ teaspoon chaat masala (substitute ground
    coriander)
1 star anise
½ stick cinnamon
1 clove
1 cup orange juice
3 tablespoons red wine vinegar

For the croutons

½ baguette, cut into ½-inch cubes
2 tablespoons light olive oil
1 teaspoon toasted ground fennel (page 287)
Salt and pepper, to taste

FOR THE SALAD

In a small bowl, combine the mint and cilantro.

In another small bowl, combine the grapes and apples, and lightly toss with the citrus-anise vinaigrette (see below).

On a large sheet pan, lay out the all the lettuce quarters (the root end holds the lettuce together). Drizzle with the citrus-anise vinaigrette, working it into the lettuce layers with your fingers.

FOR THE CITRUS-ANISE VINAIGRETTE

Heat olive oil in a sauté pan over medium heat. Add the jalapeño, ginger, and shallots, and cook until soft, about 3 minutes.

Add the chaat masala, anise, cinnamon, clove, orange juice, and vinegar, Reduce liquid to half its volume, 5–10 minutes.

Remove from heat, and remove anise, cinnamon stick, and clove. When slightly cooled, place liquid in a blender and process until smooth. Cover and refrigerate until chilled.

FOR THE CROUTONS

Preheat oven to 325°F.

Add bread cubes to a large mixing bowl. Drizzle with olive oil and toss evenly until incorporated.

Place bread cubes loosely onto a large baking sheet lined with parchment paper and bake until golden brown and crunchy all the way through, approximately 15 minutes.

Remove from oven and immediately sprinkle with fennel, salt, and pepper. Cool to room temperature.

AT SERVICE

Place lettuce wedges onto plates. Evenly distribute the grapes and apples by tucking them into the lettuce leaves and layering some on top. Garnish salads with some of the feta, croutons, and mint/cilantro mixture.

Fall Pear Salad and Aged Goat Cheese Soufflé

Sour Cherry Chutney, Cider Pear Vinaigrette

SERVES 6

Every year I look forward to pear season. I have several sources for heirloom varietals, each with its own unique flavor and texture. In this recipe, you can taste pears three different ways on one plate, all working harmoniously and pairing perfectly with a warm goat cheese soufflé. This soufflé is more dense and stable than other soufflés, and can also be prepared ahead of time and warmed up to order.

Suggested wine pairing: Off-Dry Riesling

For the pear chutney

6 cups pears, peeled, cored, and diced
   (assorted varieties)
1 cup dried cherries
1 teaspoon finely chopped ginger
¼ teaspoon salt
1 star anise
½ teaspoon chile flakes
½ cup apple juice
½ cup cider vinegar
½ cup granulated sugar

For the pear vinaigrette

2 tablespoons light olive oil
2 shallots, finely chopped
1 tablespoon minced ginger
1 small bay leaf
1 small sprig thyme
1 cup brandy
2 pears, peeled, cored, and chopped
½ cup unfiltered apple juice
1 tablespoon honey
¼ vanilla bean, split and scraped
½ cup cider vinegar
2 tablespoons walnut oil
2 tablespoons canola oil
Salt and pepper, to taste

For the pear salad

6 assorted pears, peeled, cored, and sliced
3 Belgian endive
Salt and pepper, to taste

For the soufflé

2 tablespoons butter, more for coating ramekins
¼ cup all-purpose flour
1 cup cold milk
½ cup Bûcheron goat cheese
3 egg yolks
3 egg whites
Salt and pepper, to taste

FOR THE PEAR CHUTNEY

Combine all ingredients in a large saucepot over medium-low heat; gently stirring. Reduce to a consistency of a chunky pie filling, about 1 hour.

FOR THE PEAR VINAIGRETTE

Heat oil in a medium saucepot over low heat. Add shallots, ginger, bay leaf, and thyme, and sauté until opaque, about 5 minutes.

Add brandy, pears, apple juice, honey, and vanilla bean, and keep over medium heat. Reduce vinaigrette mixture by half, stirring often to not burn, 30–45 minutes. Remove bay leaf and thyme.

Prepare an ice bath by nesting a medium bowl in a larger bowl that's partially filled with ice and water. Add vinaigrette to prepared ice bath and stir until chilled. Move vinaigrette to a blender.

Blend on low speed. Drizzle in oils, and season with salt and pepper.

Remove sauce from heat and add it to a stand mixer with whisk attachment in place. Add in the goat cheese and combine thoroughly.

Let the mixture cool slightly. At high speed, add one egg yolk at a time. When combined, season with salt and pepper and remove to a large mixing bowl

In a separate large mixing bowl, whisk egg whites until soft peaks form. Gently fold the egg whites into egg yolk mixture.

Coat six 4-ounce ramekins with butter and dust with flour. Fill the ramekins to ½-inch from the top with soufflé batter.

Place the ramekins in a shallow baking dish and pour boiling water around them until it comes about halfway up the sides of the dishes (this water bath will help the soufflés cook evenly).

Bake until soufflés are golden brown on top and have risen, about 30 minutes.

Remove soufflés from oven and place on a baking sheet; cool completely. Unmold soufflés onto a baking sheet lined with buttered parchment paper. Soufflés can be covered and refrigerated for up to 2 days.

AT SERVICE

Arrange pears on plates. Top the pears with the endive. Place 1 soufflé on each plate and top each soufflé with the pear chutney.

Chef's Tip: *Using diverse varieties and colors of pears adds interesting textures and flavors to the dish. Some of my favorite pears are Bosc, Green d'Anjou, and Red Starkrimsom.*

FOR THE PEAR SALAD

Add pears to a mixing bowl and coat with some of the vinaigrette. Season with salt and pepper.

Split endive in half, remove core, and thinly slice. Add endive to a mixing bowl and coat with some of the vinaigrette.

FOR THE SOUFFLÉ

Preheat oven to 325°F.

Melt butter in a saucepot over low heat. Add flour and whisk until incorporated. Add milk and slowly cook mixture over medium-low heat, whisking continually until it resembles a thick cream sauce, about 10 minutes.

Big-Eye Tuna Sashimi and
Shiitake Mushroom–Spaghetti Squash Salad

SERVES 6

I have been fishing waters in San Diego for many years and love the thrill of catching a diversity of fish. I especially like the dark red flesh of the bluefin tuna, which contains a little more fat than the other varieties, thus providing a richer flavor profile.

Suggested wine pairing: Dry Riesling

For the sashimi

1 (1½-pound) sushi-grade, bluefin tuna loin

For the squash

1 large spaghetti squash
3 tablespoons light olive oil
20 medium shiitake mushrooms, thinly sliced
1 tablespoon minced ginger
1 tablespoon minced garlic
3 tablespoons rice wine vinegar
Salt and pepper, to taste
½ cup scallion, shaved
1 jalapeño, seeded, halved, and thinly sliced
½ bunch cilantro, finely chopped
Sesame oil, to taste

For the soy vinaigrette

1 cup tsuyu sauce
1 cup seasoned rice wine vinegar
2 teaspoons tapioca

For the horseradish-yuzu aioli

1 egg yolk
1 teaspoon yuzu juice
1 cup light olive oil
2 tablespoons prepared horseradish, lightly
    squeezed and finely chopped

For the garnish:

1 tablespoon toasted sesame seeds
1 cup shelled edamame (green soybeans)

FOR THE SASHIMI

Cut tuna loin into 3 x 3-inch log, then slice into 18 ¼-inch-thick medallions.

FOR THE SQUASH

Preheat oven to 350°F.

Cut squash in half and place (cut side down) in a small, shallow baking sheet. Add about ½ inch of water, just enough to cover the bottom of the pan. Bake for 40-45 minutes, checking for doneness by scraping the flesh of the squash with a fork. It should easily release and look like spaghetti.

Remove from the oven and cool. Using a fork, release the spaghettilike flesh into a large bowl and reserve.

Heat olive oil in a small sauté pan over medium-high heat. Cook the mushrooms until they just start to wilt.

Add ginger and garlic and sauté for about 2 more minutes. Add vinegar and cook until evaporated, 2-3 minutes. Season with salt and pepper. Remove from heat and chill.

Add the mushrooms, scallions, jalapeño, and cilantro to the chilled spaghetti squash. Add a few drops of sesame oil and salt. Combine.

FOR THE SOY VINAIGRETTE

Combine tsuyu and vinegar in a blender on a low speed. While blender is running, add the starch and process for 15 seconds longer. Reserve.

FOR THE HORSERADISH-YUZU AIOLI

In a mixing bowl, combine egg yolk and yuzu. Slowly whisk in olive oil until emulsified. Once emulsified, whisk in horseradish. Reserve.

AT SERVICE

Spoon soy vinaigrette onto the bottom of rectangular plates. Add three pieces of tuna to each plate. On each piece of tuna, place a large pinch of the spaghetti squash salad, covering half and leaving the other half exposed. Place desired amount of aioli on exposed half of fish and sprinkle sesame seeds on top of aioli. Garnish each plate with edamame.

Chef's Tip: *Substitute your favorite tuna.*

Truffled Fettuccine Pasta Carbonara

Serrano Ham, Roasted Sweet Potatoes, Parmigiana Reggiano

SERVES 6 / MAKES 1½ POUNDS PASTA DOUGH

This is not your traditional carbonara. Serrano ham, roasted sweet potatoes, and Parmigiana Reggiano add bold flavors, making this dish anything but ordinary.

Suggested wine pairing: Pinot Gris

For the fettuccine

3½ cups all-purpose flour, more if needed
3 large eggs
¼ cup light olive oil
8 tablespoons very cold water
Salt and pepper, to taste
6 tablespoons Parmigiano Reggiano
2 tablespoons finely chopped chives

For the carbonara sauce

6 egg yolks
6 tablespoons crème fraîche
3 tablespoons bacon fat
1 cup finely chopped Spanish onions
2 tablespoons finely chopped garlic
½ cup mushroom stock (page 286)
1 cup heavy cream
¼ cup cold, diced truffle butter

For the brussels sprout petals

18 brussels sprouts
3 tablespoons light olive oil
Salt and pepper, to taste

For the roasted sweet potatoes

3 tablespoons light olive oil
1 large sweet potato, peeled and diced
Salt and pepper, to taste

For the ham

6 large slices serrano ham

FOR THE FETTUCCINE

Place flour in a stand mixer with dough-hook attachment in place. Add eggs, olive oil, and water, and process until a soft dough forms, 1–2 minutes.

Turn the dough onto a lightly floured surface and knead by hand for a minute until it's smooth, soft, and stretchy.

Wrap dough in plastic wrap, and let it rest at room temperature for 30 minutes.

If rolling pasta dough by hand, cut the dough into quarters and, using a rolling pin, roll out the dough to ⅛–1/16 inch thick. If using a pasta-rolling machine, cut the dough into quarters, press flat, and run each piece several times through the machine, adjusting the setting each time, until the pasta is ⅛–1/16 inch thick.

Cut each pasta sheet into 10-inch lengths. Brush lightly with flour, roll up sheet, and, using a sharp knife, cut into ¼-inch-wide strips; unroll.

Bring a large pot of salted water to a boil. Drop fettuccine in boiling water and cook until al dente. Drain in a colander.

Add pasta to a large bowl. Add desired amount of carbonara sauce (see page 25) to the pasta and lightly toss; season with salt and pepper. Garnish with Parmigiana Reggiano and chives.

FOR THE CARBONARA SAUCE

In a small mixing bowl, whisk the egg yolks and crème fraîche until creamy. Set aside.

Heat bacon fat, onions, and garlic in a large sauté pan over low heat. Cook, stirring frequently, until onions are soft, about 5 minutes.

Add mushroom stock and cream. Simmer over medium-low heat until mixture is thickened and coats the back of a spoon. Whisk in butter until fully incorporated.

Add the egg yolk/crème fraîche mixture and cook over low heat, whisking continuously just until egg yolks are slightly thickened (be careful not to get the pan too hot or eggs will overcook).

FOR THE BRUSSELS SPROUT PETALS

Split brussels sprouts in half, remove core, and separate all the leaves (the leaves are what you are using).

Heat olive oil in a sauté pan over high heat.

Immediately throw in the brussels sprouts leaves and add the salt and pepper. Toss the leaves and sauté until tender, 3–5 minutes. Remove pan from heat and set aside.

FOR THE ROASTED SWEET POTATOES

Preheat oven to 375°F.

Combine oil and sweet potatoes in a large ovenproof sauté pan over medium-high heat. Cook the potatoes for about 2 minutes; season with salt and pepper. Place pan in oven and cook potatoes until soft, 10–15 minutes.

AT SERVICE

Mound a pile of fettuccine into each bowl. Place brussels sprout petals over and around the fettuccine. Garnish with the sweet potatoes. Top with Parmigiana Reggiano and ham. Spoon any leftover carbonara sauce over the top.

Chef's Tip: *Substitute your favorite ham or a thick slice of Prosciutto de Parma.*

Octopus and Braised Beluga Lentils

Jalapeño-Garlic Aioli, Sautéed Broccolini

SERVES 6

Octopus and lentils pair well together. For this recipe I've taken a braised octopus favorite and added a twist with crispy fried octopus and rock shrimp paired with creamy lentils. The root vegetables add a nice depth.

Suggested wine pairing: Albariño

For the beluga lentils

2 tablespoons light olive oil
2 strips bacon, finely chopped
½ cup small diced Spanish onions
½ cup small diced celery
½ cup small diced turnips
½ cup small diced carrots
½ cup small diced red bell peppers
1 tablespoon finely chopped garlic
1 cup black beluga lentils, rinsed
1 teaspoon cumin/coriander spice blend (page 283)
½ teaspoon paprika
1 teaspoon chile powder
¼ teaspoon cayenne pepper
4 cups chicken stock (page 283)
1 bay leaf
1 sprig rosemary

For the octopus and rock shrimp

4 tablespoons light olive oil
3 cloves garlic
½ Spanish onion, peeled and sliced
½ pound whole raw octopus
½ pound rock shrimp, raw
2 cups buttermilk
3 cups all-purpose flour
2 tablespoons paprika
1 teaspoon cayenne
1 teaspoon dry mustard
Canola oil, for frying
Salt and pepper, to taste

For the sautéed broccolini

2 tablespoons light olive oil
2 teaspoons finely chopped garlic
2 bunches broccolini, roughly chopped
½ teaspoon salt

For the jalapeño-garlic aioli

3 jalapeño peppers
Light olive oil, for coating peppers
Salt and pepper, to taste
Base aioli (page 281)
¼ teaspoon smoked paprika

FOR THE BELUGA LENTILS

Heat olive oil in a medium saucepot over low heat. Add bacon and cook until the fat starts to render and the bacon is slightly crispy, 3–5 minutes.

Add onions, celery, turnips, carrots, peppers, and garlic. Stirring often, cook vegetables over medium heat until just tender, 5–10 minutes.

Add lentils, cumin/coriander, paprika, chile powder, and cayenne. Gently stir and cook for 1–2 minutes more.

Add stock, bay leaf, and rosemary. Bring to a simmer and cook uncovered until the lentils are tender, 25–30 minutes. Remove bay leaf and rosemary.

FOR THE OCTOPUS AND ROCK SHRIMP

Heat olive oil in a large saucepot over low heat. Add garlic, onion, and octopus. Cover and cook until tender, about 1 hour. To test for doneness, stick a fork in the thickest part of the octopus (it is done if the fork slides out easily).

Remove the octopus from the pot and let cool. Cut the octopus into ¾-inch rounds, skin and all.

Combine octopus rounds and rock shrimp in a large mixing bowl. Add buttermilk and toss the fish gently until fully coated.

Cover bowl with plastic wrap and place in the refrigerator for 30 minutes.

Meanwhile, combine flour, paprika, cayenne, and mustard in a large mixing bowl.

Strain the octopus and rock shrimp in a colander. Shake off any excess buttermilk and toss seafood in the seasoned flour.

Heat oil in a deep fryer to 375°F. (If using a large saucepot, add enough cooking oil to completely submerge the fish; heat to 375°F.)

In batches, add the octopus and shrimp to the hot oil. Cook until crispy and light golden brown. Turn the octopus and shrimp during frying if necessary.

Remove the fish to a plate lined with paper towels. Season with salt and pepper.

FOR THE SAUTÉED BROCCOLINI

Heat olive oil in a large sauté pan over medium heat. Add garlic and cook until just fragrant. Add broccolini and salt; toss lightly and cook until just wilted.

FOR THE JALAPEÑO-GARLIC AIOLI

Preheat oven to 400°F.

Coat peppers with olive oil, salt, and pepper. Place peppers onto a small baking sheet and roast in oven until skins are blistered, 10–15 minutes.

Remove peppers from oven, place in a small bowl, and cover with plastic wrap. Allow peppers to steam for 5–10 minutes (this makes it easier to peel the peppers). Remove outer skin, core, and seeds from peppers, and finely mince.

Add smoked paprika to base aioli, then fold in roasted peppers.

AT SERVICE

Ladle the lentils into bowls. Add the broccolini to the center, then stack the fried shrimp and octopus onto the broccolini. Finish with a drizzle of jalapeño-garlic aioli.

Chef's Tip: *You can skip the first step of cooking the octopus in this recipe by purchasing cooked octopus available at many fish and Asian markets.*

Mesquite Grilled Quail and Asian Pear Salad

Hoisin-Citrus Glaze, Fresno Chiles, Ginger-Fish Sauce Vinaigrette

SERVES 6

Celery root and Asian pears are on the scene in early fall in San Diego. An Asian pear is crunchy and sweet, but not quite as much as an apple. The grilled quail is somewhat charred and tastes slightly gamey. Paired with a clean and crisp salad, this dish is definitely complex.

Suggested wine pairing: Austrian Gruner Veltliner

For the quail

¼ cup soy sauce
¼ cup dry sherry
1 tablespoon white wine vinegar
1 tablespoon smashed garlic
1 tablespoon finely chopped ginger
1 teaspoon granulated sugar
1 teaspoon crushed red pepper flakes
6 quail, preferably boneless (your butcher
    can do this)
6 bacon slices, cut in half

For the ginger-fish sauce vinaigrette

1 cup plus 3 tablespoons light olive oil (divided)
1 jalapeño pepper, seeded and chopped
1 Serrano pepper, chopped
2 tablespoons chopped garlic
2 tablespoons chopped ginger
6 bunches scallions, roughly chopped
1 cup seasoned rice wine vinegar
¼ cup granulated sugar
¼ cup water
½ cup fish sauce
¼ cup light soy sauce
1 tablespoon fresh squeezed lime juice
1 tablespoon chile oil

For the Asian pear salad

¼ head purple cabbage, thinly sliced
¼ head green cabbage, thinly sliced
3 Asian pears, thinly sliced
1 cup thinly sliced celery root
2 Fresno chiles, seeded and cut into rounds
½ cup roughly chopped cilantro

½ cup scallions, cut into rounds
1 cup roughly chopped salt roasted peanuts, divided

For the hoisin-citrus glaze

1 tablespoon light olive oil
1 teaspoon garlic
1 teaspoon ginger
2 scallions, chopped
½ cup sweet chili sauce
¼ cup eel sauce
¼ cup hoisin sauce
½ cup orange juice

FOR THE QUAIL

Combine the soy sauce, sherry, vinegar, garlic, ginger, sugar, and red pepper flakes in a large mixing bowl. Add the quail and, with your hands, generously rub with the marinade until fully coated.

Arrange the quail in a baking dish and cover with plastic wrap. Place in refrigerator for 2–4 hours. Remove from the marinade and pat dry with paper towels.

Heat an indoor or outdoor grill to high heat. Grill the quail until just pink at the leg bones, 4–5 minutes on each side.

FOR THE GINGER-FISH SAUCE VINAIGRETTE

Heat 3 tablespoons olive oil in a sauté pan over medium heat. Add peppers, garlic, ginger, and scallions, and cook for 5 minutes.

Spread mixture onto a plate and refrigerate until chilled.

In a blender combine vinegar, sugar, water, fish sauce, soy sauce, and lime juice. Process on high speed until smooth. Lower speed and drizzle in the chile oil and remaining 1 cup of olive oil.

FOR THE ASIAN PEAR SALAD

Rinse purple cabbage under cold water in a strainer until it doesn't release any more color. Combine cabbages and pat dry or spin dry in a salad spinner.

In a large mixing bowl, combine cabbages, pears, celery root, chiles, cilantro, scallions, and ½ cup peanuts. Drizzle with some of the vinaigrette and lightly toss.

FOR THE HOISIN-CITRUS GLAZE

Heat olive oil in a sauté pan over medium-high heat. Add garlic, ginger, and scallions. Cook until garlic is just fragrant.

Add sweet chile sauce, eel sauce, hoisin sauce, and orange juice. Simmer over medium heat and reduce to a syrup consistency or until mixture coats the back of a spoon, about 30 minutes.

AT SERVICE

Place Asian pear salad in the center of each plate. Place 1 quail breast on top of each salad. Drizzle the hoisin-citrus glaze around and on top of the quail. Garnish with remaining peanuts.

Chef's Tip: *For an easier way to peel and cut celery root, place it on a cutting board, cut it in half, and cut the skin away from all sides with a sharp knife, not a vegetable peeler. Slice it thin on a slicer or mandoline, stack it into rounds, and cut it into thin strips.*

Porcini Mushroom Agnolotti with Butternut Squash Sauce

Brussels Sprout Leaves, Ham Hock, Shaved Pecorino, Lemon Oil

SERVES 6 / YIELDS 1½ POUNDS PASTA DOUGH

Porcini mushroom agnolotti paired with the smokiness from the ham hock is very hearty in this unique small plate. The natural sweetness of the butternut squash and the earthy meatiness of the porcini mushrooms paired with the saltiness of the pecorino Romano cheese make for the perfect starter to any fall main course.

Suggested wine pairing: White Burgundy

For the ham hock vegetable broth

3 smoked ham hocks
2 cups chopped Roma tomatoes
2 tablespoons tomato paste
1 cup chopped Spanish onion
½ cup chopped celery
½ cup chopped carrots
1 sprig thyme
1 bay leaf
1 teaspoon whole peppercorns

For the butternut squash sauce

3 tablespoons light olive oil
1 cup small diced butternut squash
1 Spanish onion, peeled and roughly chopped
1 leek (white part only), roughly chopped
6 cloves garlic, chopped
1 teaspoon finely chopped ginger
1 teaspoon salt
¼ teaspoon pepper
4 cups ham hock broth
1 sprig rosemary
1 bay leaf
3 tablespoons cold butter

For the mushroom filling

3 tablespoons light olive oil
6 cups porcini mushrooms, small diced (may substitute any mushroom varietal)
½ teaspoon salt
3 shallots, finely chopped
8 cloves garlic, finely chopped

3 tablespoons mascarpone cheese
2 teaspoons fines herbes (page 285)
2 tablespoons grated Parmigiana Reggiano
1 teaspoon lemon zest

For the pasta dough

3½ cups all-purpose flour, more if needed
5 large eggs, divided
¼ cup light olive oil
10 tablespoons very cold water, divided
Salt and pepper, to taste

For the brussels sprout leaves

18 brussels sprouts
3 tablespoons light olive oil
Salt and pepper, to taste

For the garnish

Small block of pecorino Romano cheese

FOR THE HAM HOCK VEGETABLE BROTH

Place ham hocks in a large saucepot and completely cover with water (at least an inch over the top of them). Bring to a boil, then reduce heat to low. Cover saucepot and simmer ham hocks for 1 hour.

Add tomatoes, tomato paste, onion, celery, carrots, thyme, bay leaf, and peppercorns. Continue to simmer on low heat for an additional hour, then strain and set ham hocks aside.

When cool, pull meat from ham hocks with your hands, trim off the fat and slice meat into large chunks.

FOR THE BUTTERNUT SQUASH SAUCE

Heat olive oil in a large sauté pan over medium-low heat. Add squash, onion, leek, garlic, ginger, salt, and pepper. Cover pan and, stirring occasionally, cook the mixture until onions become translucent, 20–25 minutes.

Add broth, rosemary, and bay leaf. Bring to a boil, then reduce heat to medium low and simmer uncovered, for 15 minutes.

Remove bay leaf and rosemary. Add mixture to a blender and process, adding in the butter, until smooth.

FOR THE MUSHROOM FILLING

Heat olive oil in a large sauté pan over medium-low heat. Add mushrooms and salt, stirring often, cook the mushrooms until very dry, about 15 minutes.

Add shallots and garlic and continue cooking for 1 minute more.

Remove mushroom mixture from heat and loosely arrange on a large baking sheet. Cool to room temperature. Once cool, combine mushrooms in a large mixing bowl with mascarpone, fines herbes, Parmigiana Reggiano, and lemon zest, and incorporate thoroughly.

FOR THE PASTA DOUGH

Place flour in a stand mixer with dough-hook attachment in place. Add 3 eggs, olive oil, and 8 tablespoons water. Process ingredients until a soft dough forms, 1–2 minutes.

Turn the dough out onto a lightly floured surface and knead by hand for a minute until it's smooth, soft, and stretchy.

Wrap dough in plastic wrap, and let it rest at room temperature for 30 minutes.

If rolling pasta dough by hand, cut the dough into quarters and, using a rolling pin, roll out the dough until it is ⅛–1/16 inch thick. If using a pasta-rolling machine, cut the dough into quarters, press flat, and run each piece of pasta dough several times through the machine, adjusting the setting each time, until the pasta is ⅛–1/16 inch thick.

In a small mixing bowl, create an egg wash by whisking the remaining 2 eggs and 2 tablespoons of water together.

TO FORM AGNOLOTTI

Cut pasta dough into 4 × 4-inch squares. Place a heaping tablespoon of mushroom filling in the center of each square. Brush all four edges of each pasta square with a thin amount of egg wash. Fold pasta in a triangle and pinch closed. Continue until pasta and filling are finished. Place agnolotti pasta on a sheet pan lined with flour-dusted parchment paper.

Bring a large pot of salted water to a boil. Drop agnolotti in boiling water and cook until floating. Drain in a colander. Set aside.

FOR THE BRUSSELS SPROUT LEAVES

Split brussels sprouts in half, remove core, and separate all the leaves (the leaves are what you are using).

Heat olive oil in a sauté pan over high heat. Immediately throw in the brussels sprouts leaves

and add the salt and pepper. Toss the leaves and sauté until tender, 3–5 minutes. Remove pan from heat and set aside.

AT SERVICE

Place 2 agnolotti onto each plate. Ladle desired amount of butternut squash sauce over the agnolotti. Garnish with brussels sprout leaves and pulled ham hock. Shave desired amount of pecorino Romano cheese over pasta with a vegetable peeler.

Chef's Tip: *To cut the butternut squash easily, slice off the neck first, then slice squash in half. Cut it into 2-inch-thick rounds. Place on a cutting board and then work around it by cutting down on the exterior part of the rounds to remove skin. Peel remaining seed pocket with a vegetable peeler; scoop, and discard the seeds.*

Duck Confit and Pink Lady Apples

Candied Kumquats, Celery Root, Huckleberry Glaze

SERVES 6

This fall duck recipe brings back memories of hunting with family and friends. The acid from the apples and tart huckleberries cuts the richness of the darker duck meat and makes for a perfect pairing.

Suggested wine pairing: White Burgundy

(Preparation 2 days in advance)

For the duck confit

6 duck legs
3 tablespoons salt
1 tablespoon pepper
4 sprigs thyme
1 sprig rosemary
4 bay leaves
2 large shallots, roughly chopped
2 bulbs garlic, peeled, and roughly chopped
8 cups duck fat (substitute 8 cups of shortening)

For the apple salad

½ cup crème fraîche
½ cup mayonnaise (page 285)
2 tablespoons apple cider vinegar
1 tablespoon granulated sugar
Salt and pepper, to taste
3 Pink Lady apples, cored and thinly sliced
1 celery root, thinly sliced
1 Serrano pepper, thinly sliced
2 tablespoons chopped cilantro

For the huckleberry glaze

2½ cups balsamic vinegar
2 cups fresh huckleberries
1½ cups cranberry juice
1 cup granulated sugar
2 sticks cinnamon
½ vanilla bean, scraped

For the candied kumquats

12 kumquats, seeds removed and sliced into rounds
1 cup granulated sugar
1 cup water

For the garnish

2 serrano peppers, thinly sliced
Micro arugula

FOR THE DUCK CONFIT

Preheat oven to 275°F.

Combine the duck legs in a large mixing bowl with salt, pepper, thyme, rosemary, bay leaves, shallots, and garlic. Mix together using your hands until thoroughly incorporated. Cover bowl with plastic wrap and refrigerate (to cure) for 2 days. (Periodically mix everything together with your hands during the 2-day process.)

Remove duck legs from the refrigerator and rinse thoroughly with cold water to remove the marinade; thoroughly dry with paper towels.

Arrange duck legs in a dutch oven and cover with duck fat. Place dutch oven on stovetop and heat until boiling, then remove from heat, cover with lid, place in oven, and bake for 2 hours.

Remove from oven and cool to room temperature.

Remove bones in duck legs by twisting the bones of the leg; remove thigh and drumstick bones.

In a large nonstick skillet over medium heat, use a little duck fat and cook duck meat until crispy, about 5 minutes per side; slice legs in half.

FOR THE APPLE SALAD

Combine crème fraîche, mayonnaise, vinegar, sugar, salt, and pepper in a mixing bowl, and whisk to incorporate. Refrigerate dressing for 1 hour.

Combine apples, celery root, pepper, and cilantro in a mixing bowl. Drizzle with dressing and coat thoroughly.

FOR THE HUCKLEBERRY GLAZE

Combine all ingredients in a saucepot over medium-low heat. Stirring frequently, reduce to a syrup consistency or until mixture coats the back of a spoon. Refrigerate.

FOR THE CANDIED KUMQUATS

Place the kumquats in a large enough bowl to accommodate 2 cups of simple syrup.

Combine sugar and water in a small saucepot. Bring to a boil and immediately pour over kumquats. Cover with plastic wrap and cool to room temperature for 1 hour. Refrigerate.

AT SERVICE

Place some of the apple salad onto each plate. Top with 1 duck leg half. Drizzle the huckleberry sauce around each plate, and garnish with serranos. Top duck leg with candied kumquats and micro arugula.

Chef's Tip: *When choosing ripe kumquats, make sure the fruit is completely firm, heavy, and orange.*

Bacon-Wrapped Pork Tenderloin and Slow-Roasted Pork Shoulder

Mole Sauce, Spiced Pepper Relish, Sweet Potato Greens, Jalapeño-Cabbage Salad

SERVES 6

In many of my entrees, I like to get creative with proteins done two different ways, especially with this recipe. The bacon and the earthy mole sauce bring the tenderloin and pork shoulder together, adding an innovative Latin twist.

Suggested wine pairing: Cabernet Franc

For the slow-roasted pork shoulder

(Prepare 24 hours in advance)

1 cup BBQ spice mix, plus more for sprinkling (page 281)
¼ cup cumin/coriander spice blend (page 283)
¼ cup chile powder
5 pounds pork butt, cut into quarters
2 cups chicken stock (page 283)
Salt and pepper, to taste
½ cup apple cider vinegar
3 tablespoons light olive oil

For the bacon-wrapped tenderloin

24 slices bacon
6 (4-ounce) pieces of pork tenderloin
Salt and pepper, to taste
3 tablespoons light olive oil

For the mole sauce

3 tablespoons light olive oil
5 cloves garlic, chopped
1 Spanish onion, peeled and chopped
1 bunch green onions, chopped
1 leek, chopped
1 pasilla pepper, seeded and chopped
1 red bell pepper, seeded and chopped
½ bulb fennel, chopped

½ bunch cilantro, chopped
1 teaspoon salt
¼ cup raisins
¼ cup toasted almonds
½ tablespoon canned, chopped chipotle peppers
1 tablespoon cumin/coriander spice blend (page 283)
1 teaspoon cocoa powder
½ teaspoon instant espresso
4 cups vegetable stock (page 288)

For the jalapeño-cabbage salad

½ cup plus 2 tablespoons light olive oil, divided
1 shallot, chopped
2 cloves garlic, chopped
½ cup white distilled vinegar
1 small bay leaf
1 teaspoon cumin/coriander spice blend (page 283)
½ teaspoon hot sauce
¼ head green cabbage, thinly sliced
¼ cup mixture of green onion and cilantro, finely chopped
2 jalapeños, seeded, halved, and thinly sliced

For the sweet potato greens

2 tablespoons light olive oil
2 teaspoons finely chopped garlic
2 bunches sweet potato greens, roughly chopped
½ teaspoon salt

For the spiced pepper relish

2 tablespoons light olive oil
1 Spanish onion, peeled and finely chopped
1 tablespoon chopped garlic
1 teaspoon salt
3 red bell peppers, cored, seeded, and roughly chopped
3 pasilla peppers, peeled and roughly chopped
2 tomatillos, roughly chopped
1¼ cups vegetable stock (page 288)
1 tablespoon BBQ spice mix (page 281)
2 tablespoons red wine vinegar

For the plantain chips

1 tablespoon granulated sugar
1 teaspoon cinnamon
½ teaspoon cayenne pepper
1 teaspoon paprika
1 teaspoon salt
1 plantain, thinly sliced

For the garnish

2 jalapeños, seeded and thinly sliced
2 scallions, thinly sliced

FOR THE SLOW-ROASTED PORK SHOULDER

Preheat oven to 325°F.

In a small mixing bowl, combine BBQ spice, cumin/coriander, and chile powder. Rub spices onto all sides of the pork, then place pork on a rack in a shallow roasting pan.

Pour chicken stock into the bottom of the roasting pan and cover pan tightly with foil. Cook pork until tender, about 3 hours.

When tender, roughly chop the pork and place it in a large mixing bowl. Season the meat with salt, pepper, and vinegar, and combine thoroughly.

Line a 1½-quart cast-iron blue terrine mold with plastic (may substitute a loaf pan of equal size). Pack the pork mixture inside the terrine and fold plastic wrap tightly over it (wrapping the plastic wrap completely around all sides of the terrine). Place a full wine bottle (or similar weight) on top of the terrine and chill in the refrigerator overnight.

Just before service, unwrap the pork from the terrine and cut it into ½-inch-thick slices. Sprinkle more BBQ spice mix over the presentation side of the tenderloin.

Heat olive oil in a large skillet over medium-high heat, add the pork slices (spice side down), and cook until slightly crispy (be careful not to burn the spices). Flip the pork slices over and continue cooking until completely warmed through, about 10 minutes.

FOR THE BACON-WRAPPED TENDERLOIN

Place 4 slices of bacon on a work surface, overlapping them slightly. Put 1 tenderloin on top of the bacon and roll up tightly. Repeat steps for the other tenderloins.

Preheat oven to 350°F.

Season the tenderloins with salt and pepper.

Heat olive oil in a large ovenproof sauté pan over high heat. Add the tenderloins, seam side down, to the pan. (This is where the bacon comes together around the pork, which helps the proteins stick to the bacon and seals it during the searing process so it won't unravel.) Turn the tenderloins and crisp the bacon all sides. Cook tenderloins to desired doneness, about 5 minutes for medium rare. Cut tenderloins into 3 pieces each.

FOR THE MOLE SAUCE

Heat olive oil in a saucepot over medium-high heat. Add garlic, onions, leek, pasilla pepper, red bell pepper, fennel, cilantro, and salt. Cook the vegetables until soft, 20–25 minutes.

Add raisins, almonds, chipotle peppers, cumin/coriander, cocoa, espresso, and stock. Cook over medium heat until thick, about 30 minutes.

Remove mixture from heat, add to a blender, and process until smooth.

FOR THE JALAPEÑO-CABBAGE SALAD

Heat 2 tablespoons of olive oil in a sauté pan over medium-high heat. Add shallot and garlic. Cook until translucent, about 5 minutes.

Add vinegar, bay leaf, cumin/coriander, and hot sauce. Simmer over low heat for about 10 minutes.

Prepare an ice bath by nesting a medium bowl in a larger bowl that's partially filled with ice and water. Place mixture into the medium bowl and stir until chilled.

FOR THE SWEET POTATO GREENS

Heat olive oil in a large sauté pan over medium heat. Add garlic and cook until fragrant.

Add greens and salt, lightly toss, and cook greens until wilted.

FOR THE SPICED PEPPER RELISH

Heat olive oil in a saucepot over medium heat. Add onion, garlic, and salt, and sauté until translucent.

Add peppers, tomatillos, vegetable stock, BBQ spice, and vinegar. Cook, stirring often, until all moisture has evaporated and vegetables are dry, 30–45 minutes.

FOR THE PLANTAIN CHIPS

In a small mixing bowl, combine sugar, cinnamon, pepper, paprika, and salt.

Heat a deep fryer to 350°F. Fry the plantain slices until crispy, remove from oil, and place on a plate lined with paper towels. Sprinkle with spices.

AT SERVICE

Ladle mole sauce onto the center of each plate. Place 1 pork slice to one side of each plate, and top it with the jalapeño-cabbage salad and jalapeños. Place 3 mounds of the sweet potato greens onto each plate, and top each with 1 tenderloin. Top tenderloins with spiced pepper relish and scallions. Garnish plate with plantain chips.

Chef's Tip: *You can find sweet potato greens seasonally at many farmers' markets. However, feel free to use any fall green, such as collard greens or swiss chard.*

Remove bay leaf, add mixture to a blender, and process until smooth. With blender set at a low speed, slowly drizzle in ½ cup olive oil. Process until smooth and set aside.

Combine cabbage, onion, cilantro, and jalapeños in a mixing bowl, add some of the vinaigrette, and lightly toss.

Pan-Roasted Local White Sea Bass with Jewel Yams

Apple and Dungeness Crab Salad, Wilted Swiss Chard,
Honey-Ginger Yam Sauce

SERVES 6

In this recipe, I like to counter the sweetness of the yams by using a tart Granny Smith apple. The acidity of the apple helps cut the richness of the braised yams. I like to use a local white sea bass for this recipe, but I also like striped bass, sustainable Chilean sea bass, hake, or Pacific white sea bass.

Suggested wine pairing: Austrian Gruner Veltiner

For the yams and honey-ginger yam sauce

6 cups apple cider
1 cup brown sugar
¼ cup honey
¼ cup maple syrup
1 (2-inch) piece ginger, cut into 4 rounds
4 cups peeled, medium diced yams
4 tablespoons cold butter, divided
Salt and pepper, to taste

For the swiss chard

1 tablespoon light olive oil
1 tablespoon butter
1 tablespoon finely minced shallots
1 tablespoon finely minced garlic
6 cups roughly chopped swiss chard leaves
Salt and pepper, to taste

For the apple and Dungeness crab salad

1½ cups fresh lump crabmeat
2 Granny Smith apples, thinly sliced
House vinaigrette, to taste (page 285)
1 tablespoon finely chopped cilantro
1 tablespoon finely chopped mint

For the sea bass

6 (5-ounce) local white sea bass fillets
Salt and pepper, to taste
3 tablespoons light olive oil

For the garnish

1 lemon, for drizzling

FOR THE YAMS AND HONEY-GINGER YAM SAUCE

Combine cider, sugar, honey, syrup, and ginger in a saucepot. Simmer on low heat for 15 minutes.

Add yams and continue simmering until yams are soft, about 20 minutes.

Remove yams to a bowl and cool to room temperature.

Remove ginger pieces from the saucepot and discard.

Over medium-high heat, reduce remaining sauce to a syrup consistency or until it coats the back of a spoon, about 30 minutes. Reserve.

Melt 2 tablespoons of butter in a large sauté pan over medium heat. Add cooked yams and ½ cup of yam sauce. Bring to a boil, then reduce to low heat.

Simmer mixture until it resembles a glaze, about 5 minutes. Stir in remaining 2 tablespoons of butter, and season with salt and pepper.

FOR THE SWISS CHARD

Heat olive oil in a large sauté pan over high heat. Add butter, shallots, and garlic, and cook until fragrant. Add chard and sauté until wilted. Season with salt and pepper.

FOR THE APPLE AND DUNGENESS CRAB SALAD

In a large mixing bowl, combine the crab and apples, Add vinaigrette and lightly toss, making sure to not break up the crabmeat. Add cilantro and mint, and gently incorporate.

FOR THE SEA BASS

Preheat oven to 350°F.

Season sea bass on both sides with salt and pepper.

Heat olive oil in a large sauté pan over high heat. Add sea bass and reduce heat to medium high. Sear until lightly golden brown, 2–3 minutes per side, or until cooked through.

AT SERVICE

Squeeze fresh lemon juice over sea bass. Forming a small mound, add swiss chard to the center of each plate and place yams on top. Place 1 piece of sea bass on top of the yams. Distribute the crab and apple salad on top of the sea bass. Drizzle some of the yam sauce around the plate.

Chef's Tip: *Depending on the size of the fish, cooking times may need to be adjusted.*

Mesquite-Grilled Venison Loin
with Roasted Pears and Gorgonzola Butter

Sautéed Italian Black Kale, Crispy Yam Cakes, Poached Pear Sauce

SERVES 6

There's no better way to prepare a venison loin than cooking it to perfection over a fire-hot mesquite grill. I recommend purchasing deer steaks that are the backstrap and tenderloin as they are lean, tender, and free of sinew. Traditionally paired with fruit, venison tastes even better when paired with roasted sweet pears.

Suggested wine pairing: Shiraz

For the venison loin chops

6 (6-ounce) venison loin chops

For the pears and poached pear sauce

1 bottle (750 ml) Gewürztraminer wine
4 cups unfiltered apple juice
1 cup cranberry juice
¼ cup honey
2 sticks cinnamon
5 star anise
1 tablespoon coriander seeds
1 teaspoon cloves
½ vanilla bean, split
¼ cup butter, diced
3 pears (firm but ripe), peeled, cored, and cut in half

For the sautéed Italian black kale

3 tablespoons light olive oil
½ cup finely chopped pork
2 bunches Italian black kale, stems and leaves
    coarsely chopped
3 cloves garlic, finely sliced
Salt and pepper, to taste

For the yam cakes

1 pound yams, peeled, medium diced
Light olive oil, for coating yams, plus more for frying
Salt and pepper, to taste
2 cups chopped cremini mushrooms
2 egg yolks
4 tablespoons grated Parmigiana Reggiano

1 tablespoon fines herbes (page 285)
1 teaspoon toasted ground fennel (page 287)
2 cups all-purpose flour
4 eggs, whisked well
2 cups panko bread crumbs
Canola oil, for frying

For the Gorgonzola butter

½ cup butter, softened and diced
Pinch of salt
½ teaspoon lemon zest
½ cup crumbled Gorgonzola
1 clove garlic, finely minced

FOR THE VENISON LOIN CHOPS

Preheat an outdoor grill (with mesquite chips) to high heat. Lay the venison chops on a grill rack coated with cooking spray. Cook chops to desired doneness.

FOR THE PEARS AND POACHED PEAR SAUCE

Add wine, juices, honey, cinnamon, anise, coriander seeds, cloves, and vanilla bean to a large saucepot. Bring to a boil and simmer for 30 minutes. Strain ingredients through a fine-mesh sieve into a large bowl. Reserve.

Preheat oven to 350°F.

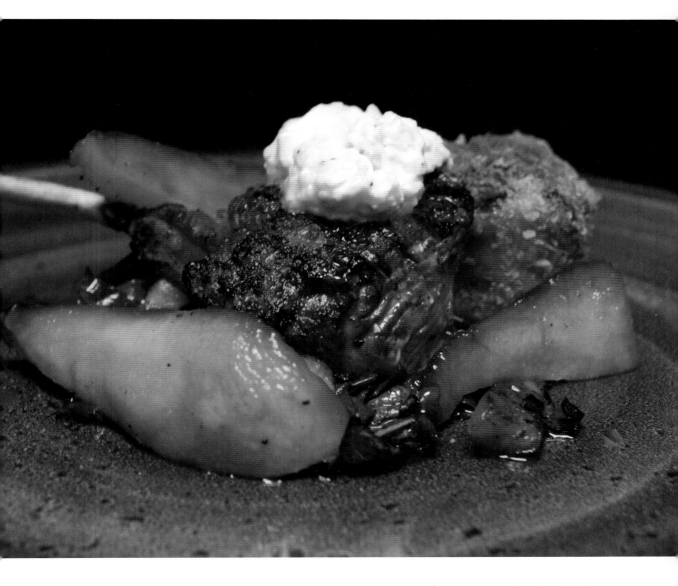

Add some of the poached pear sauce to the bottom of a large baking dish. Scatter the butter around the pear sauce. Arrange the pears, face side down, in the baking dish. Pour more of the pear sauce over the pears.

Roast pears, continuously basting, until the pears are soft. Remove pears from oven and slice each half into three slices each.

FOR THE SAUTÉED ITALIAN BLACK KALE

Heat olive oil in a large saucepan over medium-high heat. Add pork and cook until crispy.

Bring pan to high heat, add the kale, and toss to combine. Cook kale until slightly wilted, 5–10 minutes.

Add garlic and season with salt and pepper.

FOR THE YAM CAKES

Preheat oven to 350°F.

Add yams to a large mixing bowl, drizzle with olive oil, and season with salt and pepper. Arrange the yams on a large baking sheet. Roast until tender, about 15 minutes. Remove from oven and cool to room temperature.

Heat olive oil in a large sauté pan set over medium heat. Add mushrooms and cook until all moisture has evaporated, about 10–15 minutes. Remove mushrooms from heat and cool at room temperature.

In a large mixing bowl, combine yams and mushrooms. Add egg yolks, Parmigiana Reggiano, fines herbes, and fennel; gently combine. With your hands, form 6 yam cakes.

Set up 3 mixing bowls. Place flour in one, whisked eggs in another, and bread crumbs in the third.

Dredge yam cakes (one at a time) in flour, dip in egg to coat, then roll quickly in the bread crumbs.

Add enough oil for frying to a large cast-iron skillet (about 2 inches deep). Preheat the oil in the pan slowly, over a low flame to a medium heat. Fry yam cakes on each side until golden brown.

FOR THE GORGONZOLA BUTTER

Add butter to a large mixing bowl and whisk until creamy, then add salt, garlic, and lemon zest. Gently fold in the crumbled Gorgonzola, and incorporate thoroughly.

AT SERVICE

Place the Italian kale in the center of each plate. Place one yam cake to one side of the kale. Place one venison chop on top of the kale. Arrange three sliced pears around the venison chop. Top the venison chop with a dollop of Gorgonzola butter.

Chef's Tip: *To test if the oil temperature is ready for frying, take a few bread crumbs and drop them in the oil as it's heating. If the bread crumbs burn or the oil starts smoking, then it's too hot. If the bread crumbs are frying and turning light brown, the oil is ready.*

Chef's Tip: *I like to use a cast-iron pan for frying because it creates a nice and even retained heat.*

Cilantro Marinated Cabrilla Grouper and Curried Vegetable Saffron Tortellini

Sesame-Garlic Broccoli, Grilled Calamari Salad, Carrot-Coconut Emulsion

SERVES 6 / YIELDS 1½ POUNDS PASTA DOUGH

A simple salad of grilled calamari over sesame-garlic broccoli makes this light fish dish exceptionally vibrant. The coconut-carrot emulsion covers a curried vegetable tortellini for a rich and creamy dish.

Suggested wine pairing: Dry Furmint

For the cilantro marinated grouper

3 tablespoons plus ½ cup light olive oil, divided
2 scallions, roughly chopped
2 tablespoons roughly chopped garlic
1 tablespoon roughly chopped ginger
2 cups cilantro leaves
½ cup unseasoned rice wine vinegar
½ teaspoon salt
6 (5-ounce) grouper fillets

For the tortellini filling

3 tablespoons light olive oil
1 tablespoon finely chopped garlic
1 tablespoon finely chopped ginger
1 cup small diced potatoes
1 cup roughly chopped cauliflower
1 cup small diced rutabaga
½ pasilla pepper, small diced
1 teaspoon salt
½ cup coconut milk
1 teaspoon curry powder
¼ cup roughly chopped cilantro

For the saffron pasta

½ cup water plus 2 tablespoons water
½ teaspoon saffron threads
5 large eggs, divided
3 cups all-purpose flour, more if needed
¼ cup light olive oil
2 tablespoons water
Salt, to taste

For the carrot-coconut emulsion

2 tablespoons light olive oil
1 Spanish onion, peeled and sliced
1 cup roughly chopped celery
10 cloves garlic, roughly chopped
1 (2-inch) piece ginger, finely chopped
1 (3-inch) piece lemongrass, crushed
1 teaspoon cumin
1 teaspoon dark mustard seed
1 tablespoon coriander
3 star anise
½ teaspoon fenugreek
2 roughly chopped bird's eye chiles
3 cups carrot juice
1 cup coconut milk
1 tablespoon soy sauce
2 tablespoons unseasoned rice wine vinegar
1 teaspoon fish sauce
1 bay leaf

For the grilled calamari salad

1 pound calamari (tubes and tentacles)
2 tablespoons fish sauce
Juice of 1 lime
½ cup sweet chile sauce
1 tablespoon soy sauce

For the sesame-garlic broccoli

4 cups broccoli (florets and stalks)
4 tablespoons light olive oil
Salt, to taste
Pepper, to taste
Chile flakes, to taste
1 tablespoon finely minced garlic
1 teaspoon sesame oil, for drizzling
1 tablespoon toasted sesame seeds, for garnish

FOR THE CILANTRO MARINATED GROUPER

Heat 3 tablespoons of olive oil in a small sauté pan over medium heat. Add scallions, garlic, and ginger. Cook until fragrant and soft, about 2 minutes. Remove from heat and allow mixture to cool to room temperature.

Combine mixture in a blender with cilantro, remaining ½ cup olive oil, vinegar, and salt. Process until smooth.

Place fillets in a large mixing bowl, add marinade, and gently rub the marinade over all the fish until fully coated. Transfer fish to a shallow baking dish and cover with plastic wrap. Marinate fillets in the refrigerator for 1–2 hours.

Preheat an indoor or outdoor grill pan to medium high. Lay the fillets on a grill rack coated with cooking spray. Grill until fish flakes easily when tested with a fork, about 4 minutes per side.

FOR THE TORTELLINI FILLING

Heat olive oil in sauté pan over medium heat. Add garlic and ginger and, stirring constantly, sauté for 30 seconds.

Add potatoes, cauliflower, rutabaga, pepper, and salt. Stir gently and cook until tender, 10–15 minutes.

In a small mixing bowl, combine coconut milk and curry powder and whisk until thoroughly combined.

Add the coconut milk mixture and cilantro to the cooked vegetable mixture. Cook for 2–3 minutes until the vegetables have absorbed all the milk. Remove vegetables from heat and chill in the refrigerator.

FOR THE SAFFRON PASTA

In a small saucepot combine ½ cup water with saffron threads. Bring to simmer over low heat and cook until saffron is bright yellow in color.

Remove saucepot from heat, place it in a bowl of ice, and cool. Add 3 eggs into the pot and whisk vigorously until creamy.

Place flour in a stand mixer with dough hook attachment in place. Add saffron-egg mixture and olive oil. Process until a soft dough forms, 1–2 minutes.

Turn the dough onto a lightly floured surface and knead by hand until it's smooth, soft, and stretchy, 1–2 minutes.

Wrap dough in plastic wrap, and let it rest at room temperature for 30 minutes.

If rolling pasta dough by hand, cut the dough into quarters and, using a rolling pin, roll out the dough until it is ⅛–1/16 inch thick. If using a pasta-rolling machine, cut the dough into quarters, press flat, and run each piece of pasta dough several times through the machine, adjusting the setting each time, until the pasta is ⅛–1/16 inch thick.

In a small bowl, create an egg wash by whisking remaining 2 eggs and 2 tablespoons water together.

Cut the pasta sheet into rounds using a 3-inch round cutter.

Place 1 teaspoon of tortellini filling in the middle of each round of pasta. With a pastry brush, moisten edges of pasta with egg wash. Fold the dough over to form a half moon, then draw the two corners together to form a rounded bonnet shape. Continue until pasta and filling are finished. Place tortellinis on a sheet pan lined with parchment paper dusted with flour.

Bring a large pot of salted water to a boil. Drop tortellini in boiling water and cook until floating. Drain in a colander.

FOR THE CARROT-COCONUT EMULSION

Heat olive oil in a saucepot over medium-high heat. Add onion, celery, garlic, ginger, lemongrass, cumin, mustard seed, coriander, star anise, fenugreek, and chiles. Sauté until tender, 4–8 minutes.

Add carrot juice, coconut milk, soy sauce, vinegar, fish sauce, and bay leaf. Simmer on low heat for about 15 minutes.

Strain mixture through a fine-mesh sieve, add to a blender, and process until smooth. Just before serving, return emulsion to its original saucepot, warm over low heat, and immersion blend.

FOR THE GRILLED CALAMARI SALAD

In a large mixing bowl, combine all ingredients. Cover bowl with plastic wrap and refrigerate for 2 hours.

Preheat oven to broil.

Place calamari on a broiler pan and cook for about 2 minutes per side.

FOR THE SESAME-GARLIC BROCCOLI

Bring a large pot of salted water to a boil. Add broccoli florets and stalks and blanch for 2–3 minutes. Remove broccoli to a bowl of ice and water, than remove broccoli to a plate lined with paper towels.

Heat olive oil in a large sauté pan over high heat. Add broccoli and cook until caramelized.

Season the broccoli with salt, pepper, and chile flakes. Remove from heat, add garlic, and lightly toss. Drizzle with some of the sesame oil and garnish with sesame seeds.

AT SERVICE

Place broccoli on each plate. Ladle the carrot-coconut emulsion around the broccoli. Place the tortellini around the broccoli and add some more of the carrot-coconut emulsion. Place a grouper fillet on top of the broccoli and then add calamari to the top.

Chef's Tip: *Crush the lemongrass with the back of a knife on your cutting board. Hit it hard and smash it. This releases the oils and flavor.*

Chef's Tip: *For this recipe you can use any firm, meaty white fish.*

Chef's Tip: *Blanching is a great way to precook vegetables to be added to sautés and stir-fries.*

Cast-Iron-Seared Yellowtail and Crispy Shrimp Tempura

Stir-Fried Vegetables, Scallion and Sweet Pepper Salad, Ginger-Soy Emulsion

SERVES 6

For this recipe I like to use fresh local spot prawns; however, fresh Mexican white shrimp out of the Gulf of Mexico are abundant in San Diego during the season and are an excellent substitute.

Suggested wine pairing: Off-Dry German Riesling

For the yellowtail

1½ pounds yellowtail loin, cut into 18 medallions
Light olive oil, more for coating yellowtail
Salt, for seasoning
2 tablespoons togarashi spice (substitute 1 tablespoon of paprika and 1 tablespoon cayenne)

For the shrimp tempura

18 fresh Mexican white shrimp (size 26/30), peeled, tails left on
1 cup all-purpose flour
1 cup cornstarch
1 tablespoon baking powder
¼ teaspoon salt
1½ cups soda water
2 tablespoons vodka
2 cups panko bread crumbs

For the stir-fried vegetables

2 bunches broccolini, cut into 1-inch pieces
2 large carrots, finely diced
2 red bell peppers, finely diced
6 tablespoons light olive oil, divided
½ teaspoon finely chopped garlic
½ teaspoon finely chopped ginger
1 teaspoon soy sauce
Pinch of chile flakes

For the Thai chile aioli

Base aioli (page 281)
1 tablespoon hot sauce

For the ginger-soy emulsion

3 tablespoons light olive oil
5 cloves garlic, finely chopped
1 (½-inch) piece ginger
1 Spanish onion, peeled and finely chopped
3 scallions, finely chopped
½ bunch cilantro, finely chopped
½ tablespoon cumin/coriander spice blend (page 283)
1 bird's eye chile, finely chopped
4 cups tsuyu sauce
½ tablespoon unseasoned rice wine vinegar
2 cups softened butter

For the scallion and sweet pepper salad

2 bunches of scallions (green part only)
1 red bell pepper

For the garnish

Sesame oil, for drizzling

FOR THE YELLOWTAIL

Arrange the yellowtail medallions on a large baking sheet. Rub a small amount of olive oil on each side of the fish, sprinkle both sides with salt, and sprinkle the presentation side with togarashi.

Heat a large cast-iron pan over high heat. Sear yellowtail until rare, about 20 seconds per side.

FOR THE SHRIMP TEMPURA

Using a sharp knife, make 3–4 "x" marks about a quarter of the way through each shrimp. If you cut deep enough you will see the shrimp loosen up and straighten out flat. This ensures that the shrimp isn't curled up after it's deep-fried.

Combine flour, cornstarch, baking powder, and salt in a large mixing bowl. Add the water and vodka and gently whisk until just incorporated.

Dredge shrimp in the tempura, then roll in the bread crumbs. Fry in 365°F oil until golden brown, about 2–3 minutes.

FOR THE STIR-FRIED VEGETABLES

Combine broccolini, carrots, and peppers in a large mixing bowl, and toss to combine.

Heat olive oil in a large sauté pan over high heat. Add vegetables, garlic, ginger, soy sauce, and chile flakes. Toss for 1 minute. Add soy sauce, keep tossing, and remove from heat.

FOR THE THAI CHILE AIOLI

Combine aioli and hot sauce in a mixing bowl.

FOR THE GINGER-SOY EMULSION

Heat olive oil in a large saucepot over low heat. Add garlic, ginger, onions, and scallions, and cook until onions are translucent.

Add cilantro, cumin/coriander, chile, and tsuyu, and simmer for 15–20 minutes.

Add vinegar and butter and immersion blend until creamy.

FOR THE SCALLION AND SWEET PEPPER SALAD

Lay the scallions out vertically on a cutting board. Cut at a 45-degree angle to create long strips. Submerge in ice water for 15 minutes and remove to a plate lined with paper towels.

Core and remove seeds from the red bell pepper, and slice into very thin strips. Submerge peppers in ice water for 15 minutes and remove to a plate lined with paper towels.

Combine scallions and peppers in a bowl.

AT SERVICE

Place 3 small mounds of sir-fried vegetables on each plate. Top each mound with 1 yellowtail medallion. Place scallions and sweet pepper salad on top of the fish with a dollop of aioli. Drizzle ginger-soy emulsion around the plate. Place 1 shrimp on top of each yellowtail medallion and add a drizzle of sesame oil.

Chef's Tip: *Choose fresh, bright green broccolini, and store it in a tightly sealed plastic bag or container inside the refrigerator until ready to use.*

Rosemary-Roasted Game Hen
and Mushroom Duxelle–Stuffed Leg

Kabocha Squash, Wilted Swiss Chard, Sage Brown Butter Sauce

SERVES 6

Rosemary-roasted game hens paired with kabocha squash rubbed with butter and brown sugar provide the perfect fall evening meal with your family. If you get kabocha squash at the height of the season, very little needs to be done to it because it's naturally sweet, creamy, and flavorful.

Suggested wine pairing: Red Burgundy

For the kabocha squash

2 kabocha squash, quartered, seeds removed
½ cup butter, softened
½ cup brown sugar
Salt and pepper, to taste

For the game hens

3 game hens, breasts and legs removed
Salt and pepper, to taste
4 tablespoons light olive oil
2 tablespoons butter
3 sprigs rosemary
5 cloves garlic, peeled
¼ cup Dijon mustard
Mushroom duxelle (page 286)
4 tablespoons light olive oil

For the sage brown butter sauce

8 tablespoons unsalted butter
6 garlic cloves, peeled and smashed with
    the side of a knife
1 sprig sage
3 cups brown chicken stock (page 282)
1 teaspoon lemon juice
2 tablespoons fines herbes (page 285)

For the wilted swiss chard

2 tablespoons light olive oil
2 teaspoons finely chopped garlic
2 bunches swiss chard, roughly chopped
½ teaspoon salt

For the garnish

Light olive oil, for coating pan
18 sage leaves
Salt and pepper, to taste

FOR THE KABOCHA SQUASH

Preheat oven to 350°F.

Rub cut surfaces of the squash liberally with butter and sprinkle with sugar, salt, and pepper.

Roast skin side down until soft, about 1 hour.

Remove squash from oven, scoop the flesh into a small bowl, and lightly mash with the back of a fork (adjust to taste with butter, salt, and pepper). Cover with foil and reserve.

FOR THE GAME HENS

Preheat oven to 350°F.

Season game hen breasts with salt and pepper. Heat olive oil in a large ovenproof sauté pan over high heat. Place breasts in pan, skin side down, and sear until golden brown, but not cooked through.

Flip the breasts over, reduce heat to low, and add butter, rosemary, and garlic to the pan. Baste the breasts with the butter-oil-herb mixture for 3-5 minutes, then place in oven and bake until cooked through, about 10 minutes.

Remove from pan and allow meat to rest, about 5 minutes. Cut the breasts into slices.

Remove bones from the game hen legs without cutting through the meat or skin.

Smear mustard into the thigh cavity, season with salt and pepper, and stuff the thigh cavity with mushroom duxelle.

Pull the thigh skin and meat around the duxelle. Using butcher twine, tie the legs together to prevent them from opening.

Heat olive oil in a large ovenproof sauté pan over high heat. Place legs in pan and brown on all sides, about 5 minutes.

Place pan in oven and bake legs until cooked through, 10–15 minutes. Slice the duxelle-stuffed boneless portion of each leg into 3 medallions.

FOR THE SAGE BROWN BUTTER SAUCE

Prepare an ice bath by nesting a medium bowl in a larger bowl that's partially filled with ice and water.

Combine butter, garlic, and sage in a small sauté pan over high heat. Heat butter until it turns a dark golden brown color and exudes a nutty aroma (don't burn).

Quickly strain the brown butter through a fine-mesh sieve into the prepared mixing bowl on ice. Stir until the butter hardens.

Add stock to a small saucepot over medium-high heat and reduce by half its volume.

Add the brown butter a little at a time, and immersion blend until all the butter is added and emulsified.

Add lemon juice and fines herbes, and thoroughly incorporate.

FOR THE WILTED SWISS CHARD

Heat olive oil in a large sauté pan over medium heat. Add garlic and cook until just fragrant.

Add swiss chard and salt. Toss lightly and cook until just wilted.

FOR THE GARNISH

Heat olive oil in a small sauté pan (about 2 inches from the bottom) to 375°F.

Add sage leaves and fry until they stop bubbling. Remove to a plate lined with paper towels and season with salt and pepper.

AT SERVICE

Using two large spoons quinelle the kabocha squash. Arrange to the left of each plate. On the right side of the plates, add a line of swiss chard. Shingle 4 slices of game hen breast against the kabocha squash. Shingle 3 mushroom duxelle medallions on top of the swiss chard. Spoon the brown butter sauce over breast and medallions. Garnish with sage leaves.

Chef's Tip: *This recipe would also be great with squab or quail.*

Braised Beef Cheek and Mac 'n' Cheese

Cavatappi Pasta, Beef Cheek Reduction, Sautéed Broccolini

SERVES 6

The name "beef cheek" refers to the facial cheek muscle of a cow. Since it is a very tough and lean cut of meat, I like to slow cook it in the oven at low heat for a rich, deep flavor and a meltingly fork-tender result. Since it's often necessary to order beef cheeks ahead of time, I suggest checking with your local butcher before planning this dish.

Suggested wine pairing: Barolo

For the braised beef cheek and reduction

6 beef cheeks (about 5 pounds), large diced
Salt and pepper, to taste
5 tablespoons light olive oil
2 cups roughly chopped Spanish onion
1 cup roughly chopped carrots
2 cups roughly chopped celery
2 bottles red wine
6 cups demi-glace (page 284)
1 herb sachet (page 285)

For the mac 'n' cheese

½ cup finely chopped bacon
1½ cup small diced onion
1 tablespoon finely minced garlic
1 cup white wine
1 bay leaf
16 ounces cavatappi pasta, cooked according to labeled instructions
4 cups heavy cream
1 tablespoon Aleppo pepper flakes (substitute chile flakes)
1 cup shredded gruyère cheese
2 cups shredded fontina cheese
1 cup shredded aged white cheddar
Salt, to taste
3 tablespoons fines herbs (page 285)

For the breadcrumb topping

2 cups panko bread crumbs
½ cup finely grated Parmigiana Reggiano
Zest of 1 lemon

1 tablespoon paprika
¼ cup melted butter
Salt and pepper, to taste

For the sautéed broccolini

2 tablespoons light olive oil
2 teaspoons finely chopped garlic
2 bunches broccolini, roughly chopped
½ teaspoon salt

FOR THE BRAISED BEEF CHEEK AND REDUCTION

Preheat oven to 275°F.

Using a very sharp knife, trim the extra fat and the tough silverskin from the beef cheeks and season with salt and pepper.

Warm olive oil in a large ovenproof saucepot over high heat. Sear beef cheeks on both sides until golden brown. Remove to a large bowl and reserve.

Pour out half the fat from the saucepot and return pot to high heat.

Add onions, carrots, and celery and sauté vegetables until slightly caramelized.

Add beef cheeks back to the pot and combine with the wine, demi-glace, and sachet. Bring to a boil. Cover, remove from heat, and braise beef cheeks in the oven until fork tender, about 3 hours.

Remove the cheeks from the liquid to a large plate and reserve.

Place the saucepot over medium heat; reduce remaining liquid to a sauce consistency or until it coats the back of a spoon.

FOR THE MAC 'N' CHEESE

Cook the bacon in a large saucepot pot over medium heat until it starts releasing some of its fat. Add onions and cook until translucent.

Add garlic and cook until fragrant, about 2 minutes. Add the wine and bay leaf, and cook for 5 minutes or until liquid is reduced by half its volume.

Add the pasta and toss until well combined.

Add the cream and pepper flakes and bring to a boil.

Add the cheeses and reduce to low heat. Using a wooden spoon, gently combine cheeses until fully melted.

Season with salt and garnish with fines herbes.

FOR THE BREADCRUMB TOPPING

Preheat oven to 325°F.

Combine bread crumbs in a large mixing bowl with Parmigiana Reggiano, lemon zest, and paprika. Add butter, salt, and pepper. Spread mixture onto a baking sheet lined with parchment paper. Bake until golden brown and crispy, 10–15 minutes.

FOR THE SAUTÉED BROCCOLINI

Heat olive oil in a large sauté pan over medium heat. Add garlic and cook until just fragrant. Add broccolini and salt, and toss lightly. Cook until just wilted.

AT SERVICE

Place a small mound of mac 'n' cheese in the center of each plate. Top each mound with 1 beef cheek. Spoon some of the reduction on top of each beef cheek, and top that with the broccolini. Sprinkle with bread crumbs.

Pumpkin Bread Pudding Soufflé

Pepita-Oat Streusel, Brown Sugar Bourbon Ice Cream,
Raisin Puree with Caramel Sauce

SERVES 8

In this dessert I combine the comfort of bread pudding with the lightness of a soufflé, while adding a staple fall ingredient—pumpkin. Incorporating crunch to the pudding with the pepita streusel is a great way to add a completely different complementary flavor profile. The spike of bourbon in the ice cream plays well with the spices and gives an added appreciation of being warm on a chilly night. Try this dish as a break from your pumpkin pie routine next holiday season.

Suggested wine pairing: Bual Madeira

For the pumpkin bread pudding soufflé

1 medium sugar pumpkin
Butter and granulated sugar, for dusting bowls
8 slices challah or brioche bread, cut into
    ½-inch cubes
1 cup whole milk
1 cup heavy cream
¼ cup, plus 3 tablespoons butter
¾ cup brown sugar
⅛ teaspoon kosher salt
1 teaspoon ground cinnamon
⅛ teaspoon ground cardamom
⅛ teaspoon ground cloves
⅛ teaspoon ground nutmeg
4 egg yolks
2 egg whites
1 tablespoon granulated sugar

For the pepita-oat streusel

¼ cup all-purpose flour
¼ cup rolled oats
¼ cup pepitas
¼ cup light brown sugar
¼ teaspoon ground cinnamon
¼ teaspoon kosher salt
3 tablespoons cold butter, cut into ½-inch squares

For the brown sugar bourbon ice cream

3 cups whole milk
1 cup heavy cream
12 egg yolks
1¼ cups dark brown sugar
1 teaspoon vanilla extract
Pinch of kosher salt
3 tablespoons bourbon

For the raisin puree

½ cup dark raisins
½ cup water

For the caramel sauce

½ cup granulated sugar
1 tablespoon corn syrup
3 tablespoons water
6 tablespoons heavy cream
2 teaspoons butter
¼ teaspoon kosher salt

FOR THE PUMPKIN BREAD PUDDING SOUFFLÉ

Preheat oven to 400°F.

Cut pumpkin in half from top to bottom, remove seeds, and place pumpkin on a baking sheet lined with parchment paper. Roast until very soft, 30–40 minutes.

Cool slightly. Remove the flesh with a large spoon and discard skin. Add pumpkin flesh to a food processor while it's still warm, and process until smooth. Reserve 1 cup for recipe.

Turn oven temperature down to 350°F.

Butter and sugar eight 8-ounce bowls; shake out any excess sugar.

Add bread cubes to a small mixing bowl.

In a small saucepot, combine milk and cream. Bring to a simmer over low heat. Remove from heat and pour half of the liquid over the bread cubes.

In a mixer with paddle attachment in place, mix the butter, brown sugar, and salt until light and fluffy, about 5 minutes.

Add cinnamon, cardamom, cloves, nutmeg, and egg yolks. Beat well, scraping bowl twice.

Add pumpkin puree and remainder of the heated cream and milk. Stir slowly until well combined. Fold the soaked bread cubes into the pumpkin mixture.

In a large mixing bowl, combine the egg whites and sugar. Beat until stiff peaks form, then gently fold into the pumpkin batter.

Divide the batter into the prepared bowls. Place the bowls into a pan with sides big enough to hold puddings and pour enough hot water to come halfway up sides of bowls. Carefully transfer to oven and bake until puddings have slightly risen and tops are browned, 35–40 minutes. Serve warm.

FOR THE PEPITA-OAT STREUSEL

Preheat oven to 350°F.

In a food processor, combine flour, oats, pepitas, brown sugar, cinnamon, and salt. Pulse three or four times until mixture is roughly chopped, about 3 seconds.

Transfer mixture to an electric mixer with paddle attachment in place. Add cold butter and mix on medium speed until mixture starts to combine in a crumbly texture.

Sprinkle streusel onto a baking sheet lined with parchment paper. Bake streusel until it turns golden brown and toasted, about 15 minutes, but move it with a spatula every 4 minutes to prevent it from clumping together.

Remove from oven and cool to room temperature.

FOR THE BROWN SUGAR BOURBON ICE CREAM

Make an ice bath by nesting a medium bowl in a larger bowl that's partially filled with ice and water.

Combine milk and cream in a medium saucepot and bring just to boiling point and then reduce heat to scald.

In a mixing bowl, whisk together egg yolks and brown sugar, about 1 minute. Gradually add some of the hot cream/milk mixture while continually whisking.

Scrape the yolk mixture back into the saucepot containing the remaining cream/milk mixture, and cook on low heat, stirring with a wooden spoon, until mixture slightly thickens and coats the back of the spoon.

Remove from heat and whisk in vanilla and salt. Immersion blend for 10 seconds, then strain through a fine-mesh sieve into a prepared ice bath.

Stir mixture gently until fully chilled, then add in bourbon and transfer to refrigerator to rest overnight.

Freeze mixture in an ice-cream maker according to the labeled instructions.

FOR THE RAISIN PUREE

Combine raisins and water in a small saucepot. Bring to boil over medium heat, cover, and turn down to a simmer. Cook until raisins are very soft, about 20 minutes.

Remove cover and slightly reduce liquid for 5 minutes.

Let cool to room temperature, then transfer to a blender and puree until very smooth, scraping down sides if needed. Chill in the refrigerator.

FOR THE CARAMEL SAUCE

Bring sugar, corn syrup, and water to a boil over medium heat. Brushing sides of pot with water, clear sugar from the sides of the pot twice. Continue to boil until sugar starts to caramelize and turns a medium/dark amber color.

Slowly whisk in cream in three stages. Whisk in butter and salt, bring to a boil, and immediately remove from heat. Cool to room temperature.

AT SERVICE

Place one warm pudding soufflé on a plate; pour 1½ tablespoons of caramel sauce on top. Sprinkle pepita streusel over caramel. Spread raisin puree on plate and top with a scoop of brown sugar bourbon ice cream.

Chef's Tip: *Don't be alarmed if the ice cream base breaks slightly during the final seconds of cooking. It will come together easily when mixed with immersion blender.*

Chef's Tip: *Roasting your own pumpkin to make a puree is always better, but in a pinch, feel free to substitute a canned version.*

Sweet Potato Caramelized Apple Tart

Pecan Crust, Cinnamon Ice Cream, Stewed Cranberries, Vanilla Meringue

SERVES 6

This dish came from my love of sweet potatoes with brown sugar, butter, and salt, which is essentially what part of the filling is. What you don't see when you are served this dish are the soft juicy caramelized apples underneath. That, combined with a pecan shortbread crust and toasted soft meringue on top, makes this tart a celebration of everything autumn. The tart is great served alone or dressed up with homemade cinnamon ice cream and stewed cranberries for a more composed dessert. All components can be made ahead of time and put together last minute with the exception of the meringue.

Suggested wine pairing: Pedro Ximenez Sherry

For the pecan crust

½ cup pecans
2 cups all-purpose flour
¾ cup plus 2 tablespoons unsalted butter, room temperature
½ cup plus 1 tablespoon powdered sugar
½ teaspoon kosher salt
1 egg
1 egg yolk
½ teaspoon vanilla extract
6 (4-inch) shallow tart pans

For the caramelized apples

2 large Granny Smith apples, peeled and chopped into ½-inch cubes
¼ cup light brown sugar
Pinch of kosher salt
¼ teaspoon cinnamon
2 teaspoons unsalted butter
3 tablespoons apple cider

For the sweet potato filling

1 large sweet potato (approximately 1 pound)
½ cup light brown sugar
2 tablespoons unsalted butter
⅛ teaspoon kosher salt

For the cinnamon ice cream

1½ cups heavy cream
1½ cups whole milk
½ cup plus 2 tablespoons granulated sugar
1 tablespoon honey
6 large cinnamon sticks, broken up with mortar and pestle
¼ teaspoon ground cinnamon
Pinch of kosher salt
8 egg yolks

For the stewed cranberries

1½ cups fresh cranberries, washed
½ cup plus 2 tablespoons fresh orange juice (no pulp)
½ cup granulated sugar
Pinch kosher salt
½ teaspoon orange zest, finely chopped
¼ vanilla bean, scraped

For the vanilla meringue

2 egg whites
½ cup plus 1 tablespoon granulated sugar
¼ teaspoon cream of tarter
1 teaspoon vanilla extract
Pinch kosher salt

FOR THE PECAN CRUST

Preheat oven to 350°F.

Place pecans on a baking sheet and toast until fragrant, 6–8 minutes. Remove from the oven, cool to room temperature, and finely chop. Add to a large bowl and combine with flour.

In an electric mixer with paddle attachment set at low speed, combine the butter, sugar, and salt for 1 minute. Increase mixer to medium speed and mix for 5 minutes, scraping mixture off the sides of the bowl twice.

Turn mixer down to a slow speed and add egg, egg yolk, and vanilla. Continue to mix, scraping down bowl, until mixture is fully incorporated and smooth.

Add half the flour mixture on low speed until just incorporated. Scrape bowl and add remaining flour mixture until incorporated. Scrape bowl and mix a few seconds more.

Remove dough, flatten between plastic wrap, and chill in the refrigerator for at least 1 hour or up to 3 days.

On a flat work surface, remove dough from plastic wrap and carefully soften by folding over and kneading a few times. Lightly dust surface with all-purpose flour and roll dough evenly out to ⅛ inch.

Cut out six 6-inch rounds and line shallow tart pans. Trim any excess dough off tops of pans.

Place the tart shells in the refrigerator for 30 minutes. Remove, prick with a fork 3 times each, and bake at 350°F. until golden brown, 12–15 minutes. Cool in tart pan to room temperature.

FOR THE CARAMELIZED APPLES

In a large bowl, combine apples, sugar, salt, and cinnamon.

Heat butter in a stainless sauté pan on medium-high heat until melted and bubbling. Add apples, toss to coat with butter, and cook until juices start to release from the apples. Continue cooking without stirring until juices reduce and apples start to caramelize slightly. Toss and continue to cook until apples are evenly and lightly caramelized. Add apple cider and toss; continue to cook until juices have reduced to a syrup consistency. Remove mixture from pan, place in a bowl, and cool to room temperature. Cover with plastic wrap and chill in the refrigerator.

FOR THE SWEET POTATO FILLING

Preheat oven to 400°F.

Clean and dry sweet potato, poke several times with a fork, and place on baking sheet lined with foil. Bake potato in oven for 30 minutes, flip it over, and continue to bake until soft, approximately 20 minutes more. Remove potato from oven and let rest for 10 minutes.

Cut baked sweet potato in half and remove all the flesh; discard the skin.

In a food processor, combine potato with brown sugar, butter, and salt. Puree, scraping down sides twice, until smooth, about 2 minutes.

Place in a bowl, cover with plastic wrap, and chill for 1 hour and up to 3 days.

FOR THE CINNAMON ICE CREAM

Make an ice bath by nesting a medium bowl in a larger bowl that's partially filled with ice and water.

In a medium saucepan, combine cream, milk, sugar, honey, cinnamon stick pieces, ground cinnamon, and salt. Bring just to boiling, then reduce heat to scald. Remove from heat, cover, and let steep for 1 hour. Bring back to a scald and remove cinnamon sticks with a slotted spoon.

In a large mixing bowl, continually whisk the egg yolks while gradually adding some of the cinnamon-infused cream mixture. Scrape the egg yolk mixture into pan with remaining cinnamon cream and cook on low heat, stirring with a wooden spoon, until mixture slightly thickens and coats the back of the spoon.

Quickly remove from heat and strain ice-cream base through a fine-mesh sieve into chilled ice bath. Stir gently until fully chilled. Transfer ice cream to refrigerator to rest overnight. Freeze the ice cream base in an ice-cream maker according to labeled instructions.

FOR THE STEWED CRANBERRIES

Combine all ingredients in a small saucepan and cook over medium heat until mixture comes to boil. Reduce heat and let simmer 10 minutes, swirling a few times during process, until berries are soft and their juices have released. Cover and chill.

FOR THE VANILLA MERINGUE

Create a water bath by bringing a small saucepan filled a third of the way with water to a simmer.

In a mixing bowl, whisk together egg whites, sugar, and cream of tarter until just slightly bigger than the diameter of saucepan.

Gently warm egg white mixture over simmering water, slowly whisking, until mixture reaches a temperature of 165°F.

Transfer mixture to an electric mixer with whisk attachment. Whip on high speed until meringue forms stiff peaks and is room temperature.

Turn off mixer and add vanilla extract and salt. Whisk another 10 seconds to fully incorporate, scraping down bowl once.

AT SERVICE

Fill each pecan tart shell halfway with caramelized apples. Spoon the sweet potato puree on top to just above level of the tart shells. Place meringue in a piping bag and pipe in a circular design starting from the center. With a blowtorch or broiler, gently toast top of meringue. Serve with a scoop of cinnamon ice cream and small spoonful of stewed cranberries.

Green Apple "Creamsicle"

Warm Apple Fritter, Huckleberry Compote, Apple Chips

SERVES 8 / MAKES 8 APPLE FRITTERS

This is a twist on the classic vanilla/orange version usually served on a stick. The tart green apple sorbet plays well off the smooth cream cheese ice cream and is a fresh, light way to showcase apples in the fall. The warm apple fritter is a nice contrast to the cold creamsicle, and is also great on its own. Since it adds a brightness in flavor and color, it's worth the effort to juice the apples fresh when making the sorbet for this dish. Look for apples that are dark green with good acid.

Suggested wine pairing: Late Harvest Riesling

For the green apple sorbet

8–10 large Granny Smith apples
4 tablespoons granulated sugar
3 tablespoons water
3 tablespoons glucose syrup or light corn syrup
1–2 tablespoons lemon juice
Kosher salt, to taste

For the cream cheese ice cream

1 cup whole milk
½ cup plus 1 tablespoon granulated sugar
5 egg yolks
1 teaspoon vanilla paste
¾ cup cream cheese
¾ cup crème fraîche

For the warm apple fritters

2 Granny Smith apples, peeled and diced into
    ½-inch cubes
¼ cup light brown sugar
1 cup all-purpose flour
¼ cup granulated sugar
½ teaspoon kosher salt
½ teaspoon ground cinnamon
1½ teaspoons baking powder
⅓ cup buttermilk
1 egg
Grape seed oil, for frying

For the fritter glaze

1 tablespoon butter
3 tablespoons evaporated milk
¾ teaspoon vanilla extract
1 cup powdered sugar, sifted
Pinch of kosher salt

For the huckleberry compote

1½ cups huckleberries, washed, stems removed,
    divided
3 tablespoons granulated sugar
3 tablespoons water
1 teaspoon lemon juice
Kosher salt, to taste

For the apple chips

2 tablespoons powdered sugar, divided
1 Granny Smith apple, cored, sliced ¹⁄₁₆-inch thin
    (recommend a mandoline)

FOR THE GREEN APPLE SORBET

Line an 8 × 8 × 2-inch pan with parchment paper and place in freezer.

Wash and core the apples. Cut them into pieces small enough to fit through a juicer and quickly extract 2½ cups of juice before apples oxidize and turn color.

In a small stainless steel pot, combine sugar, water, and syrup. Bring to a boil, remove from heat, and chill.

Combine apple juice with sugar mixture and add lemon juice and salt. Strain through a fine-mesh sieve.

Freeze in ice cream machine according to labeled instructions. Smooth sorbet level into prepared pan. Wrap tightly with plastic wrap and place back in freezer.

FOR THE CREAM CHEESE ICE CREAM

Make an ice bath by nesting a medium bowl in a larger bowl that's partially filled with ice and water.

In a medium saucepot, combine milk and sugar and bring just to a boiling point, then reduce heat to scald.

Whisk egg yolks in a large mixing bowl. While continually whisking, add in some of the hot cream/milk mixture. Scrape the yolk mixture into saucepot with remaining cream/milk mixture, and cook on low heat, stirring with a wooden spoon until mixture thickens slightly and coats the back of the spoon.

Quickly remove from heat and whisk in vanilla, cream cheese, and crème fraîche. Immersion blend to break up any cream cheese lumps.

Strain the ice cream base through a fine-mesh sieve into prepared ice bath; stir gently until fully chilled. Transfer to refrigerator to rest overnight.

Freeze the ice cream base in ice-cream maker according to the labeled instructions. Spread evenly in prepared pan on top of green apple sorbet. Wrap with plastic wrap and place in freezer.

FOR THE WARM APPLE FRITTERS

In a large sauté pan, combine apples with brown sugar and cook over medium heat, tossing often, until apples are tender and slightly caramelized, about 5 minutes. Cover and chill.

Sift flour, sugar, salt, cinnamon, and baking powder together.

In a mixing bowl, whisk together buttermilk and egg. Stir very gently into sifted flour mixture until just combined. Fold in apples and chill in the refrigerator for 30 minutes.

Heat a deep fryer to 350°F. Drop rounded tablespoon-size portions of batter carefully into grape seed oil and fry for 1 minute on each side until fritters are cooked throughout. Remove fritters with slotted spoon and place on a plate lined with paper towels to remove excess oil. While still warm, dip the top half in glaze (see below).

FOR THE FRITTER GLAZE

In a saucepot, combine butter, milk, and vanilla, and warm slightly to melt butter. Whisk in sugar and salt. Keep warm in preparation for fritters.

FOR THE HUCKLEBERRY COMPOTE

In a small saucepot, combine 1 cup huckleberries, sugar, and water. Bring to a simmer over low heat and continue to cook until berries break down and liquid slightly reduces, about 7 minutes.

Cool slightly, add to a blender, and puree until sooth. Strain the mixture through a fine-mesh sieve into a bowl.

Add lemon juice, salt, and remaining ½ cup huckleberries. Gently stir, cover with plastic wrap, and chill in the refrigerator.

FOR THE APPLE CHIPS

Preheat oven to 225°F.

Sprinkle 1 tablespoon powdered sugar on a
half-sheet pan lined with a silicone baking mat.
Place apples flat on mat, making sure they are
not touching each other. Sprinkle remaining
1 tablespoon powdered sugar on top of the sliced
apples.

Immediately place apples in oven to dry for about
3 hours (chips are done when they are crisp
when removed and cooled for 1 minute at room
temperature).

AT SERVICE

Remove creamsicles from freezer. Cut, ice-
cream-side-down into eight 2 × 2-inch squares.
Spoon huckleberry compote over and serve with
warm glazed apple fritter and an apple chip for
garnish.

Chef's Tip: *To make the green apple sorbet even
greener in color, add a few baby spinach leaves
while juicing the apples. This won't affect the taste
and will make the color pop.*

Market Bar

Peanut Crunch and Chocolate Mousse Cake with Chocolate Glaze, Caramel Corn,
Peanut Butter Ice Cream, and Caramel Sauce

SERVES 8–10

If this dish reminds you of a combination of things from a movie concession stand, then you understand where it gets its roots. Chocolate, peanut butter, and caramel corn are what gave me the inspiration for this popular staple dessert at Market. Adding the comfort flavors of banana and malt ice cream with textures of roasted peanuts and panko bread crumbs takes this dish out of the movie theater and into a dining room. Although there are many steps to making this layer cake, it can be kept in the freezer for up to two weeks. Just save the glazing with chocolate ganache to right before serving. Since bittersweet chocolate is the focal point of this dish, it is important to use a high-quality chocolate brand with 60 to 72 percent cocoa solids.

Suggested wine pairing: Tawny Port

For the cocoa chiffon cake

⅓ cup all-purpose flour
⅓ cup plus 2 tablespoons granulated sugar, divided
2 tablespoons cocoa powder
½ teaspoon baking powder
2 egg yolks
3 tablespoons plus, 1 teaspoon buttermilk
1 tablespoon plus 2 teaspoons grape seed oil
1 teaspoon vanilla extract
Pinch of kosher salt
2 egg whites
2 tablespoon granulated sugar

For the peanut crunch layer

1 cup panko bread crumbs
¾ cup smooth, natural, and salted peanut butter
⅓ cup (2½ ounces) chopped milk chocolate
2 tablespoons butter
¼ cup roasted chopped peanuts

For the chocolate mousse

6 ounces (70 percent) chocolate
1¼ cups heavy cream

For the chocolate glaze

3 ounces (60 percent cocoa) chocolate, chopped
    into small pieces
¼ cup plus 2 tablespoons heavy cream

For the caramel corn

3 tablespoons granulated sugar
2 teaspoons water
1 teaspoon corn syrup
1 teaspoon butter
Pinch of kosher salt
2 cups plain popped popcorn

For the salted peanut butter ice cream

½ cup heavy cream
1½ cups milk
½ cup granulated sugar
⅛ teaspoon kosher salt
6 egg yolks
½ cup smooth, natural, and salted peanut butter

For the caramel sauce

½ cup granulated sugar
1 tablespoon corn syrup
3 tablespoons water
6 tablespoons cream
2 teaspoons butter
¼ teaspoon kosher salt

For the garnish

1 banana, peeled and chopped

FOR THE COCOA CHIFFON CAKE

Preheat oven to 350°F.

Grease and line a 9 × 13-inch pan with parchment paper.

In a large bowl, sift together the flour, ⅓ cup sugar, cocoa, and baking powder.

In a separate bowl, combine the egg yolks, buttermilk, grape seed oil, vanilla, and salt, and gently stir into the flour mixture until combined. Set aside.

In another large mixing bowl, beat egg whites until frothy; sprinkle in the sugar. Continue to beat egg whites until stiff peaks form, then gently fold egg whites into batter.

Spread evenly onto prepared pan and bake until cake springs back when gently touched in center, 12–15 minutes. Cool to room temperature.

FOR THE PEANUT CRUNCH LAYER

Preheat oven to 350°F.

Place bread crumbs on a baking sheet and toast until slightly browned, 3-4 minutes. Cool to room temperature.

Line a 9 × 13-inch baking sheet with parchment paper.

Over a simmering pot of water, combine and melt the peanut butter, milk chocolate, and butter. When mixture is melted, stir in the toasted panko bread crumbs and peanuts. Spread onto baking sheet. Place in the freezer until frozen.

FOR THE CHOCOLATE MOUSSE

In a small saucepot, melt chocolate to 120°F.

In a large mixing bowl, whip cream to a soft mound. Whisk ¼ cream into melted chocolate. Fold the remaining cream in gently. Over folding will result in a broken mousse, so be careful to be efficient with your technique.

FOR THE CHOCOLATE GLAZE

Place chocolate in small bowl. Scald heavy cream over medium-high heat and pour over chocolate. Let sit for 30 seconds and gently whisk together until smooth and shiny. Cover and set aside.

FOR THE CARAMEL CORN

Preheat oven to 350°F.

In a medium pot, combine sugar, water, and corn syrup, and caramelize over medium-low heat to a medium amber color. Stir in butter and salt with a wooden spoon.

Over low heat, fold in popcorn quickly and gently. Separate on parchment paper and place in oven for 30 seconds to rewarm and to help separate (if needed).

FOR THE SALTED PEANUT BUTTER ICE CREAM

Make an ice bath by nesting a medium bowl in a larger bowl that's partially filled with ice and water.

Combine cream, milk, sugar, and salt in a medium saucepan and scald.

Whisk the egg yolks in a mixing bowl and gradually add some of the cream mixture while continually whisking. Scrape the yolk mixture into pan with remaining cream mixture and cook on low heat, stirring with a wooden spoon, until mixture slightly thickens and coats the back of the spoon.

Quickly remove from heat and mix in peanut butter. Immersion blend until smooth.

Strain the ice cream base through a fine-mesh sieve into chilled ice bath bowl. Stir gently until fully chilled. Transfer mixture to the refrigerator, cover, and allow to rest overnight.

Freeze the ice cream base in ice-cream maker according to labeled instructions.

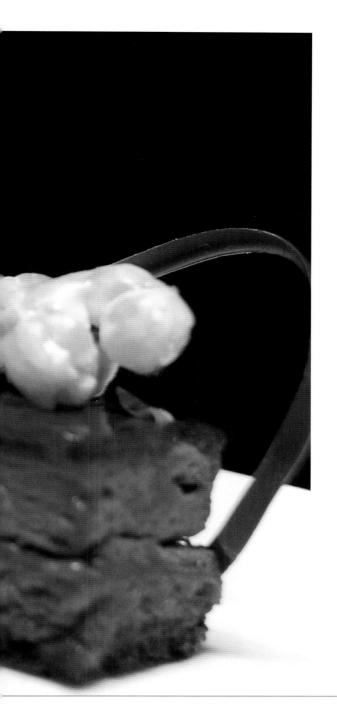

FOR THE CARAMEL SAUCE

Bring sugar, corn syrup, and water to a boil over medium heat. Brushing sides of the pot with the water, clear sugar from the sides twice. Continue to boil until sugar starts to caramelize and turns a medium/dark amber color.

Slowly whisk in cream in three stages.

Whisk in butter and salt, and bring to a boil. Immediately remove from heat and cool to room temperature.

AT SERVICE

Spread a third of the mousse on top of the cake in the pan. Remove the peanut crunch layer from the freezer and invert onto mousse layer. Peel off parchment paper. Spread remaining mousse over peanut layer. Freeze until firm.

Remove the cake from the pan, peel off parchment paper on bottom, and pour warm glaze over top. Quickly spread evenly. Let set 5 minutes.

Cut cake into 4½ × 1-inch bars. Defrost to room temperature and serve with caramel sauce, chopped banana, caramel popcorn, and peanut butter ice cream.

WINTER

There aren't many plants that like the cold weather besides the ones that grow underground. I feel very lucky here in San Diego because our winters are mild, giving me access to local ingredients year-round. My favorite winter produce includes all the local citrus, namely blood oranges and tangerines. In addition, winter is all about braising meats and creating hearty rustic soups. I think you will especially enjoy my recipes for Local Melogold Grapefruit and Avocado Salad or Braised Beef Tongue with Petite Winter Vegetable Roast.

Citrus Kumquat

SERVES 2

4 kumquats
3 ounces Hangar One Mandarin vodka
1 ounce Lillet Blanc
4 pieces candied kumquats (page 283)
½ ounce kumquat syrup (page 283)
6 drops orange bitters
2 orange wedges

Muddle the kumquats in a martini shaker. Add remaining ingredients, shake, and strain into prechilled martini glasses. Garnish with 2 candied kumquats per glass.

Blood Orange Hemingway

SERVES 2

4 ounces 10 Cane Rum
2 ounces Luxardo Maraschino Liqueur
2 ounces lime juice
2 ounces blood orange juice
1 ounce simple syrup
4 dashes Angostura Bitters
2 round lime slices

Shake all ingredients in a martini shaker and strain into martini glasses. Garnish each with one lime.

Curried Root Vegetable Soup and Saffron Basmati Rice

Winter Vegetable Roast, Garlic Sausage, Shaved Scallions

SERVES 6

The roasting process for the yam in this recipe is a dry-cooking technique. The yam is steamed in its own skin, which allows its sugars to caramelize, lending a nice depth to the soup. Pops of spicy sausage paired with the unique textures of root vegetables and basmati rice bring their own characteristics and flavor.

Suggested wine pairing: Alexander Valley Semillon

For the winter vegetable roast and sausage

8 cups vegetable stock (page 288)
1 large carrot, peeled and medium diced
2 large turnips, peeled and medium diced
2 large rutabagas, peeled and medium diced
4 tablespoons light olive oil
¼ cup fully cooked spicy sausage (lamb or pork), medium diced

For the soup

1 large jewel yam
4 tablespoons light olive oil
1 Spanish onion, finely sliced
1 leek (white part only), chopped
1 tablespoon salt
6 cloves garlic, finely minced
1 (¾-inch) piece ginger, finely minced
2 Roma tomatoes, chopped
1 bay leaf
1 tablespoon red curry paste
½ teaspoon chile powder
1 teaspoon cumin
1 teaspoon coriander
1 bay leaf
¼ teaspoon oregano
1 teaspoon paprika
1 (13½-ounce) can coconut milk

For the saffron basmati rice

1 cup basmati rice
1 tablespoon light olive oil
1 clove garlic, peeled and smashed
Small pinch saffron
2 cups chicken stock (page 283)
Salt and pepper, to taste

For the garnish

¼ cup scallions (green part only), cut on a bias
¼ cup red pepper, thinly sliced

FOR THE WINTER VEGETABLE ROAST AND SAUSAGE

Heat vegetable stock in a large saucepot over high heat. Add carrots and cook until just tender. Remove carrots with a hand strainer to a baking sheet lined with paper towels. Repeat this process with remaining vegetables. Cool all to room temperature. Reserve the vegetable stock.

Just before serving, heat olive oil in a large sauté pan over high heat. Add vegetables and sausage. Cook vegetables until caramelized.

FOR THE SOUP

Preheat oven to 350°F.

Place the yam on a small baking sheet and roast until very soft, about 1 hour. Remove and cut a slit from the top to the bottom, pushing on the sides to open it. Cool to room temperature, then scoop out the flesh and discard skin.

Heat olive oil in a large saucepot over medium heat. Add onion, leek, and salt. Cover, reduce heat to medium low, and cook onions and leeks until translucent, about 15 minutes.

Add garlic, ginger, tomatoes, bay leaf, and all the spices. Continue to cook, stirring with a wooden spoon repeatedly to ensure the spices don't burn, for about 3 minutes.

Add the reserved vegetable broth and roasted yam and bring to a boil. Reduce to medium-low heat and simmer for 15–20 minutes.

Remove bay leaf and add coconut milk. Bring to a boil and remove from heat. Pass mixture through a fine-mesh sieve.

FOR THE SAFFRON BASMATI RICE

Rinse the rice under cold water until it runs clear. Heat olive oil in a saucepot over medium heat. Add rice, garlic, and saffron. Stir the rice until fragrant, 2–3 minutes.

Add stock, bring to a boil, then reduce heat to medium low. Cover and simmer for 15 minutes.

Remove saucepot from heat and let rice rest for 5 minutes. Then, using a fork, fluff the rice and season it with salt and pepper.

AT SERVICE

Ladle soup into large flat-bottom bowls. Distribute root vegetables and sausage into each bowl of soup. Place a large, packed spoonful of rice in the center of each bowl. Garnish with scallions and red peppers.

Chef's Tip: *Substitute your favorite rice in this recipe.*

Maine Lobster and Seafood Chowder

Shrimp, Cod, Andouille Sausage

SERVES 6

Nothing is better on a cold winter night than a creamy bowl of seafood chowder. I like to purchase local black cod and Mexican white shrimp when they are in season. The richness of this broth comes together with the potatoes and sausage and is brightened by the acidity of the wine.

Suggested wine pairing: Albariño

For the potatoes

4 medium russet potatoes, peeled and medium diced
1 bay leaf
Salt, to taste

For the vegetables and Andouille sausage

4 tablespoons light olive oil
4 stalks celery, small diced
1 pasilla pepper, seeded and small diced
½ fennel bulb, small diced
½ teaspoon salt
¾ cup small diced andouille sausage

For the chowder

3 tablespoons light olive oil
2 slices bacon
2 Spanish onions, peeled and sliced
1 leek, roughly chopped
10 cloves garlic, roughly chopped
½ bulb fennel, sliced
¼ teaspoon toasted ground fennel (page 287)
1 tablespoon salt
2 tablespoons all-purpose flour
¼ dry white wine
7 cups fish stock (page 285)
1 herb sachet (page 285)
1 cup heavy cream
1 teaspoon hot sauce
1½ cups cooked lobster
12 large cooked Mexican White Shrimp (or your favorite variety)
1 pound cooked local black cod or true cod

For the garnish

¼ cup finely chopped parsley leaves
Lemon oil, for drizzling

FOR THE POTATOES

Place potatoes in a medium-size saucepot covered with water (2 inches from the bottom). Add bay leaf and salt, and bring to a boil. Reduce to low heat, and cook potatoes until fork tender. Strain potatoes in a colander and spread on a large sheet pan; cool to room temperature.

FOR THE VEGETABLES AND ANDOUILLE SAUSAGE

Heat olive oil in a sauté pan over medium heat. Add celery, pepper, and fennel, and sauté until tender, 3–5 minutes.

Season vegetables with salt and remove from heat. Add vegetables to the same large sheet pan as the potatoes; cool to room temperature.

Just before serving, warm the sausage over low heat in a large sauté pan with the potato and vegetable mixture.

FOR THE CHOWDER

Heat oil in a large saucepot over medium-low heat. Add bacon and render until some of the fat is released, about 5 minutes. Add onion, leek, garlic, fennel, ground fennel, and salt. Cover and,

stirring often, cook for about 15 minutes (do not caramelize).

Add flour, stir until incorporated, and cook for 2 minutes.

Add wine, then slowly incorporate the stock, whisking gently as you pour. Add the sachet and, stirring often, simmer over medium-high heat. Reduce heat to low and simmer for 20–30 minutes.

Slowly stir in cream, then remove from heat and stir in hot sauce.

Strain the mixture through a fine-mesh sieve, add to a blender, and process until smooth.

Just before serving, return chowder to its original saucepot, warm over low heat, and immersion blend.

AT SERVICE

Distribute the vegetable and sausage mixture into soup bowls. Distribute lobster, shrimp, and cod evenly into each bowl. Ladle warm chowder into each bowl, then garnish with the parsley and a drizzle of lemon oil.

Chef's Tip: *To make a low-fat version of this soup, reserve 1 cup of the vegetables strained from the colander. Add soup to a blender with these vegetables and process until smooth. Skip the heavy cream. This will give the soup broth its depth and body.*

Roasted Chile Posole

Avocado, Corn Crisps, Lime Crème Fraîche

SERVES 6

When it's cold outside this is a great one-pot soup to prepare for a crowd that wants to venture to your house for a football game or party. This wintery "comfort soup" is not only extremely hearty, but also offers a rich depth. The tortilla chips add texture, and I leave all the garnishes off to the side so people can create their desired experience.

Suggested wine pairing: New Zealand Sauvignon Blanc

For the posole

1½ pounds pork shoulder, cut into 1-inch cubes
Salt and pepper, to taste
4 tablespoons light olive oil, divided
2 strips bacon
1 white onion, small diced
18 cloves garlic, finely chopped
2 tablespoons chile powder
1 tablespoon paprika
1 tablespoon cumin/coriander spice blend
   (page 283)
1 stick cinnamon
8 cups chicken stock (page 283)
8 cups canned whole tomatoes in juice, chopped
2 bay leaves
1 teaspoon hot sauce
4 large carrots, peeled and small diced
2 celery stalks, small diced
1 bunch scallions (white bulbs only), roughly
   chopped (reserve green tops)
2 red bell peppers, cored, seeded, and small diced
2 green bell peppers, cored, seeded, and small diced
2 pasilla peppers, small diced
2 cups prepared hominy

For the lime crème fraîche

1 cup sour cream
1 teaspoon freshly squeezed lime juice
Pinch of salt

For the corn crisps

Canola oil, for frying
6 corn tortillas, cut into strips
BBQ spice mix (page 281)

For the garnish

½ bunch cilantro, finely chopped
3 avocados, peeled, pitted, and sliced
1 jalapeño, thinly sliced
Scallion tops, sliced (reserved from posole)

FOR THE POSOLE

Season pork cubes with salt and pepper.

Heat 2 tablespoons of olive oil in a large saucepot over high heat. Add pork and sear on all sides until golden brown, about 10 minutes. Remove pork and set aside.

In the same saucepot heat 2 tablespoons of olive oil over low heat. Add bacon, onion, and garlic and cook for about 5 minutes.

Add chile powder, paprika, cumin/coriander, and cinnamon stick, and simmer until fragrant.

Add the pork back into the saucepot. Add stock, tomatoes, bay leaves, and hot sauce. Simmer on low heat for about 20 minutes.

Add the carrots, celery, white scallion bulbs, peppers, and hominy. Simmer soup on low heat for 1 hour, occasionally stirring and making sure not to break up the pork cubes.

FOR THE LIME CRÈME FRAÎCHE

Combine all ingredients in a mixing bowl and whisk until creamy.

FOR THE CORN CRISPS

Heat a deep fryer or a pot filled with oil (3 inches from the bottom) to 375°F. Fry the tortillas until crispy and golden brown. Remove tortillas to a plate lined with paper towels. Season with BBQ spice.

FOR THE GARNISH

Finely chop the reserved green scallion stems from the posole and combine them in a small mixing bowl with the cilantro. Slice avocados and jalapeños.

AT SERVICE

Ladle soup into bowls. Add the avocado slices and a dollop of the lime crème fraîche. Garnish with jalapeños and scallion/cilantro mixture. Serve corn crisps alongside.

Chef's Tip: *This soup is also great served over rice.*

Potato Leek Soup and Pesto-Grilled Shrimp

Pasilla Peppers, Caramelized Fennel, Lemon Croutons

SERVES 6

Living in California, we have many nice days during the winter. Often, I like to fire up my barbecue and grill fresh shrimp. I've elevated this soup from a simple winter dish to a light and more interesting creation. The pasilla and chopped Serrano peppers add a little spice and complexity, while the basil-grilled shrimp add texture, pairing perfectly with the potatoes and leeks.

Suggested wine pairing: Austrian Grüner Veltliner

For the soup

2 tablespoons light olive oil
2 tablespoons butter
4 leeks (white part only), chopped
3 cups thinly sliced Spanish onions
1 russet potato, peeled and thinly sliced
1 fennel bulb, coarsely chopped
10 garlic cloves, roughly chopped
1 tablespoon salt, more to taste
4 cups chicken stock (page 283)
4 cups vegetable stock (page 288)
2 bay leaves
1 sprig thyme
2 cups heavy cream
Pepper, to taste

For the basil marinade

2 cups basil leaves
1 clove garlic
1 cup light olive oil
¼ cup grated Parmigiana Reggiano
1 teaspoon salt

For the shrimp

12 large raw shrimp, peeled and deveined

For the croutons

¼ loaf of a baguette, cut into ½-inch cubes
½ cup light olive oil
Lemon pepper, for sprinkling (substitute salt and pepper)

For the caramelized fennel

2 tablespoons light olive oil
1 fennel bulb, tops removed, cut in half, diced
2 pasilla peppers, cut in half, seeds removed, diced
Salt and pepper, to taste

For the garnish

2 Serrano peppers, finely sliced
3 scallions, finely chopped

FOR THE SOUP

Heat olive oil and melt butter in a large saucepot over medium-low heat. Add leeks, onions, potato, fennel, garlic, and salt. Cover saucepot and cook over low heat for about 20 minutes (checking and stirring every 5 minutes until all vegetables are very soft).

Add stocks, bay leaves, and thyme. Bring to a boil, then reduce to medium heat, cover, and simmer for 15 minutes.

Remove soup from heat and add the cream.

In small batches, add soup to a blender and process until smooth. Season with salt and pepper.

Just before serving, return soup to its original saucepot, warm over low heat, and immersion blend.

FOR THE BASIL MARINADE

Bring a small saucepot of water to a boil. Add basil and blanch for 3 minutes. Remove basil and submerge in a bowl of ice and water. Once chilled, remove basil and squeeze out all excess water.

In a blender, combine basil, garlic, olive oil, Parmigiana Reggiano, and salt. Process until smooth, approximately 3 minutes.

FOR THE SHRIMP

In a mixing bowl, combine shrimp with some of the basil marinade and toss until fully coated. Using an outdoor grill or sauté pan over medium-high heat, cook shrimp, about 2 minutes per side. Cut shrimp in halves.

FOR THE CROUTONS

Preheat oven to 325°F.

Add bread cubes to a mixing bowl, drizzle with olive oil, and toss until evenly coated.

Arrange bread cubes loosely on a baking sheet lined with parchment paper. Bake until golden brown and crunchy, about 15 minutes. Remove bread cubes and season with lemon pepper. Cool to room temperature.

FOR THE CARAMELIZED FENNEL

Heat olive oil in a large sauté pan over high heat. Add fennel and sauté until caramelized, about 2 minutes.

Add pasilla peppers and cook until soft, about 1 minute. Season with salt and pepper.

AT SERVICE

Ladle soup into bowls, and add some of the fennel/pasilla pepper mixture. Add 4 shrimp halves to each bowl. Garnish with some of the Serrano peppers, scallions, and croutons.

Chef's Tip: *When selecting peppers, make sure they are firm with tight skin and very fragrant.*

Star Crimson Pear Salad and Spice-Braised Pear "Strudel"

Lemon Vinaigrette, Walnut Streusel, Belgian Endive

SERVES 6

Cooking the puff pastry in this nontraditional way gives you the best things about a strudel. You get a flaky, crispy puff pastry with a warm filling. This dish is a great interplay between a cold pear salad and the texture and warmth of a "strudel."

Suggested wine pairing: Loire Valley Chenin Blanc

For the pear chutney

6 firm, ripe pears, peeled and medium diced
¾ cup granulated sugar
¼ cup brown sugar
½ cup orange juice
2 tablespoons lemon juice
1 cup pear brandy
1 teaspoon minced ginger
2 sticks cinnamon
3 star anise

For the puff pastry and pear strudel

1 (12 × 8½-inch) puff pastry sheet (store bought)
2 eggs
2 tablespoons water
Salt and pepper, to taste

For the walnut streusel

2 tablespoons unsalted butter, softened
2 tablespoons brown sugar
2 tablespoons all-purpose flour
¼ cup chopped walnuts

For the pear salad

3 heads red Belgian endive
3 star crimson pears
1 cup lemon vinaigrette (page 285)
10 cups petite field lettuces
Salt and pepper, to taste

For the port reduction

2 cups high-quality port wine
2 cups balsamic vinegar
1 stick cinnamon
2 star anise

FOR THE PEAR CHUTNEY

Combine ingredients in a saucepot over medium heat and bring to a boil. Reduce heat to low and simmer chutney until thickened to the consistency of pie filling, about 1 hour. Remove star anise and cinnamon. Reserve.

FOR THE PUFF PASTRY AND PEAR STRUDEL

Preheat oven to 350°F.

Cut puff pastry into 6 rectangles roughly 2 × 7½ inches. Roll out the last 2 inches very thin.

Wrap a 2-inch ring mold with 5–6 layers of plastic wrap, tucking excess into the middle (this keeps puff pastry from sticking to the metal and will not melt in the oven). Spray the plastic wrap with nonstick cooking spray.

Wrap puff pastry rectangle around the ring mold until the ends meet and overlap by about 2 inches.

In a small mixing bowl, whisk eggs and water to make an egg wash. Seal the seam of the puff pastry (where the two sides meet) with egg wash and press together firmly.

Lightly brush each pastry with egg wash around entire exterior, and sprinkle with salt and pepper. Bake for about 10–15 minutes; remove from oven.

Reduce oven heat to 250°F.

Slide metal ring molds from puff pastry (pastry should hold the shape of the ring mold). Place pastry back in oven and continue to cook until the pastry is crispy and golden brown, 15–20 minutes.

FOR THE WALNUT STREUSEL

Preheat oven to 350°F.

In a small mixing bowl, combine butter, sugar, and flour. Mix until well incorporated. Add walnuts and incorporate.

Crumble the streusel onto a small sheet pan lined with parchment paper; bake for 15–20 minutes. Remove and cool to room temperature.

FOR THE PEAR SALAD

Split the Belgian endive lengthwise and remove core, release individual leaves, and slice thin.

Cut pears in half, remove cores, slice each half into ¼-inch-thick slices, and drizzle with some of the vinaigrette.

In a large mixing bowl, combine field lettuce and endive. Drizzle with vinaigrette and lightly toss. Season with salt and pepper.

FOR THE PORT REDUCTION

Heat wine in a small saucepot over medium-high heat, then reduce heat to low and simmer until reduced to about 1 cup.

Add vinegar, cinnamon, and star anise, and simmer until reduced to a syrup-like consistency.

AT SERVICE

Take lettuce leaves and stack them one after another until you have a pile (like a deck of cards). Place a pile on each plate, allowing the stack to expand while supporting it on either side with both hands (salad will be organized in an accordion shape). Working carefully, slide the pear slices into the stacks of lettuce, distributing evenly throughout the stack (use one-half pear per salad). Garnish the top of the salads with endive.

Place one puff pastry ring next to each salad. Fill each pastry to the top with the pear chutney, and sprinkle with desired amount of walnut streusel. Sprinkle remaining streusel over salads. Drizzle port reduction in a circle around the salad.

Chef's Tip: *When making a reductions such as the pear chutney and port, stir often. During the cooking process be sure to adjust the heat as necessary. Some fruits drop more moisture and need to be simmered for longer. Toward the end of the simmering process, watch carefully and check often to be sure not to burn the liquid.*

Satsuma Tangerine with Butternut Squash and Crispy Vegetable Fritters

Citrus Vinaigrette, Feta Cheese, Purple Cabbage Slaw

SERVES 6 / MAKES 24 SERVINGS

Cabbage and citrus is a classic combination. Cabbage, with its texture, earthiness, and crunch, is brightened by the acidity of the citrus. In most of my dishes, I like to add texture and a high level of acidity to brighten the palate.

Suggested wine pairing: Spanish Loureira

For the citrus vinaigrette

- 2 tablespoons plus 1 cup light olive oil, divided
- 2 tablespoons shallots, minced
- 1 tablespoon minced ginger
- 1 cup fresh-squeezed orange juice
- ½ cup lemon juice
- ½ cup lime juice
- 1 teaspoon Dijon mustard
- 1 teaspoon sherry vinegar
- Pinch salt
- ¼ teaspoon pepper

For the vegetable fritters

- 1½ cups garbanzo flour
- ½ teaspoon baking soda
- 2 tablespoons fines herbes (page 285)
- 1½ teaspoons cumin/coriander spice blend (page 283)
- ¾ teaspoon garlic powder
- ½ teaspoon onion powder
- ¾ teaspoon salt
- 1 tablespoon lemon juice
- ½ cup hot water
- 1 egg
- ¼ cup finely shredded carrot
- ¼ cup diced red bell pepper
- 3 cups panko bread crumbs
- Canola oil, for frying

For the slaw

- 2 cups butternut squash, thinly sliced
- 2 cups purple cabbage, shaved very thin
- 2 cups green cabbage, shaved very thin
- ¼ cup cilantro finely chopped
- ¾ cups feta cheese, crumbled
- Citrus vinaigrette (see above)
- Salt and pepper, to taste

For the garnish

- 8 Satsuma tangerines, peeled and cut into ¼-inch rounds
- ¾ cups feta cheese, crumbled

FOR THE CITRUS VINAIGRETTE

Prepare an ice bath by nesting a medium bowl in a larger bowl that's partially filled with ice and water.

Heat 2 tablespoons olive oil in a small saucepot over medium heat. Add shallots and cook for about 1 minute.

Add ginger and fruit juices, bring to a boil over high heat, reduce to medium heat, and simmer until reduced by half its volume, 15–20 minutes.

Pour into the medium mixing bowl over ice, and whisk until chilled. Remove from the ice bath and whisk in mustard, vinegar, and remaining 1 cup olive oil. Season with salt and pepper.

FOR THE VEGETABLE FRITTERS

In a large mixing bowl, combine flour, baking soda, fines herbes, cumin/coriander, garlic powder, onion powder, and salt. Stir in lemon juice, water, and egg. Add the peppers and carrots and incorporate thoroughly.

Heat a deep fryer to 375°F.

Place the bread crumbs in a large mixing bowl. Roll rounded, tablespoon-size portions of batter carefully into the bread crumbs, shaking off any excess crumbs.

Carefully drop into the oil, and fry for 2 minutes.

Remove fritters with a slotted spoon and place onto a plate lined with paper towels to remove excess oil.

FOR THE SLAW

In a large mixing bowl combine squash, both cabbages, and cilantro. Add the feta and just enough citrus vinaigrette to coat. Season with salt and pepper.

AT SERVICE

Place a small mound of slaw on each plate, followed by a tangerine. Repeat until you have a long linear salad of alternating slaw and tangerines. Garnish with feta and a drizzle of remaining vinaigrette over the top and onto the plate. Place 3 warm fritters next to the salads.

Chef's Tip: *In place of tangerines, use whatever citrus you like best. Blood oranges and cara cara oranges are great choices.*

Chef's Tip: *For the fritters, fold in whatever seasonal ingredient you like, including especially zucchini, squash, or carrots. You can also add different herbs and spices. Customize the fritter to almost any season or dish. The panko breading, gives it a super crispy exterior.*

Local Melogold Grapefruit and Avocado Salad

Dashi-Yuzu Vinaigrette, Petite Red Swiss Chard

SERVES 6

For this salad I like to use locally grown Melogolds or Ruby Red grapefruits. This is a traditional winter salad with a twist. The acidity in this dish comes from the in-season yuzu crop. The dashi broth adds depth and character to the vinaigrette, elevating the traditional pairing of avocado with grapefruit.

Suggested wine pairing: Sauvignon Blanc

For the dashi-yuzu vinaigrette

¼ cup plus 3 tablespoons light olive oil, divided
1 tablespoon minced ginger
1 tablespoon minced garlic
¼ cup chopped scallions
1 teaspoon cumin/coriander spice blend (page 283)
1 teaspoon chile flakes
2 cups dashi broth (page 284)
3 tablespoons yuzu juice (substitute fresh
    lemon juice)
2 tablespoons soy sauce
1 tablespoon sesame oil

For the avocado salad

3 avocados, peeled, pitted, and halved
3 grapefruits, peeled and divided into segments
2 cups red petite swiss chard

For the garnish

Maldon sea salt, to taste

FOR THE DASHI-YUZU VINAIGRETTE

Heat 3 tablespoons of olive oil in a saucepot over medium-low heat. Add ginger, garlic, and scallions and cook until fragrant, 2–3 minutes.

Add cumin/coriander and chile flakes.

Add dashi broth and bring mixture to a boil. Reduce heat to medium low and simmer until mixture is reduced by half its volume.

Prepare an ice bath by nesting a medium bowl in a larger bowl that's partially filled with ice and water.

Remove mixture from heat and add to the medium bowl. Stir until chilled.

Combine mixture in a blender with yuzu juice and soy sauce; process until smooth. With blender set on low speed, slowly drizzle in remaining ¼ cup olive oil and sesame oil.

FOR THE AVOCADO SALAD

Cut avocado halves into 5 slices per half. Gently arrange grapefruit segments and avocado slices onto a large sheet pan. Drizzle with dashi-yuzu vinaigrette.

Place swiss chard in a small bowl, add some of the vinaigrette, and lightly toss until leaves are coated.

AT SERVICE

Arrange 5 avocado wedges on each plate. Distribute grapefruit segments on top of the avocados, interlaying segments with the avocado slices. Add swiss chard leaves to the avocado and grapefruit salad. Season salad with sea salt.

Chef's Tip: *I like to use Maldon sea salt because it's not overly salty. Maldon sea salt melts quickly on hot food so it should be added at the last minute. It's also great on cold preparations where, its thin flakes stay crispy and crunchy.*

Organic Baby Beet and Local Citrus Salad

Shaved Fennel, Bûcheron Goat Cheese, Candied Walnuts

SERVES 6

During the winter, the harvest of baby beets, ranging in color from red-violet to yellow, is abundant. Loaded with powerful antioxidants, these subtly sweet roasted beets offer fresh and vibrant flavors that come to life when mingled with the citrus of local grapefruits and blood oranges.

Suggested wine pairing: White Burgundy

For the beets

30 baby beets, assorted colors
8 cups water
¾ cup granulated sugar
¼ cup cider vinegar
1 tablespoon salt
Mustard vinaigrette (page 286)

For the citrus salad

3 cups roughly chopped arugula lettuce
1½ cups roughly chopped frisée lettuce (optional)
2 bulbs fennel, thinly sliced
Mustard vinaigrette (page 286)
2 grapefruits, peeled, seeded, and cut into segments
3 blood oranges, peeled, seeded, and cut into
 segments
1 cup goat cheese (or your favorite cheese)

For the candied walnuts

½ cup granulated sugar
1½ cups walnuts

FOR THE BEETS

Wash beets under cold water. Cut the tops off, leaving the skin on and leaving an inch from the stalk (this ensures that the beets retain their nutrients and bright color). Leave the bottom part of the beet attached.

In a large saucepot combine water, vinegar, sugar, and salt. Place the beets in the water, bring to a boil, then reduce heat to medium low. Simmer the beets until knife tender, about 20–30 minutes.

Remove with a slotted spoon onto a sheet pan and allow beets to cool to room temperature.

Using a paper towel or dish towel, rub the skins off. Cut into quarters and refrigerate until cool.

In a large mixing bowl, combine beets with some of the mustard vinaigrette.

FOR THE CITRUS SALAD

In a large mixing bowl combine arugula, frisée, and fennel. Drizzle with mustard vinaigrette and lightly toss.

FOR THE CANDIED WALNUTS

Preheat oven to 350°F.

Heat sugar in a small saucepot over medium heat. Cook, stirring occasionally, until melted.

Add walnuts to sugar mixture and coat evenly. Place on a baking sheet and toast in oven for 10 minutes. Remove from oven and cool.

AT SERVICE

Distribute beets onto plates. Place lettuce mixture on top of the beets, making sure that some of the beets are exposed. Garnish with grapefruit and orange segments, walnuts, and goat cheese. Drizzle the mustard vinaigrette around the plate.

Chef's Tip: *Even though beets are rinsed thoroughly, any remaining dirt from the outer skin falls to the bottom of the pot while cooking. If you strain the cooked beets with the water in a colander, you pour out all the dirt with the beets. For this reason, it is best to remove the cooked beets from the water with a slotted spoon.*

Chef's Tip: *Candied walnuts can be stored in an airtight container at room temperature up to one week.*

Crispy Wonton Kampachi Tostadas

Green Papaya Salad, Avocado Puree, Jalapeño Dressing, Pickled Ginger

SERVES 6

Traditionally, Thai restaurants serve papaya salad with fish sauce and vinegar. I made it more of a creamy slaw by adding mayonnaise, which adds richness and makes for a smoother taste on the palate. Although a bit richer, my version contains the great flavors of a Thai salad. Paired with crispy wontons and chilled fish, this dish is a great start to any meal.

Suggested wine pairing: Torrontes

For the wonton wraps

18 wonton wrappers (store bought)
Salt and pepper, to taste

For the kampachi sashimi

¾ pound kampachi fillet (skin and bones removed)

For the jalapeño dressing

3 tablespoons light olive oil
5 jalapeños, seeds removed, finely minced
1 tablespoon finely minced garlic
1 tablespoon finely minced ginger
1 cup mayonnaise (page 285)
1 tablespoon lime juice
1 tablespoon granulated sugar
1 tablespoon fish sauce
Salt and pepper, to taste

For the green papaya salad

½ green papaya
1 red bell pepper, cored, seeded, and thinly sliced
4 tablespoons finely chopped cilantro
2 tablespoons finely chopped mint

For the cabbage

3 cups green cabbage, finely shredded

For the avocado puree

½ avocado, pitted and peeled
1 tablespoon lemon juice
¼ teaspoon salt
1 teaspoon green hot sauce

For the garnish

¼ cup thinly sliced pickled ginger

FOR THE WONTON WRAPS

Heat a deep fryer or a pot filled with 3 inches of oil (from the bottom) to 375°F. Fry wonton wrappers until crispy and golden brown, Remove to a plate lined with paper towels and season with salt.

FOR THE KAMPACHI SASHIMI

Thinly slice kampachi into 18 pieces.

FOR THE JALAPEÑO DRESSING

Heat olive oil in a small sauté pan over medium heat. Add jalapeños, garlic, and ginger, and cook until fragrant, about 2 minutes, then cool to room temperature.

Combine jalapeño mixture in a bowl with remaining ingredients, and whisk until incorporated. Season with salt and pepper.

FOR THE GREEN PAPAYA SALAD

Remove top portion of green papaya (about 1 inch from the top) and nip the bottom. Using a vegetable peeler, remove skin. Split in half lengthwise and remove all seeds. Using a mandoline, finely shred papaya (until you have 3 cups).

In a large mixing bowl, combine papaya with red pepper, cilantro, and mint. Drizzle with the jalapeño dressing and lightly toss.

FOR THE AVOCADO PUREE

Combine all ingredients in a blender, process until smooth, and place in a squeeze bottle.

AT SERVICE

Place a small amount of green cabbage down the center of each rectangular plate. Place 3 wonton wrappers on top. Add the kampachi sashimi, avocado puree, and papaya salad. Top with pickled ginger.

Chef's Tip: *When introducing wontons to hot oil, lay them as flat as possible (one at a time) to ensure a flat surface. Have a few extra on hand so you have the right size and amount.*

Alderwood Smoked Black Cod and Garlic Mashed Potatoes

Soft-Poached Egg, Lemon-Marinated Olives, Sourdough Toast

SERVES 6

This is a super rustic yet controlled and elegant dish. It's a twist on a dish known as "Brandade," in which very moist local black cod is brined, smoked, and cooked perfectly.

Suggested wine pairing: Godello

For the garlic mashed potatoes

3 whole garlic bulbs
2 tablespoons light olive oil
1 tablespoon salt, more to taste
Pepper, to taste
3 russet potatoes, peeled and roughly chopped
4 tablespoons butter, room temperature
1 tablespoon hot sauce
¼ cup crème fraîche, room temperature
1 cup heavy cream, warmed

For the lemon-marinated olives

1 cup picholine olives, pitted
1 cup kalamata olives, pitted
1 cup extra-virgin olive oil
1 lemon, zested and finely chopped
½ teaspoon chile flakes
½ tablespoon Spanish paprika

For the smoked cod

4 tablespoons granulated sugar
3 tablespoons salt
1 cup hot tap water
1 pound black cod

For the poached egg

6 eggs
2 tablespoons salt
1 tablespoon distilled white vinegar
Pepper, to taste

For the sourdough toast

12 (½-inch) slices sourdough baguette (cut on a diagonal)
Light olive oil, for coating
Salt and pepper, to taste

For the garnish

2 tablespoons chives, finely chopped

FOR THE GARLIC MASHED POTATOES

Preheat oven to 400°F.

Remove outer skins of garlic bulbs, keeping cloves intact. Cut ¼–½ inch off the top of bulbs. Place on a piece of aluminum foil, drizzle with olive oil, and sprinkle with salt and pepper. Close foil tightly, forming a pouch. Roast cloves in oven until soft, about 30 minutes. Cool to room temperature. Using your hand, squeeze the bulb from the bottom, pushing the cloves out onto a cutting board where you should roughly chop them.

In a medium saucepot combine potatoes with enough water to cover. Season with salt and bring to a boil. Reduce heat to medium low and simmer potatoes until tender, about 15 minutes.

Strain potatoes in a colander and return them to the pot. Add butter, hot sauce, crème fraîche, and roasted garlic,

Mash potatoes with a potato masher or the back of a fork until smooth. Add in the cream, 1 tablespoon at a time, until the potatoes are smooth and creamy. Season with salt and pepper.

FOR THE LEMON-MARINATED OLIVES

Strain the brine from olives, pat dry using paper towels, and cut into ¼-inch-thick circles.

Slowly warm the olive oil in a small saucepot over low heat, being careful not to get the oil too hot. Add olives, lemon zest, chile flakes, and paprika. Remove from heat and cool to room temperature.

FOR THE SMOKED COD

In a mixing bowl, whisk sugar and salt into the hot water until dissolved. Add 3 ice cubes and stir until dissolved. Add the fish, cover bowl with plastic wrap, and refrigerate for 3 hours.

Remove fish from brine, pat dry with absorbent paper towels, and place on a rack on a baking sheet. Refrigerate until a sticky surface has formed, 4–5 hours (preferably overnight).

Smoke cold fish in a smoker according to labeled instructions (while this recipe calls for alderwood, applewood could also be used). Remove from smoker and reserve.

Preheat oven to 375°F.

Cook fish until done, 10–15 minutes.

FOR THE POACHED EGG

Crack 6 eggs into 6 individual cups.

Fill a large pot with water and add salt and vinegar. Bring water to a low simmer and turn off heat. Stir the pot using a spoon and create a slow whirlpool. Working quickly, drop eggs in one at a time in a rapid, fluid succession.

Cook eggs for 3–4 minutes, or until desired doneness.

Remove using a slotted spoon onto a plate lined with paper towels. Remove any excess white strands until you have a nice, round, poached egg. Season with salt and pepper.

FOR THE SOURDOUGH TOAST

Brush both side of bread with olive oil and season with salt and pepper. Griddle until golden brown and crispy.

AT SERVICE

Spoon potatoes into the center of each bowl. Using the back of a spoon, create a divot in the middle of the potatoes. Place the smoked fish inside the divot and top with one poached egg. Spoon olives and olive oil over the plate. Garnish with chives and two pieces of toast.

Chef's Tip: *Feel free to substitute any fatty fish traditionally used for smoking, including Wild King salmon, trout, or East Coast haddock.*

Chef's Tip: *I like to keep the egg moving during the cooking process. Keep the water moving in a whirling fashion at the very top (above the eggs). This will cook the eggs evenly. To check the egg, lift with a slotted spoon and check for doneness by feeling with your hand to see how set the egg is (keeping in mind there's always a little carry over after cooking).*

Chocolate Clams and Caviar

Angel-Hair Pasta, Crème Fraîche, Chives, Quail Egg Yolk

SERVES 6

Chocolate Baja clams are big and meaty with sweet and delicate meat. They are great eaten on the half shell, raw with a little bit of lemon juice, or in a dish like this one during the winter months.

Suggested wine pairing: Sonoma Coast Chardonnay

For the pasta and sauce

3 tablespoons butter
3 tablespoons light olive oil
4 cloves minced garlic
1 shallot, minced
1 cup dry white wine
1 sprig thyme
6 jumbo clams (about 8 ounces each) rinsed, shell on
1½ cups heavy cream
3 tablespoons crème fraîche
½ teaspoon Aleppo chile flakes (substitute chile flakes)
Zest of one lemon
½ pound angel-hair pasta, cooked al dente according to package
Salt and pepper, to taste
2 tablespoons chopped fresh chives
½ cup grated Parmigiana Reggiano

For the quail yolks

6 quail eggs
1 ounce osetra caviar
Freshly ground black pepper, to taste

FOR THE PASTA AND SAUCE

Melt butter and oil in a saucepot over medium heat. Add garlic and shallot, and sauté until fragrant (do not allow the garlic to brown).

Add white wine and thyme, and bring to a strong boil.

Add clams and cover saucepot (clams should be in a single layer on the bottom of the pot). Cook clams until just steamed open. Carefully remove and reserve.

Reduce remaining liquid by half its volume. While reducing, remove the meat from the clamshells using a paring knife, cutting close to the shell to detach the muscle. Break the top and bottom of the shell apart. Discard the top shell (the bottom shell will be used as the serving vessel). Roughly chop the clam meat and reserve.

Reduce heat to medium, stir in cream, and simmer until reduced to a sauce consistency, about 10 minutes.

Remove thyme sprig and reduce heat to low. Whisk in crème fraîche.

Add the chopped clams, chile flakes, lemon zest, and pasta to the sauce. Completely coat the pasta with the sauce and season with salt and pepper.

Using a large entree fork, spin the pasta around the fork to appropriate size for the shell. Repeat this until all 6 shells are filled with the desired amount of pasta. Spoon remaining sauce from the pot over each pasta serving. Garnish with chives and Parmigiana Reggiano.

FOR THE QUAIL YOLKS

Working quickly while your pasta is still hot, crack the quail eggs open one at a time into your hand. Separate the white from the yolk. Discard

the white. Place one yolk on top of each pasta serving and season with black pepper. Top with a dollop of osetra caviar.

AT SERVICE

Slightly dampen six white paper towels with water. Twist and circle each paper towel into a ring shape, slightly smaller than the clamshell. Place one ring in the center of each plate. Place each pasta filled clam on each paper towel ring, using the ring to stabalize the shell from tipping over.

Chef's Tip: *Substitute any jumbo clam in this recipe, but when you are opening them, be sure to do it over a bowl in order to catch needed clam juice.*

Chef's Tip: *To stabilize the shells while filling, place a 2-foot-long piece of aluminum foil on a plate. Slightly crumple the foil to allow all 6 clamshells to sit level and not roll to the side. Fill the shells with all the components while stabilized by the foil.*

Sugar Pumpkin Gnocchi with Chile-Cured Pork

Wilted Kale, Mushrooms and Scallions, Mushroom Sauce

SERVES 6

The saltiness and richness of pork belly paired with pumpkin gnocchi are what I love best about this dish. It's nice to take seasonal ingredients and work them into pasta and gnocchi.

Suggested wine pairing: Tempranillo

For the gnocchi

1 tablespoon light olive oil
1 tablespoon garlic
1 tablespoon ginger
1 sugar pumpkin
Butter, for seasoning pumpkin
Salt and pepper, to taste
1 tablespoon egg yolk
2 tablespoons finely grated Parmigiana Reggiano
1 teaspoon cumin/coriander spice blend (page 283)
¼ teaspoon sage, chopped very fine
¾ cup bread flour

For the kale

2 tablespoons light olive oil
2 teaspoons finely chopped garlic
2 bunches black kale, roughly chopped
½ teaspoon salt

For the pork belly and cure

½ pound salt
½ pound granulated sugar
½ cup brown sugar
4 Guajillo chiles, roughly chopped
6 cloves garlic
1 (4-inch) sprig rosemary, roughly chopped
2 sprigs thyme, roughly chopped
1 tablespoon black peppercorns
1 pound pork belly
4 tablespoons light olive oil

For the mushroom sauce

3 tablespoons light olive oil
½ Spanish onion, peeled and sliced
½ cup chopped green scallions
8 cloves garlic, roughly chopped
1½-inch piece ginger, roughly chopped
1 bunch cilantro stems
1 cup roughly chopped mushroom stems
2 cups chicken stock (page 283)
1 small piece of kombu
3 tablespoons soy sauce
1 teaspoon chile flakes
2 tablespoons white distilled vinegar
1 tablespoon hoisin sauce

For the mushrooms and scallions

4 tablespoons light olive oil
5 cups assorted mushrooms, sliced
30 scallions (2-inch pieces of the white part of the onion)
2 tablespoons chopped garlic
Salt and pepper, to taste

FOR THE GNOCCHI

Heat olive oil in a small sauté pan over medium-high heat. Add garlic and ginger and cook until just fragrant. Remove from heat and reserve.

Preheat oven to 350°F.

Cut pumpkin in half and scoop out the seeds. Using your hand, smear the butter liberally over the flesh side of the pumpkin and season with a little salt and pepper.

Roast the pumpkin (cut side up) until very soft, about 1 hour.

Scoop out pumpkin flesh and process in food processor until smooth (you will need 1 cup puree when done).

Spread pumpkin onto a baking sheet lined with a nonstick baking mat.

Place pumpkin back in oven, stirring every 5 minutes until slightly dry and a thick paste consistency, about 15 minutes. Cool to room temperature, and refrigerate for about 20 minutes.

In a large mixing bowl, combine pumpkin, garlic/ginger mixture, egg yolk, Parmigiana Reggiano, cumin/coriander, sage, salt, and pepper. Work in flour by kneading and forming a dough.

Roll dough into ½-inch logs and cut into 1-inch pieces (you can just leave them in this shape or press and roll on a gnocchi paddle).

Bring a medium pot of salted water to a boil.

Add gnocchi and cook until they float to the top. Using a slotted spoon, remove gnocchi from the water into a bowl of ice and water. Cool and remove to a baking sheet lined with paper towels.

FOR THE KALE

Heat olive oil in a large sauté pan over medium heat. Add garlic and cook until just fragrant. Add kale and salt, and toss lightly. Cook until just wilted.

FOR THE MUSHROOM SAUCE

Heat a small saucepot over high heat. Add olive oil, onion, scallions, garlic, ginger, cilantro, and mushroom stems, and sauté over high heat, stirring often, for 5 minutes.

Add stock, kombu, soy sauce, chile flakes, vinegar, and hoisin sauce. Bring mixture to a boil, reduce to low heat, and simmer for 5 minutes.

Remove from heat and let steep for 15–20 minutes. Strain mixture through a fine-mesh sieve, and reserve.

FOR THE MUSHROOMS

Heat a large sauté pan over high heat. Add oil, mushrooms, and scallions; sauté, stirring often, for about 2 minutes. Add garlic, season with salt and pepper, and sauté for another 2 minutes.

FOR THE PORK BELLY

Combine all ingredients (except pork belly and olive oil) in a food processor; pulse until well incorporated.

Line a perforated hotel pan with a double layer of cheesecloth. With your hands, spread a thin layer of cure to create a flat bed just big enough to accommodate the pork belly.

Place the pork belly on top of cure and pour the excess cure on top of pork belly, pressing the salt into it (belly slices should be completely covered with cure). Place another pan on top and weigh it down with about 10 pounds of weight.

Allow pork to cure for 1 day, then remove from the salt by rinsing all the cure off with cold water.

Cut pork belly into ½-inch-thick slices across the meat grain, then slice across the belly strips about ½ inch to create small pieces.

Heat a large sauté pan over medium-high heat. Add olive oil and the pork belly pieces. Cook the pork belly until caramelized, about 5 minutes.

Remove belly from the pan and pour off half the fat.

Add gnocchi and cook until slightly caramelized, about 2 minutes. Add mushrooms, kale, and scallions and heat until warm.

AT SERVICE

Distribute the gnocchi into bowls. Add the pork belly pieces, kale, mushrooms, and scallions and pour desired amount of mushroom sauce into each bowl.

Chef's Tip: *Substitute kabocha squash, sweet potatoes, or yams for the pumpkin.*

Housemade Cavatelli Pasta and Fennel Spiced Sausage

Chanterelle Mushroom, Mushroom-Leek Jus

SERVES 6 / YIELDS 1½ POUNDS PASTA DOUGH

I like to choose small chanterelle mushrooms that have a firmer texture to complement this hearty and meaty pasta. The in-season leeks add a sweet and earthy component.

Suggested wine pairing: Alsatian Pinot Blanc

For the cavatelli pasta

3½ cups all-purpose flour, more if needed
Pinch of salt
3 large eggs, divided
¼ cup light olive oil
8 tablespoons very cold water

For the sausage

3 tablespoons light olive oil
2 pounds ground pork butt
1 teaspoon coriander
1 teaspoon chile flakes
¼ teaspoon caraway seeds
½ teaspoon granulated sugar
¼ teaspoon black pepper
1 tablespoon cracked fennel seed
6 tablespoons ice water
1 tablespoon salt
1 teaspoon onion powder
1 teaspoon garlic powder

For the mushroom leek jus

4 tablespoons light olive oil, divided
4 cups chanterelle mushrooms, cut in half
2 tablespoons finely chopped chives
2 tablespoons finely minced garlic, divided
2 tablespoon finely minced shallots, divided
Salt and pepper, to taste
2 large leeks (white part only), cut into
    ½-inch squares
1 teaspoon chile flakes
¼ cup dry sherry

2 cups chicken stock (page 283)
1 cup black truffle butter (substitute cold butter),
    large diced
2 tablespoons fines herbes

For the garnish

Lemon olive oil, for drizzling
1 small block Parmigiana Reggiano cheese

FOR THE CAVATELLI PASTA

Place flour in a stand mixer with dough-hook attachment in place. Add salt, eggs, olive oil, and water. Process ingredients until a soft dough forms, 1–2 minutes.

Turn the dough out onto a lightly floured surface and knead by hand for a minute until it's smooth, soft, and stretchy. Wrap dough in plastic wrap, and let it rest at room temperature for 30 minutes.

Cut dough into quarters. Working with one quarter at a time, roll the dough on a lightly floured surface, into a ¼-inch-diameter rope. Cut rope into ½-inch pieces. With your index and third fingers held together, gently press down on each piece, beginning at the top and moving down toward the bottom, dragging your fingers toward you and causing the pasta to roll over on itself. Transfer the formed pasta to a lightly floured baking sheet.

Bring a large pot of salted water to a boil, add the pasta, and cook until they float to the surface.

Strain pasta and add to a large bowl, add the mushroom-leek jus (see below), and toss to combine.

FOR THE SAUSAGE

Combine all ingredients in a large mixing bowl. Work vigorously with your hands until well mixed and slightly sticky.

Heat olive oil in a large sauté pan over medium-high heat, brown the sausage, breaking it into large pieces. Cook until done. Reserve.

FOR THE MUSHROOM LEEK JUS

Heat 2 tablespoons olive oil in a large sauté pan over high heat. Add mushrooms and chives; sauté until slightly wilted, about 3 minutes. Add 1 tablespoon each of garlic and shallots, and continue to cook for about 1 minute. Season with salt and pepper to taste. Remove mushrooms from pan and reserve.

Wipe out the pan and return it to high heat. Add remaining olive oil, leeks, remaining garlic and shallots, and chile flake. Cook until fragrant, about 1 minute. Add the sherry, and allow mixture to cook down until almost dry.

Add the chicken stock, bring to a boil, and reduce to a strong simmer. Allow to simmer for 2–3 minutes.

Add reserved mushrooms and fennel-spiced sausage and turn heat to medium.

Stir in diced butter, and reduce to sauce consistency, 3–5 minutes. Finish with herbs.

Toss pasta in sauce and heat through.

AT SERVICE

Distribute pasta among plates. Drizzle with lemon oil and grated Parmigiana Reggiano cheese.

Chef's Tip: *The best way to tell if pasta is done is to remove a piece and taste it.*

Crispy Abalone and Shaved Vegetables

Horseradish Vinaigrette, Meyer Lemon Aioli, Serrano Chiles

SERVES 6

When I was a kid we would always have our abalone knives on us on our weight belts when we were spearfishing. We would dive under the rocks where they attach themselves. Abalone is good marinated ceviche-style or, as in this recipe, breaded and pan-fried.

Suggested wine pairing: Albariño

For the horseradish vinaigrette

1 cup house vinaigrette (page 285)
1 tablespoon lemon juice
8 tablespoons prepared horseradish
1 tablespoon Dijon mustard

For the shaved vegetables

3 carrots, peeled
1 large Chioggia beet, peeled
2 bulbs fennel
Salt and pepper, to taste

For the abalone

4 eggs
2 cups all-purpose flour
4 teaspoons smoked paprika
2 teaspoons cayenne pepper
2 teaspoons poultry seasoning
2 teaspoons onion powder
2 teaspoons garlic powder
2 teaspoons dry mustard powder
2 teaspoons salt
1 pound abalone, sliced, pounded, and cut
    into 18 pieces
Light olive oil, for frying
Salt and pepper, to taste

For the Meyer lemon aioli

¼ cup base aioli (page 281)
1 teaspoon finely grated Meyer lemon zest
1 teaspoon fresh Meyer lemon juice

For the garnish

1 Serrano pepper, thinly sliced
2 tablespoons finely chopped chives

FOR THE HORSERADISH VINAIGRETTE

In a small mixing bowl, combine all ingredients; whisk until incorporated.

FOR THE SHAVED VEGETABLES

Using a mandoline, shave the vegetables very thin and combine in a mixing bowl. Season with horseradish vinaigrette and salt and pepper.

FOR THE ABALONE

In a mixing bowl, whisk eggs thoroughly.

In another large mixing bowl, combine flour, paprika, cayenne, poultry seasoning, onion powder, garlic powder, mustard powder, and salt.

Dip the abalone in eggs (shaking off excess) and then coat all sides with seasoned flour.

Heat olive oil (½ inch from the bottom) in a large sauté pan over medium-high heat. Fry abalone until crispy and golden brown, 2–3 minutes. Season with salt and pepper.

FOR THE MEYER LEMON AIOLI

In a small mixing bowl, combine all ingredients; whisk until incorporated.

AT SERVICE

Place a small amount of shaved vegetables at one end of each plate, and add a piece of abalone. Repeat the pattern until a long narrow salad is nicely formed and there are 3 pieces of abalone on the plate. Drizzle plate with some of the horseradish vinaigrette. Spoon some of the aioli onto each piece of abalone and top with 1 slice of Serrano pepper. Garnish with some of the chives.

Chef's Tip: *Abalone is a large and very flavorful mollusk, but the muscular texture is a challenge for any cook. One of the best techniques for preparing the flesh for any recipe is to wield a very sharp knife and filet into thin slices, followed by a light tenderizing with a mallet or other flat instrument.*

Braised Beef Tongue

Horseradish Whipped Potatoes and Petite Winter Vegetable Roast

SERVES 6

Beef tongue is an extremely moist cut of meat. Some of my favorite dishes when I was visiting Japan were made with braised beef tongue. When braised properly, it's delicate in texture and is a great alternative to other more traditional braised items.

Suggested wine pairing: Red Bordeaux Blend

For the beef tongue

1 (3-pound) cow or calf tongue

For the braising liquid

2 tablespoons light olive oil
2 slices of bacon, chopped
2 yellow onions, peeled and chopped
1 large carrot, chopped
1 rib celery, chopped
8 cups demi-glace (page 284)
1 bottle cabernet wine
2 bay leaves
¼ bunch fresh thyme, chopped
¼ bunch fresh parsley, chopped
Salt and pepper, to taste

For the horseradish whipped potatoes

3 russet potatoes, peeled and diced
1½ cups heavy cream, warmed
¾ cup butter, room temperature
½ cup fresh grated horseradish
Salt and pepper, to taste

For the petite winter vegetable roast

24 baby carrots, peeled
24 turnips, cleaned and quartered
24 baby beets, cleaned and quartered
4 bunches broccolini, roughly chopped
2 tablespoons light olive oil
Salt, to taste

For the garnish

1½ cups crumbled blue cheese

FOR THE BEEF TONGUE

Submerge beef tongue in a large pot of cold water. Bring to a boil, then to a simmer over low heat. Cook tongue for 1½–2 hours, then remove and let cool. Using a sharp knife, carefully remove and discard the skin.

FOR THE BRAISING LIQUID

Preheat the oven to 350°F.

Heat olive oil in a large saucepot over high heat, Add bacon, and cook until the fat of the bacon is released.

Add onions, carrot, and celery, and cook until onions are translucent.

Add demi-glace, wine, bay leaves, thyme, and parsley; season with salt and pepper. Cook over medium-low heat uncovered until liquid is reduced by half it volume, about 20 minutes.

Add beef tongue to a large baking dish, cover with braising liquid, and tightly seal dish with aluminum foil. Braise the beef tongue in the oven for 3–4 hours, or until fork tender.

Slice beef tongue into 24 ½-inch-thick segments. Reserve the braising liquid.

Heat an indoor or outdoor grill pan over high heat. Cook beef tongue until slightly caramelized; season with salt and pepper.

FOR THE HORSERADISH WHIPPED POTATOES

Place potatoes in a large saucepot filled with salted, cold water, and bring to a boil.

Reduce heat to low and simmer potatoes until fork tender.

Drain potatoes in a colander.

In a food mill or food processor, combine potatoes with cream, butter, and horseradish. Process until smooth; season with salt and pepper.

FOR THE PETITE WINTER VEGETABLE ROAST

Preheat oven to 400°F.

In a large mixing bowl, combine carrots, turnips, beets, and broccolini. Drizzle with olive oil and salt, and toss to incorporate.

Place vegetables on a baking sheet and roast until tender, occasionally tossing during the cooking process, 30–40 minutes.

AT SERVICE

Ladle braising liquid onto plates, place horseradish whipped potatoes to the side, and distribute some of the broccolini onto each plate. Arrange 4 beef tongue segments on each plate, and ladle braising liquid over them. Distribute winter vegetables over the top of that. Garnish with blue cheese.

Chef's Tip: *When choosing horseradish, look for something that is very firm and doesn't yield when pressed hard with your thumb.*

Chef's Tip: *Freshly grated horseradish is very hot and pungent. If you want a milder version, just add less.*

Duck Breast and Crispy Leg Confit

Orange Confit, Brandy-Whipped Yams, Vegetable Stir-Fry, Cranberries

SERVES 6

When I was growing up, I remember my grandfather was the president of Duck's Unlimited for many years. When he came back from a hunting trip, my grandmother would prepare a traditional Duck à l'Orange–style dinner for the entire family. Of course, this was really old school, but I loved the taste of citrus and the standard orange marmalade paired with the duck. This recipe is a more modern and eclectic version, reflecting my travels. It has a little Asian flare, a little classic à l'orange, and kind of an after-the-hunt wintery take to it.

Suggested wine pairing: California Pinot Noir

For the duck confit

6 duck legs
3 tablespoons salt
1 tablespoon pepper
4 thyme sprigs
4 bay leaves
1 sprig rosemary
2 bulbs garlic, roughly chopped
2 large shallots, roughly chopped
8 cups duck fat (may substitute 8 cups of shortening)

For the brandy whipped yams

1 apple
¼ pound plus 1 tablespoon butter
1 large yam
1 banana, with peel
¾ cup heavy cream
2 teaspoons Chinese five-spice powder
1 teaspoon ground cinnamon
1½ tablespoons brown sugar
Pinch of salt
3 tablespoons brandy

For the cranberries

2 cups fresh cranberries
½ cup freshly squeezed orange juice
2 cups granulated sugar
3 star anise

For the orange confit

2 oranges, peeled and sliced into thin rounds (seeds removed)
2½ cups granulated sugar
1½ cups water
1 stick cinnamon
5 cloves
5 cardamom pods
½ vanilla bean pod, scraped

For the duck breast

6 duck breasts
Salt and pepper, to taste
Chinese five-spice powder, to taste

For the duck jus

2 tablespoons light olive oil
1 white onion, roughly chopped
1 celery stalk, roughly chopped
1 large carrot, roughly chopped
12 cups red wine
3 cups dry white wine
8 cups chicken stock (page 283)
3 star anise
1 stick cinnamon
1 (2-inch) sprig rosemary
1 sprig thyme
2 teaspoons whole peppercorns
2 teaspoons whole coriander

For the vegetable stir-fry

3 tablespoons light olive oil
½ head cabbage, thinly sliced
1 large carrot, peeled and thinly sliced
1 large red bell pepper, seeds removed, thinly sliced
1 tablespoon finely minced garlic
1 tablespoon finely chopped ginger
2 tablespoons light soy sauce
2 tablespoons red wine vinegar

For the broccolini

2 tablespoons light olive oil
3 bunches broccolini
Salt and pepper, to taste

FOR THE DUCK CONFIT

Preheat oven to 275°F.

In a large mixing bowl, combine the duck legs, salt, pepper, thyme, bay leaves, rosemary, garlic, and shallots; mixing together using your hands. Cover bowl with plastic wrap and refrigerate (to cure) for 2 days. Periodically mix everything together with your hands during the 2-day process.

Remove duck legs from refrigerator and rinse thoroughly with cold water to remove the marinade, then thoroughly dry with paper towels.

Arrange duck legs in a Dutch oven and completely cover with duck fat. Place Dutch oven on stovetop and heat until boiling, then remove from heat, cover with lid, and place in oven.

Bake duck legs for 2 hours, then remove from oven and allow them to cool.

Twist the bones of the leg to remove thigh and drumstick bones.

In a large nonstick skillet set on medium heat, place duck meat with skin side down and cook until crispy. Remove duck legs to a cutting board and cut in halves. The legs can be stored covered in the refrigerator for up to two days.

FOR THE BRANDY WHIPPED YAMS

Peel apple, remove core and seeds, and cut into cubes. Place cubes in aluminum foil with 1 tablespoon of butter on top. Close foil tightly.

Preheat oven to 350°F.

Place apple, yam, and banana (with peel) on a baking sheet and place in oven. After 15 minutes remove the banana and let cool. After 30 minutes, remove apple. After 1 hour, remove yam. Allow all to cool.

Peel skin away from yam and banana. Place yam, banana, and apple in a bowl and mash well with a hand masher or food mill (according to labeled instructions) until very smooth.

Combine remaining ¼ pound of butter and cream to a saucepot over medium-low heat until just simmering and butter is completely melted. Stirring constantly, add Chinese five-spice powder, cinnamon, brown sugar, and salt. Remove from heat and set aside.

Reheat the cream at low heat and add the mashed yam, banana, and apple mixture to the same saucepot. With a wooden spoon, fully incorporate. Add brandy, continue to incorporate, and remove from heat.

FOR THE CRANBERRIES

Combine all ingredients in a small saucepot over medium heat; cook until mixture is reduced to desired thickness, 10–15 minutes. Set aside.

FOR THE ORANGE CONFIT

Arrange the oranges in a baking dish.

In a saucepot, combine sugar, water, cinnamon, cloves, cardamom, and vanilla (bean and pod). Bring to a boil over high heat, then pour over oranges and incorporate by tossing very gently (be careful not to break apart the oranges). Cool to room temperature. Oranges can remain in the refrigerator, covered, for up to 2 weeks.

FOR THE DUCK BREAST

Place duck breasts skin side up on a cutting board. With a sharp knife, lightly score the skin of the duck breast in a crisscross pattern, not deep enough to hit the meat, but just into the fat layer.

Season both sides of the duck breasts with salt and pepper, and liberally sprinkle with Chinese five-spice powder evenly on the non-skin side.

Preheat oven to 350°F.

In a large nonstick ovenproof skillet over medium heat, place duck breasts skin side down. Cook duck breasts until the skin is lightly brown and rendered of its fat, about 10 minutes.

Flip duck breasts over, place the pan in the oven, and bake for 10–12 minutes.

Remove duck breasts and allow to rest at room temperature. Before serving, cut duck breasts into even slices.

FOR THE DUCK JUS

Heat olive oil in large sauté pan over medium heat. Add onion, celery, and carrots, and cook until softened, about 10 minutes.

Add red and white wines and cook uncovered, reducing volume to 2 cups, about 20 minutes.

Add the stock, anise, cinnamon, rosemary, thyme, peppercorns, and coriander, and bring heat to a medium-low simmer. Reduce the liquid to a light syrup consistency or until it coats the back of a spoon, about 1 hour.

Strain liquid through a fine-mesh sieve, place back into the pan, and cover with lid.

FOR THE VEGETABLE STIR-FRY

Heat olive oil in a large skillet over high heat until it starts to smoke. Add cabbage, carrots, peppers, garlic, and ginger. Continually stirring, cook the vegetables for about 1 minute. Turn heat off and add soy sauce and vinegar; stir to incorporate.

FOR THE BROCCOLINI

Heat olive oil in a large skillet over medium heat; add broccolini and sauté until tender, about 5 minutes. Season with salt and pepper.

AT SERVICE

Place 2 dollops of whipped yams on each dinner plate. Add the vegetable stir-fry to the tops of the yams, followed by a duck leg half. Top each duck leg with an orange slice. Place broccolini in front of yams. Place the duck breast slices on top of the broccolini. Top the duck breast with cranberries. Drizzle the au jus around the plate.

Chef's Tip: *Take advantage of the fact that many of the steps for this dish can be made well ahead of time so dinner can be relaxing and fun for you and your guests.*

Grilled Marinated Skirt Steak and Twice-Baked Potato

Spaghetti Squash, Worcestershire Butter, Braised Cippolini Onions

SERVES 6

The flavor profile of skirt steak in this recipe is deeply enhanced when it is marinated, grilled, and finished with Worcestershire butter. The rich textures of a twice-baked potato with spaghetti squash and cippolini onions offer an invigorating yet hearty balance of richness that further complements the grilled meat.

Suggested wine pairing: Napa Valley Cabernet

For the steak

½ cup light olive oil
½ cup red wine vinegar
2 tablespoons Dijon mustard
3 cloves garlic, finely chopped
1 tablespoon chopped rosemary
1 teaspoon salt
1 teaspoon black pepper
6 (6-ounce) skirt steak fillets

For the spaghetti squash

1 large spaghetti squash
3 tablespoons light olive oil
1 Spanish onion, peeled and thinly sliced
1 bay leaf
2 tablespoons butter
1 tablespoon garlic
1 tablespoon fines herbs (page 285)
Salt and pepper, to taste

For the crispy bacon discs

¼ slab bacon, room temperature

For the twice-baked potatoes

4 large russet potatoes, peeled and diced into
    1-inch pieces
Salt
1 bay leaf
½ cup sour cream
2 cups grated white cheddar cheese, divided
3 tablespoons finely chopped chives
3 tablespoons reserved bacon fat
6 (3-inch-round) ring molds

For the braised cippolini onions

6 tablespoons light olive oil
2 strips bacon, chopped
10 cloves garlic
2 sprigs rosemary
18 cippolini onions, peeled
Salt and pepper, to taste
2 cups chicken stock (page 283)

For the broccolini

2 tablespoons light olive oil
2 teaspoons finely chopped garlic
2 bunches broccolini, roughly chopped
½ teaspoon salt

For the Worcestershire butter

3 cloves garlic, tops sliced
Light olive oil, for drizzling
Salt, to taste
Black pepper, to taste
½ pound butter, room temperature
¼ cup Worcestershire sauce

For the garnish

1 cup sour cream
3 tablespoons finely chopped chives

FOR THE STEAK

Combine all ingredients, except the steaks, in a blender, and process until smooth.

Add steaks to a large mixing bowl, cover with marinade, and rub the marinade into each steak. Cover the bowl with plastic wrap and marinate the steaks in the refrigerator for 2–3 hours.

Heat an indoor or outdoor gill pan over high heat. Cook steaks until caramelized, about 5 minutes per side or until desired doneness.

FOR THE SPAGHETTI SQUASH

Preheat oven to 350°F.

Cut squash in half and place (cut side down) in a small shallow baking sheet. Add just enough water to cover the bottom of the pan about a ½-inch deep. Bake squash for 40–45 minutes, checking for doneness by scraping the flesh of the squash with a fork. It should easily release and look like spaghetti when it's done. Remove from oven and cool. Using a fork, release the spaghettilike flesh and reserve.

Heat olive oil in a large sauté pan over medium heat. Add onion and bay leaf, and reduce heat to medium low. Slowly cook onions until most of their moisture has evaporated and they intensify in flavor, about 30 minutes (do not caramelize). Add butter, garlic, and squash, and sauté until onions and squash are fully incorporated and hot, about 2 minutes. Season with fines herbes, salt, and pepper.

FOR THE CRISPY BACON DISCS

Preheat oven to 350°F.

Roll the bacon slab into a log and tie it tightly with butcher twine. Place bacon on a baking sheet and freeze in the freezer until solid.

Using an electric slicer or sharp knife, cut bacon into thin, round slices.

Place bacon slices, about an inch apart, onto a sheet pan lined with parchment paper. Place another sheet pan on top of the bacon to prevent it from curling.

Place bacon in oven and cook until golden brown and crispy, about 25 minutes. Reserve the bacon fat.

FOR THE TWICE-BAKED POTATOES

Place potatoes in a large saucepot and cover with water. Add salt and bay leaf. Bring to a boil then reduce to low heat, simmering the potatoes until soft but not falling apart. Strain the potatoes in a colander and remove the bay leaf.

Preheat oven to 350°F.

Arrange potatoes on a large baking sheet and place in oven for 10 minutes.

In a large mixing bowl, combine potatoes with sour cream, 1 cup of cheddar cheese, chives, and bacon fat.

Evenly divide the potato mixture into ring molds, about 1½ inches from the bottom. Arrange potato ring molds on a large baking sheet lined with parchment paper. Evenly distribute the remaining cheddar cheese over the tops of potato ring molds. Place in oven and bake until warmed through and cheese on top is melted, about 15 minutes.

FOR THE BRAISED CIPPOLINI ONIONS

Heat olive oil in a large saucepot over high heat. Add bacon, garlic, and rosemary, and cook until fragrant, about 30 seconds.

Add onions, and season with salt and pepper. Cook until onions are golden brown and caramelized on each side.

Add chicken stock and simmer onions until soft, but somewhat tender, 5-7 minutes per side.

FOR THE BROCCOLINI

Heat olive oil in a large sauté pan over medium heat. Add garlic and cook until just fragrant. Add broccolini and salt, lightly toss, and cook until wilted.

FOR THE WORCESTERSHIRE BUTTER

Preheat oven to 350°F.

Drizzle garlic with olive oil, salt, and pepper. Place garlic in foil, and wrap tightly.

Place in oven and cook until soft, 25-30 minutes.

Remove from oven and squeeze flesh into a small mixing bowl. Add butter, Worcestershire, 1 teaspoon of salt, and ½ teaspoon of black pepper; whisk vigorously until combined.

AT SERVICE

Mound spaghetti squash onto the center of each plate. Slice each steak fillet into slices and place over the top of the spaghetti squash. Using a spatula, position the twice-baked potatoes onto each plate just behind the fillet and carefully remove the ring molds. Top potatoes with dollops of sour cream and some of the chives. Place broccolini alongside the potatoes. Garnish fillet with the cippolini onions and insert one bacon disc into the twice-baked potatoes. Spoon Worcestershire butter over and around the steaks.

Chef's Tip: *Flank steak can also be used in this recipe.*

Veal Schnitzel and Sausage

Root Vegetable Puree, Porcini Mushroom and Leek Ragout, Apple Chutney

SERVES 6

A porcini mushroom ragout with a splash of sherry adds signature flavoring to this crispy breaded and pan-fried veal schnitzel. The apple chutney gives the sausage a decadent twist. It's a classic dish that never gets old, and my customers love it. Sometimes great classics stand on their own.

Suggested wine pairing: Shiraz

For the veal schnitzel medallions

2 cups flour
4 eggs, whisked well
3 cups panko bread crumbs
12 (2-ounce) veal medallions, lightly pounded
    to about ¼ inch thick
Canola oil, for frying
Salt and pepper, to taste

For the pork and veal sausage

2 tablespoons light olive oil
½ cup diced onions
2 tablespoons garlic
1 pound ground pork
2 pounds ground veal
1½ teaspoons ground fennel
1½ teaspoons coriander
2 teaspoons salt
½ teaspoon black pepper
½ teaspoon chile flakes
1 teaspoon dry mustard
½ teaspoon thyme
½ teaspoon paprika
½ teaspoon onion powder
½ teaspoon garlic powder
1 tablespoon Dijon mustard
1½ teaspoons hot sauce
2 tablespoons water
6 pork casings

For the root vegetable puree

4 tablespoons light olive oil
½ Spanish onion, peeled and thinly sliced
10 cloves garlic, peeled and roughly chopped
1 tablespoon salt
2 rutabagas, peeled and large diced
2 large purple top turnips, peeled and diced
Vegetable stock, as needed (page 288)
1 bay leaf
1 cup cream
¼ pound butter, diced

For the porcini mushroom and leek ragout

4 tablespoons butter
4 large leeks (white part only), sliced
1 teaspoon salt
Pinch of black pepper
3 tablespoons light olive oil
12 small porcini mushrooms, halved
1 tablespoon minced shallots
Splash of sherry

For the braised red cabbage

½ cup finely chopped bacon
1 Spanish onion, peeled and thinly sliced
2 apples peeled, cored, small diced
2 tablespoons minced garlic
1 red cabbage, thinly sliced
1 sprig thyme
1 bay leaf
½ cup apple cider
½ cup apple cider vinegar
1 cup chicken stock (page 283)
Salt and pepper, to taste

For the apple chutney

6 Granny Smith apples, peeled, cored, and diced
    into ½-inch pieces
½ cup brown sugar
1 cup raisins
1 teaspoon finely minced ginger
¼ teaspoon salt
1 star anise
½ teaspoon chile flakes
1 cup orange juice
½ cup cider vinegar

For the eggs

Butter, for coating pan
6 eggs

FOR THE VEAL SCHNITZEL MEDALLIONS

Set up 3 mixing bowls, placing flour in one, whisked eggs in the second, and bread crumbs in the third.

Dredge the medallions (one at a time) first in flour, then dip in egg to coat, then roll quickly in the bread crumbs.

Heat about ¼ inch of canola oil in a large sauté pan over medium-high heat. In batches, add schnitzel to the pan, replacing oil as needed. Cook until golden brown, about 1 minute per side. Remove to a baking sheet lined with paper towels and season liberally with salt and pepper.

FOR THE PORK AND VEAL SAUSAGE

Heat olive oil in a small sauté pan over medium-high heat. Add onions and garlic and cook until onions are translucent.

In a large mixing bowl, combine remaining ingredients (except the pork casings) with onion/garlic mixture.

Using the sausage attachment on a mixer, stuff the meat into the casings. Twist and tie off to make 4-inch sausages. Grill 3–5 minutes on each side.

FOR THE ROOT VEGETABLE PUREE

Heat olive oil in a large sauté pan over medium heat. Add onions, garlic, and salt. Cook onions until translucent.

Add rutabagas, turnips, and enough vegetable stock to just cover the vegetables. Add bay leaf, cover pot, and simmer until the vegetables are very soft and almost falling apart.

Warm cream and butter in a small saucepot until butter is melted.

Strain the vegetables through a colander, reserving some of the vegetable stock. Remove the bay leaf, and add mixture to a blender with warm cream and butter mixture; process until smooth (if needed, add a little of the vegetable broth).

FOR THE PORCINI MUSHROOM AND LEEK RAGOUT

Melt butter in a large saucepot over medium-low heat. Add leeks and sauté until very soft, 15–20 minutes (do not allow to color). Season with salt and pepper.

Heat olive oil in a large sauté pan over high heat. Add mushrooms and cook until caramelized. Add shallots and sherry, and cook until all liquid has evaporated.

Add mushroom mixture to the leek mixture and reserve.

FOR THE BRAISED RED CABBAGE

Cook bacon in a large pot over medium heat, stirring constantly until bacon is crispy. Add onion, apples, and garlic, and cook until fragrant, about 2 minutes. Add remaining ingredients and cook covered for 30 minutes. Remove bay leaf and thyme, and cool to room temperature.

FOR THE APPLE CHUTNEY

Combine all ingredients in a medium saucepot over medium-low heat. Stirring gently, cook until all moisture has evaporated and mixture is a chunky pie-filling consistency, about 1 hour.

FOR THE EGGS

Just before serving: Melt butter in a nonstick pan over medium-high heat. Add eggs and cook sunny side up.

AT SERVICE

Spread root vegetable puree across the center of each plate. Add the braised cabbage on top of the puree (left of center). Top with 1 sausage and garnish with apple chutney. Add more root vegetable (right of center). Top with porcini mushroom and leek ragout. Top the ragout with 2 veal schnitzel medallions. Top the schnitzel medallions with 1 egg per plate.

Chef's Tip: *Feel free to substitute your favorite store-bought sausage.*

Braised Lamb Shank and Mushroom-Barley Risotto

Roasted Baby Root Vegetables, Savoy Spinach

SERVES 6

Meaty lamb dishes like this wine-braised lamb shank are the perfect comfort food dish on a chilly winter's day. The ideal accompaniments of roasted beets, turnips, rutabagas, and Savoy spinach pair perfectly with a cold-weather barley risotto.

Suggested wine pairing: Châteauneuf du Pape Rouge

For the lamb shanks

4 tablespoons light olive oil
6 (1-pound) lamb shanks
Salt and pepper, for seasoning
6 cloves garlic
1 Spanish onion, peeled and chopped
1 leek (white part only), chopped
1 (750-milliliter) bottle dry red wine
1 cup demi-glace (page 284)
1 cup water
1 bay leaf
10 peppercorns

For the mushroom-barley risotto

3 tablespoons light olive oil
½ cup finely chopped Spanish onions
1 leek (white part only), small diced
2 cups crimini mushrooms, small diced
½ cup barley
2 cups chicken stock (page 283)
1 bay leaf
1 sprig thyme
1 teaspoon salt
2 tablespoons softened butter
1 teaspoon lemon zest
1 tablespoon fines herbes (page 285)

For the roasted baby root vegetables

3 large red beets, peeled and diced
3 large turnips, peeled and diced
3 rutabagas, peeled and diced
3 tablespoons light olive oil
Salt and pepper, to taste

For the Savoy spinach

3 tablespoons butter
1 tablespoon minced garlic
1 tablespoon minced shallots
16 cups Savoy spinach
Salt, to taste

FOR THE LAMB SHANKS

Preheat the oven to 325°F.

Heat olive oil in a large enameled cast-iron casserole dish over medium-high heat. Season the lamb shanks with salt and pepper. Add shanks to the pan and brown on all 3 sides, about 4 minutes per side.

Add garlic, onions, leeks, wine, and demi-glace, and bring to a boil. Reduce heat to medium low.

Add bay leaf and peppercorns, cover the casserole dish tightly, and transfer to the oven. Braise the lamb shanks, turning once, until tender, 1½–2 hours.

Cut the lamb shanks into pieces.

FOR THE MUSHROOM-BARLEY RISOTTO

Heat olive oil in a saucepot over medium heat. Add onions and leeks, and sauté until translucent. Stir in barley and cook, stirring, for about 30 seconds. Add the stock, bay leaf, thyme, and salt.

Bring to a boil, then reduce heat to medium low. Cover and simmer for about 25 minutes, then uncover and continue to simmer for another 5 minutes or until all excess moisture has evaporated.

Remove from heat and stir in butter, lemon zest, and fines herbs.

FOR THE ROASTED BABY ROOT VEGETABLES

Preheat oven to 400°F.

Place vegetables on a baking sheet and toss with olive oil. Roast for 35–40 minutes, turning once or twice with a spatula, until the vegetables are tender. Remove from oven and season with salt and pepper.

FOR THE SAVOY SPINACH

Melt butter in a large sauté pan over medium-high heat. Add garlic and shallots, and cook until fragrant. Add spinach and salt, toss lightly, and cook until wilted.

AT SERVICE

Spoon barley risotto into the center of each plate. Spoon roasted baby root vegetables on top of the risotto. Add spinach and lamb shank pieces.

Chef's Tip: *To select the best tasting beets, look for firm roots, smooth skin, and deep color. This will ensure the highest nutritional value.*

Sautéed Petrale Sole and Braised Leek Ravioli

Turnip Greens, Chopped Egg and Caper Relish, Potato Cream, Caviar

SERVES 6 / MAKES 12 RAVIOLI

Petrale sole is a flatfish or flounder found in the Pacific Ocean from Alaska to central California. The best time to buy it is in the winter, when supplies are most abundant. This medium-firm, fish boasts a mild and delicate flavor.

Suggested wine pairing: White Burgundy

For the Petrale sole

6 (5-ounce) Petrale sole fillets
Salt and pepper, to taste
1 cup all-purpose flour
2 tablespoons light olive oil
2 tablespoons butter
Juice of 1 lemon, for drizzling

For the ravioli filling

4 tablespoons butter
4 cups small diced leeks (white part only)
1 bay leaf
1 teaspoon salt
2 tablespoons minced garlic
½ cup bread crumbs
¼ teaspoon fennel seed, ground
Zest from 1 lemon
2 tablespoons chopped chives
3 tablespoons mascarpone cheese
¼ cup grated Parmigiana Reggiano

For the ravioli

1¾ cups all-purpose flour, plus more for dusting
¼ cup semolina flour
¼ teaspoon salt
5 eggs, divided
½ teaspoon extra-virgin olive oil
3 teaspoons water, divided

For the chopped egg and caper relish

3 eggs (hard boiled), chopped
2 tablespoons finely chopped parsley
¼ cup chopped capers
2 tablespoons lemon juice
2 tablespoons light olive oil
Salt, to taste

For the turnip greens

3 tablespoons light olive oil
2 teaspoons finely chopped garlic
8 cups turnip green tops
½ teaspoon salt

For the potato cream

1 medium russet potato, peeled, large diced
½ Spanish onion, peeled and thinly sliced
1 bay leaf
1 sprig thyme
4 cloves garlic
1 teaspoon chile flakes
4 cups heavy cream
1 teaspoon salt

For the garnish

1 ounce of your favorite caviar

FOR THE PETRALE SOLE

Season both sides of fish with salt and pepper, and dust both sides with flour.

Heat olive oil in a large sauté pan over medium-high heat and add butter. When butter just begins to brown, add fish and quickly sauté on each side for about 1 minute. Remove fillets onto a plate line with paper towels, and drizzle with lemon juice.

FOR THE RAVIOLI FILLING

Melt butter in a medium saucepot over medium-low heat. Add leeks, bay leaf, and salt. Cook uncovered until all moisture has evaporated, about 1 hour.

Add garlic and cook until fragrant, 1–2 minutes. Stir in bread crumbs and fennel seed.

Remove mixture from heat and chill in refrigerator.

Add lemon zest, chives, mascarpone, and Parmigiana Reggiano, and stir until incorporated.

FOR THE RAVIOLI

In a large bowl, combine flours and salt. In another bowl, whisk 3 eggs together with oil and 1 teaspoon water.

Form a well in the flour and add egg mixture. Slowly start forming a dough, adjusting flour and/or water as needed.

Turn the dough onto a lightly floured surface and knead by hand until smooth, soft, and stretchy, 1–2 minutes.

Wrap dough in plastic wrap and let sit at room temperature for 30 minutes.

If rolling pasta dough by hand, cut the dough into quarters and, using a rolling pin, roll out the dough until ⅛–1/16 inch thick. If using a pasta-rolling machine, cut the dough into quarters, press flat, and run each piece of pasta dough several times through the machine, adjusting the setting each time, until the pasta is ⅛–1/16 inch thick.

In a small bowl, whisk 2 eggs and remaining 2 teaspoons of water to create an egg wash.

Roll out the pasta and cut into 4 × 5-inch rectangles.

Put a heaping tablespoon of filling on half of the rectangle, fold over and use a pastry brush to seal edges with egg wash. Continue until pasta and filling are finished.

Place raviolis on a sheet pan lined with parchment paper and dusted with flour.

Bring a large pot of salted water to a boil. Drop ravioli in boiling water and cook until floating. Drain in a colander.

FOR THE CHOPPED EGG AND CAPER RELISH

Combine all ingredients in a mixing bowl, and stir until thoroughly incorporated. Season with salt to taste.

FOR THE TURNIP GREENS

Heat olive oil in a large sauté pan over medium-high heat. Add garlic and cook until just fragrant. Add turnip greens and salt, and, tossing lightly, cook greens until just wilted.

FOR THE POTATO CREAM

In a medium saucepot bring all ingredients just to a boil, reduce heat to medium low and simmer potatoes until soft, about 15 minutes.

Strain mixture through a fine-mesh sieve, gently pressing the mixture to allow all liquid to pass (do not press the potato chunks through).

Discard potato chunks, and season to taste with salt. Add liquid to a blender, and process until frothy.

AT SERVICE

Place 2 ravioli in the center of each plate. Place turnip greens next to the ravioli, and place 1 sole fillet on top of the turnip greens, leaning it onto the ravioli. Ladle the potato cream over everything. Top with some of the chopped egg and caper relish and garnish with the caviar.

Chef's Tip: *You want the texture of the potato cream to coat the back of a spoon. You can achieve this by simmering the strained cream for a few more minutes, than processing it in the blender. Be sure to blend the cream just before serving.*

Pan-Seared Chilean Sea Bass

Sriracha-Whipped Potatoes and Crispy Brussels Sprouts

SERVES 6

Chilean sea bass is a white fish loaded with omega-3 unsaturated oils. It boasts a mild flavor and a distinctive large-flake texture. It's very easy to pan sear and pairs nicely with hot and spicy whipped potatoes and crispy deep-fried brussels sprouts.

Suggested wine pairing: Loire Valley Sauvignon Blanc

For the sea bass

6 (5-ounce) center cut Chilean sea bass fillets
Salt and pepper, to taste
4 tablespoons light olive oil

For the sriracha whipped potatoes

3 russet potatoes, peeled and quartered
¼ cup butter
2 tablespoons minced garlic
1 tablespoon minced ginger
3 scallions, minced
2 cups heavy cream
6 tablespoons sriracha (or to taste)
Salt and pepper, to taste

For the crispy brussels sprouts

24 brussels sprouts, trimmed and halved
Salt and pepper, to taste

FOR THE SEA BASS

Season sea bass with salt and pepper.

Heat olive oil in a large sauté pan over medium heat to a slight smoke. Add sea bass and cook to desired doneness, 3–4 minutes per side.

FOR THE SRIRACHA WHIPPED POTATOES

Place potatoes in a large saucepot of cold salted water and bring to a boil.

Melt butter in a small saucepot over medium-low heat and add garlic, ginger, and scallions. Cook until onions are slightly translucent and soft. Remove from heat and stir in cream.

In a food mill or food processor, combine potatoes with the onion/cream mixture, and process until smooth.

Season with sriracha, salt, and pepper.

FOR THE CRISPY BRUSSELS SPROUTS

Heat a deep fryer to 350°F.

Working in small batches, deep-fry the brussels sprouts until the edges begin to curl and brown, about 1–2 minutes. Remove onto a large baking sheet lined with paper towels and season with salt and pepper.

AT SERVICE

Place a mound of potatoes on each plate. Top with sea bass and garnish with brussels sprout halves.

Chef's Tip: *I always use sustainably caught Chilean sea bass.*

Almond Lemon Poppy-Seed Cake with Lavender Whipped Cream

Cirtus Salad, Candied Almonds

SERVES 6-8

Recently, while teaching a pastry class that focused on tea breads and cakes, we made a lemon almond poppy cake. During the next few days, I found myself snacking on slices of this cake until it was gone. I came up with this simple dessert showcasing the wonderful texture and flavor of that cake. Playing with the inherent flavors, I added a fresh citrus salad and crunchy candied almonds for textural contrast. The lavender cream adds a floral note and brings it all together. This is an unexpected seasonal winter dessert that is best made when the citrus fruits are at their peak.

Suggested wine pairing: V.T. Gewurztraminer

For the glaze

4 tablespoons lemon juice
2 tablespoons water
⅔ cup plus 1 tablespoon granulated sugar

For the lavender whipped cream

1½ tablespoons granulated sugar
2 teaspoons dried culinary lavender
1 cup heavy cream

For the cake

¾ cup plus 1 tablespoon cake flour, more for
    dusting cake pan
½ teaspoon baking powder
2 teaspoon poppy seeds
¾ cup plus 1 tablespoon almond paste, room
    temperature
1 cup granulated sugar
Zest of 1 medium lemon
⅛ teaspoon kosher salt
1 cup unsalted butter, room temperature
5 eggs, room temperature
1 teaspoon vanilla extract
½ teaspoon almond extract

For the vanilla custard sauce

½ cup milk
½ cup heavy cream
½ vanilla bean, scraped
3 egg yolks
¼ cup granulated sugar

For the citrus salad

1 lemon, cut into ⅛-inch slices
1 cup granulated sugar
½ vanilla bean, scraped
1 cup water
2 cara cara oranges
2 mandarin oranges
1 pink grapefruit
1 Asian pear, cut into ⅛-inch strips
1 tablespoon pomegranate seeds
3 mint leaves, cut into very thin strips

For the candied almonds

2 teaspoons egg white
½ cup sliced blanched almonds
1 tablespoon granulated sugar
⅛ teaspoon kosher salt

FOR THE GLAZE

In a small bowl, combine juice, water, and sugar, and mix until combined. Transfer to small stainless saucepot and bring to a boil. Remove from heat being careful not to reduce mixture.

FOR THE LAVENDER WHIPPED CREAM

In a small saucepot, combine sugar and lavender with cream and bring to a boil. Remove from heat, cover, and let rest for 3 minutes. Strain the mixture through a fine-mesh sieve, pressing well to remove lavender. Chill well in refrigerator, about 1 hour. Whip to form medium-stiff peaks. Keep chilled.

FOR THE CAKE

Preheat oven to 350°F.

Butter a 9 × 5-inch loaf pan and coat with cake flour. Gently knock any excess flour out of pan. Set aside.

Sift remaining cake flour and baking powder together into a large mixing bowl. Add poppy seeds and set aside.

In an electric mixer with paddle attachment in place, break the almond paste into small pieces and combine with sugar, lemon zest, and salt. Mix on low and gradually increase to medium speed until mixture breaks up and is crumbly, about 3 minutes.

Add tablespoon-size pieces of butter slowly, and continue to mix with paddle attachment on medium speed for 5 minutes, scraping bowl twice during the process (mixture should be light and smooth without any lumps of almond paste or butter).

Turn speed to low and incorporate eggs, one at a time, scraping down bowl before next addition. Continue until all eggs are combined and mixture is smooth and light, about 3 minutes.

Add vanilla and almond extracts to mixture and combine.

Add flour mixture in three stages, on low speed, scraping mixture down after each addition.

Transfer cake batter into prepared loaf pan and smooth over the top. Bake until a knife inserted in center comes out clean, 50–60 minutes.

Let cake rest in pan for 5 minutes, then carefully invert onto a wire cooling rack.

While cake is hot, brush glaze on top and on all sides until all glaze is absorbed. Cool to room temperature.

FOR THE VANILLA CUSTARD SAUCE

In a small saucepot, combine milk, cream, and vanilla, and bring mixture just to boiling point and reduce heat to scald.

In a mixing bowl, whisk egg yolks and sugar until smooth, about 20 seconds. Add in the hot cream mixture 1 tablespoon at a time, whisking gently between each addition. Repeat until you have added 4 tablespoons of hot cream mixture to yolks.

Pour yolk mixture into remaining cream mixture in pan. With a wooden spoon and stirring continuously over low heat, cook sauce until it gently coats the back of the spoon. Quickly strain through a fine-mesh sieve and chill covered for 3 hours or up to 3 days.

FOR THE CITRUS SALAD

Preheat oven to 300°F.

Lay lemon slices in an 8 × 8-inch pan.

In a saucepot, combine sugar, vanilla and water, and bring to a boil. Pour mixture over lemons, and cover with aluminum foil, poking a few small holes in the top to vent. Place in oven for 90 minutes until lemons are tender. Cool to room temperature and chill for 1 hour before cutting into thin wedges.

Cut segments from oranges and grapefruit (being careful to remove all the white pith), and place in a bowl with pear, pomegranate seeds, and mint. Gently toss all the fruit with 1 tablespoon of lemon syrup from candied lemons.

FOR THE CANDIED ALMONDS

Preheat oven to 350°F.

In a small bow, whisk egg whites until frothy, about 20 seconds. Combine with almonds, sugar, and salt, and toss well until almonds are evenly coated.

Spread almonds onto a baking sheet lined with parchment paper coated with nonstick cooking spray. Toast in oven, stirring every 4 minutes, until golden brown, about 12 minutes. Cool to room temperature.

AT SERVICE

Drag one tablespoon of custard sauce across each plate. Cut a 1-inch slice of lemon almond poppy-seed cake and place it on top of the custard sauce. Arrange the citrus salad across the cake. Sprinkle with some of the candied almonds and garnish with some of the lavender whipped cream.

Chef's Tip: *This cake can be made 3 days ahead if refrigerated and covered with plastic wrap.*

Poached Pear and Cream Cheese Mousse Crepes with Kabocha Squash Puree

Pear Sorbet, Pistachio, and Crisp Kataifi

SERVES 6-8

I have done many crepe variations at Market, but this one seems to be my favorite so far. It came together rather quickly once I had these beautiful squash on my cutting board, looking for an excuse to be highlighted in a dessert. This dish has such a satisfying balance of delicate fall flavors and textures without being heavy.

Suggested wine pairing: Late Harvest Riesling

For the crepes

1 cup milk
¼ cup cream
2 large eggs
3 tablespoons granulated sugar
½ cup plus 2 tablespoons all-purpose flour
½ teaspoon vanilla
Butter for pan

For the cream cheese mousse

¼ cup granulated sugar
1 cup cream cheese
1 cup cream
1 teaspoon vanilla paste

For the poached pears

2 cups water
2 cups dry white wine
½ cup granulated sugar
¼ cup honey
1 star anise
1 stick cinnamon
1 vanilla bean, scraped
1 (½-inch) slice ginger
Zest of ¼ large orange
1 tablespoon lemon juice
4 Bosc pears

For the kabocha squash puree

2 cups kabocha squash, cut into ¾-inch cubes
2 tablespoons granulated sugar
1 small stick cinnamon
⅓ cup water
Pinch of kosher salt

For the pear sorbet

4 ripe pears (Comice, French Butter, or Bartlett), peeled, cored, and roughly chopped
¾ cup dry white wine
½ cup plus 1 tablespoon granulated sugar
½ vanilla bean, scraped
1¼ cups water
2 tablespoons pear brandy
2 tablespoons lemon juice

For the crisp kataifi

1½ cup loose kataifi
1 tablespoon plus 1 teaspoon butter, melted
1 tablespoon granulated sugar
Pinch of kosher salt
Powdered sugar, for dusting

FOR THE CREPES

Combine all ingredients in a blender, and mix on high speed 10 seconds. Strain through a fine-mesh sieve, cover, and chill for 2 hours.

Heat a nonstick pan over medium heat. Grease lightly with butter, and pour in crepe batter, being sure to cover the pan very thinly while swirling pan. Cook until edges are golden brown and bubbles form on surface of crepe. Gently flip and cook for only 5-10 seconds, being careful not to dry out the crepe.

FOR THE CREAM CHEESE MOUSSE

In an electric mixer with paddle attachment in place, mix sugar and cream cheese on medium-high speed (scraping down sides often) until very smooth.

With whip attachment in place, add cream and vanilla paste, and whip to a medium-stiff peak. Keep chilled.

FOR THE POACHED PEARS

In a saucepot, combine all ingredients except pears. Cover, bring to a boil, then lower heat to a simmer.

Peel pears, cut in half lengthwise, and remove core. Add to the simmering poaching liquid. Bring to a boil and then turn heat down to maintain a simmer. Continue cooking pears until tender throughout (a knife can pierce through easily).

Remove pears with a slotted spoon and chill. Reduce poaching liquid to 1½ cups, then add back to poached pears. Chill in refrigerator.

FOR THE KABOCHA SQUASH PUREE

Combine all ingredients in a saucepan and bring to a boil. Turn heat down to a simmer, cover, and cook until squash is very tender, about 20 minutes.

Uncover and let liquid reduce by a quarter of its volume.

Add mixture to a blender, and puree until very smooth. Chill in refrigerator.

FOR THE PEAR SORBET

In a large mixing bowl, combine pears, wine, sugar, vanilla, and water. Bring to a boil, then reduce heat to a simmer. Cover and let cook for 20 minutes until pears are very soft. Cool to room temperature. Add mixture to a high-speed blender, and puree until smooth.

Strain through a fine-mesh sieve, then stir in brandy and lemon juice. Chill in refrigerator for at least 2 hours.

Churn in ice cream machine according to labeled instructions.

FOR THE CRISP KATAIFI

Preheat oven to 350°F.

Place kataifi in bowl and pull apart to separate. Drizzle with melted butter and toss evenly to coat.

Add sugar and salt, and toss until evenly coated. Spread thinly and evenly onto a baking sheet lined with parchment paper. Cover with parchment paper and another flat pan to weigh it down. Bake 15-20 minutes until golden brown. Cool to room temperature and store in airtight container.

TO ASSEMBLE

Place 6 crepes (golden brown side down) on clean work surface. Place mousse in a piping bag and pipe a 1¼-inch tube across top ⅓ of each crepe. Dice poached pears into ½-inch pieces and place some along the mousse. Roll up crepes from top to bottom and cut into thirds.

AT SERVICE

Spread kabocha puree on each plate and place 1 prepared crepe cut into thirds on top. Sprinkle with more diced pears and toasted chopped pistachios. Place two small scoops of pear sorbet and two pieces of kataifi. Dust kataifi with powdered sugar.

Chef's Tip: *You can substitute kabocha squash for butternut squash with similar results. If you can't find kataifi, substitute by slicing phyllo dough into very thin strips in equal amounts. When making your crepes, take care in getting them as thin as possible.*

Date Toffee Pudding

Coconut Sorbet, Black Pepper Walnuts, Candied Kumquats, Charred Dates

SERVES 6

What started out as a favorite homemade trail mix of coconut, walnuts, and dates has turned into my version of this classic traditional-style pudding that has a texture like a moist cake rather than a creamy custard. The pudding is baked in a steam bath and served warm with toffee sauce poured over it to soak in slightly. The combination of spices, dates, and brown sugar gives this dessert a rich depth of flavor that is balanced with the addition of coconut sorbet and tart candied kumquats. Since this dish has a comfort quality to it, I find it best served on a chilly evening.

Suggested wine pairing: Malmsey Madeira

For the puddings

4 dried dates
1 tablespoon dry sherry
½ teaspoon baking soda
¼ cup plus 1 tablespoon unsalted butter, more
    for buttering ramekins
¾ cup brown sugar
1 egg
¾ teaspoon vanilla extract
½ cup all-purpose flour
1 teaspoon ground cinnamon
Pinch of ground cloves
Pinch of ground nutmeg
Pinch of ground cardamom
½ teaspoon baking powder
¼ teaspoon kosher salt

For the coconut sorbet

2 (14-ounce) cans coconut milk
⅓ cup plus 1 tablespoon granulated sugar
⅓ cup unsweetened shredded coconut
½ vanilla bean, scraped with pod and seeds
1 tablespoon coconut rum
2 tablespoons light agave syrup
Pinch of kosher salt

For the black pepper walnuts

1 cup walnut pieces
2 tablespoons pure maple syrup
Pinch of kosher salt
Large pinch of black pepper

For the toffee sauce

¾ cup dark brown sugar
⅓ cup light corn syrup
2 tablespoons plus 1 teaspoon unsalted butter
½ cup plus 2 tablespoons heavy cream, divided
Pinch of kosher salt
1 teaspoon vanilla extract

For the candied kumquats

12 kumquats
1 cup granulated sugar
1 cup water

For the charred dates

½ teaspoon cooking oil
6 dried dates

FOR THE PUDDINGS

Preheat oven to 350°F.

Butter the inside of six 4-ounce ramekins and set aside.

Bring a small pot of water to a boil. Add dates and blanch for 4 minutes. Add dates to a bowl of ice and water, and chill. Remove, peel off skins, and remove pits. Add prepped dates to a small pot and cover with water. Bring to a boil, then remove from heat.

Combine mixture in a blender with sherry and baking soda, and puree until smooth. Cool to room temperature.

In an electric mixer with paddle attachment in place, cream butter and brown sugar until smooth and light, about 5 minutes. Add egg and mix until well incorporated. Add vanilla, scrape down bowl, and mix a few more seconds.

Sift together flour, spices, baking powder, and salt. Add a third of this mixture into butter mixture, and mix until incorporated. Add half the date mixture, and mix until incorporated. Scrape down bowl and repeat steps until all date and flour mixtures are combined and smooth.

Fill each prepared ramekin just a bit over half with batter, place them in a flat pan with sides taller than the ramekins. Pour enough hot tap water into pan to be almost halfway up the sides of the ramekins. Cover tightly with aluminum foil and bake in the oven for 45 minutes. Remove foil and cool to room temperature.

FOR THE COCONUT SORBET

In a medium saucepot combine coconut milk, sugar, and shredded coconut. Bring to a low boil over medium heat. Remove from heat and cover for 30 minutes. Strain coconut mixture through a fine-mesh sieve, pushing to get as much liquid out as possible. Discard solids.

Combine mixture with rum, agave syrup, and salt. Chill for at least 3 hours and freeze in an ice cream machine according to labeled instructions.

FOR THE BLACK PEPPER WALNUTS

Preheat oven to 350°F. Line a baking sheet with aluminum foil coated with nonstick cooking spray.

In a bowl, toss all ingredients together until evenly coated. Spread on prepared foil and toast for 15 minutes, stirring every 5 minutes until slightly caramelized and golden brown. Cool to room temperature on pan. Store airtight container.

FOR THE TOFFEE SAUCE

In a heavy bottom saucepot, combine sugar, corn syrup, butter, and ½ cup of the cream. Bring to a boil over medium heat and stir. Turn heat to medium low and cook to 234°F.

Remove from heat and add remaining 2 tablespoons of the heavy cream. Strain through a fine-mesh sieve and cool to room temperature. Rewarm sauce if it gets too cool and thick before serving.

FOR THE CANDIED KUMQUATS

Cut kumquats in quarters and remove any seeds. In a small saucepot, combine sugar and water, and bring to a rolling boil. Turn heat down to a low boil and add kumquats. When mixture returns to a low boil, continue to cook for 3 minutes. Remove from heat and let kumquats cool (in syrup) to room temperature, then chill in refrigerator.

FOR THE CHARRED DATES

Heat a stainless sauté pan over high heat until very hot. Add oil and dates, and stir until evenly coated. Allow dates to slightly burn evenly on the outside as you toss them (the pan will smoke a little so be careful). Remove dates from pan and cool to room temperature, then slice into thin strips.

AT SERVICE

Run a knife around warm pudding and invert one onto each plate. Pour toffee sauce on top, letting it run over. Place dates and black pepper walnuts on top of sauce. Place a scoop of coconut sorbet to the side and garnish with candied kumquats.

Chef's Tip: *At all costs, avoid the temptation to open the oven and peak at the puddings while they are steaming. They bake best undisturbed for the full 45 minutes.*

Chef's Tip: *For a simpler version of this recipe, serve pudding and sauce with whipped cream flavored with bourbon.*

Chocolate Butterscotch Tasting

Malted Milk Ice Cream, Pretzel Streusel, Whipped Crème Fraîche

SERVES 6

Butterscotch is one of those comfort flavors that speaks to many grown-ups who have a fond memory of scraping that leftover pudding out of a cup as a child. Many of my desserts at Market are renditions of these types of classics. Elevated with different textures and embellishments, this dessert is a great example. By adding flavors of malt, pretzels, bittersweet chocolate, and different temperature contrasts, this dish takes on a life of its own while still remaining a comfort dessert. It can be eaten all together or as individual little desserts since they all stand on their own.

Suggested wine pairing: Vintage Port

For the butterscotch custard

½ cup milk
1 cup heavy cream
2 tablespoons dark brown sugar
⅓ cup granulated sugar
2 tablespoons water
3 egg yolks
½ teaspoon vanilla
⅛ teaspoon kosher salt

For the whipped crème fraîche

⅓ cup heavy cream
⅓ cup crème fraîche
1 tablespoons granulated sugar

For the malted milk ice cream

1½ cups milk
1½ cups heavy cream
½ cup plus 3 tablespoons granulated sugar
Pinch kosher salt
8 egg yolks
1½ teaspoons vanilla extract
¾ cup malted milk powder

For the pretzel streusel

1¾ cups chopped salted thin pretzels
¾ cup all-purpose flour
¾ cup light brown sugar
1 tablespoon malt powder
½ cup unsalted butter, melted warm

For the bittersweet chocolate soufflé cake

⅓ cup butter, plus extra for greasing
2 teaspoons cake flour, plus extra for dusting
    ramekins
¾ cup (70 percent) bittersweet chocolate, chopped
3 eggs (room temperature)
¼ cup granulated sugar
1 teaspoon vanilla extract
¼ teaspoon kosher salt

For the chocolate sauce

2 tablespoons unsalted butter
2 tablespoons light corn syrup
2 tablespoons water
2 tablespoons granulated sugar
2 tablespoons cocoa powder
2 tablespoons chocolate (70 percent), finely
    chopped
¼ teaspoon vanilla extract
Pinch of kosher salt

FOR THE BUTTERSCOTCH CUSTARD

Preheat oven to 300°F.

Heat milk, cream, and brown sugar in a saucepot until mixture is warm and the brown sugar is dissolved; set aside.

In a separate stainless steel medium pan, combine sugar and water, and cook over medium-high heat until sugar caramelizes and has a medium-dark amber color. Turn off heat and carefully add the warm cream mixture. Whisk slowly until all is incorporated.

In a mixing bowl, gently whisk the egg yolks and slowly add the warm caramel cream mixture. Add in vanilla and salt and then strain mixture through a fine-mesh sieve.

Place six 3-ounce ramekins in a roomy pan with tall sides and fill with custard. Pour enough hot water in the outer pan to come halfway up the sides of ramekins. Cover tightly with foil.

Carefully transfer ramekins to oven, and bake until custards have set and slightly jiggle when moved, about 45 minutes. Cool to room temperature, then chill covered in the refrigerator.

FOR THE WHIPPED CRÈME FRAÎCHE

In a mixing bowl, whip all ingredients together to a medium peak. Cover bowl with plastic wrap and chill in the refrigerator.

FOR THE MALTED MILK ICE CREAM

Prepare an ice bath by nesting a medium bowl in a larger bowl that's partially filled with ice and water.

In a medium saucepan combine milk, cream, sugar, and salt. Bring just to a boiling point, then reduce heat to scald.

In a large mixing bowl, whisk the egg yolks, and gradually add the hot cream/milk mixture while continually whisking. Scrape the yolk mixture into pan with remaining cream/milk mixture and cook on low heat, stirring with a wooden spoon, until mixture slightly thickens and coats the back of the spoon.

Quickly remove mixture from heat and whisk in vanilla and malt powder. Immersion blend for 10 seconds to break up any lumps.

Strain the ice cream base through a fine-mesh sieve into the chilled ice bath bowl. Stir gently until fully chilled.

Transfer to the refrigerator to rest overnight. Freeze the ice cream base in an ice-cream maker according to labeled instructions.

FOR THE PRETZEL STREUSEL

Preheat oven to 325°F.

Combine all ingredients in a food processor, and pulse until mixed and it resembles a course crumble. Spread crumble on a baking sheet lined with parchment paper, and bake for 15-20 minutes, tossing every 5 minutes until golden brown and crisp. Cool to room temperature and wrap airtight.

FOR THE BITTERSWEET CHOCOLATE SOUFFLÉ CAKE

Grease the inside of six 3-ounce ramekins well with the extra butter and coat with extra cake flour, tapping out any excess. Set aside.

In a mixing bowl, combine chocolate and ⅓ cup butter. Melt carefully over a pan with simmering water. Cool to just slightly warm.

In an electric mixer, combine eggs, sugar, cake flour, vanilla, and salt on high speed for 5 minutes until mixture has reached full volume.

Gently fold in melted chocolate/butter mixture with a large rubber spatula until incorporated and there are no more chocolate streaks.

Pour batter into prepared ramekins and chill in refrigerator until ready to bake.

FOR THE CHOCOLATE SAUCE

In a stainless steel pan over medium heat, combine butter, corn syrup, water, sugar, and cocoa powder. Whisk continuously until mixture comes to a rolling boil. Turn off heat and add chocolate, vanilla, and salt; gently whisk to combine. Cool to room temperature and warm before serving.

AT SERVICE

Preheat oven to 375°F.

Place prepared chocolate cakes on center rack and bake until still slightly undercooked in the center, 12–15 minutes. Remove and gently invert onto plates. Serve with chocolate sauce alongside malted milk ice cream rolled in pretzel streusel and butterscotch custard with whipped crème fraîche and a few cocoa nibs.

Chef's Tip: *The butterscotch can be made on its own and baked in four 4-ounce ramekins. Use the same temperature but cook them for 10–15 minutes longer. Serve with whipped crème fraîche, chocolate sauce, and pretzel streusel for a simplified version.*

SPRING

When spring rolls around, there's energy in the air of all things new. This is the time of year when I think of myself as an artist with a whole array of colors to work with for my canvas. Springtime is when my mind is even more focused on the farm-to-table concept and what's available. We have artichokes, golden pea shoots, asparagus, and mangos to name a few. I think the recipes you will find especially exciting in this chapter are the Sweet Pea Salad and Creamy Pepper Vinaigrette or the Sandabs with Braised Baby Artichokes.

Sparkling Sangria

SERVES 6

9 ounces blueberry flavored Vodka
6 ounces St. Germain liqueur
12 ounces Prosecco or dry sparkling wine
1½ cups (equal parts) diced strawberries,
    blueberries, and halved raspberries
1 tablespoon finely chopped fresh mint

For the sorbet

1 cup elderflower cordial
1½ cups water
2 tablespoons Grand Marnier
1 tablespoon simple syrup (page 286)

Process all ingredients in an ice-cream machine according to labeled instructions or freeze in a baking dish, scraping with a fork every 10–15 minutes until frozen to make a granita.

TO ASSEMBLE

In a large martini shaker, shake Stoli and St. Germain and strain equally into 6 pre-chilled coupe glasses. Top off each cocktail with Prosecco. Distribute fruit and small scoops of sorbet amongst the glasses. Garnish with mint. Serve immediately.

Basil Martini

SERVES 2

2 ounces Vodka
2 ounces house-made Velvet Falernum (page 288)
2 wedges lime, squeezed
2 wedges orange, squeezed
1 ounce basil agave nectar (page 281)
1½ ounces sweet and sour (page 287)
6 edible flowers, for garnish (nasturtium suggested)

In a large martini shaker, shake and strain all ingredients into pre-chilled martini glasses, and garnish with flower.

Chardonnay Braised Artichoke Soup and Spring Onion Bread Pudding

SERVES 6

You know how you eat soup and dip bread into it? In this soup, I do the work for you by pairing a super fresh artichoke soup with a little bread pudding that adds depth, creating an all-in-one experience.

Suggested wine pairing: New Zealand Sauvignon Blanc

For the artichoke soup

4 tablespoons light olive oil
1 Spanish onion, peeled and finely chopped
1 leek, finely chopped
5 cloves garlic, peeled and minced
1 tablespoon salt
3 large artichokes
¾ cup white wine (chardonnay)
Pinch of chile flakes
1 herb sachet (page 285)
1 teaspoon toasted ground coriander (page 287)
1 teaspoon toasted ground fennel (page 287)
5 cups vegetable stock (page 288)
½ cup fresh spinach
½ cup heavy cream

For the bread pudding

Olive oil for sautéing
1 cup diced spring onions
½ teaspoon toasted ground fennel (page 287)
¼ teaspoon dry oregano
1 teaspoon salt
1 cup half and half
3 eggs
2 tablespoons sour cream
1½ cups medium diced sourdough bread
½ cup crumbled goat cheese

For the vegetables

Salt, to taste
1 cup diced green zucchini
1 cup diced yellow squash
1 cup asparagus, cut into ¼-inch pieces
½ cup small diced carrots
½ cup small diced celery
½ cup diced red bell pepper

For the garnish

¼ cup finely chopped chives
½ cup peas
Basil oil, for drizzling
Borage flowers, for garnish (optional)

FOR THE ARTICHOKE SOUP

Heat olive oil in a large saucepot over medium-low heat. Add onion, leek, garlic, and salt. Cover saucepot and cook onions until translucent, about 20 minutes.

Remove the dark green exterior of the artichoke stem along with any dark green leaves. Cut into quarters and remove the choke. Add chokes to the cooked onion mixture. Stir to coat well.

Add wine, stirring constantly and tossing the artichoke wedges (this keeps the acid from the wine from overbrowning the artichokes). Bring to a boil over high heat, then immediately

reduce to medium heat. Cover and cook for about 15 minutes.

Add a pinch of chile flakes to the herb sachet, then add the sachet to the mixture along with coriander, fennel, and stock. Return the mixture to a boil, then reduce to medium heat and simmer for about 25 minutes.

Gently stir in the spinach and cream. Remove from the heat.

Add mixture to a blender and process until smooth. Strain through a fine-mesh sieve. Season to taste with salt.

Just before serving, return soup to its original saucepot, warm over low heat, and immersion blend.

FOR THE BREAD PUDDING

Preheat oven to 350°F.

Heat olive oil in a sauté pan over medium-high heat. Add onions, fennel, oregano, and salt, and cook until fragrant and wilted, 5-6 minutes.

Remove mixture from the pan and cool at room temperature.

In a large mixing bowl, add the half and half, eggs, and sour cream, and whisk vigorously until fully incorporated. Gently fold in the bread and onion mixture until fully incorporated, being careful to not break up the bread. Soak for about 1 hour.

Fill six 3-ounce ramekins, coated with nonstick cooking spray, about ¾ full with the bread pudding mixture, top with goat cheese, and place on a baking sheet. Cook for about 45 minutes.

FOR THE VEGETABLES

In a pot of boiling salted water, blanch the zucchini and squash until tender. Using a slotted spoon, remove vegetables from the water onto a sheet pan lined with paper towels. Repeat this blanching process with all the other vegetables (one type of vegetable at a time). Add all the vegetables to the sheet pan to cool together.

AT SERVICE

Remove bread puddings from the ramekins and place them in the center of each of 6 wide, flat bowls. Ladle the soup around each pudding, then scatter the vegetables on top. Garnish with chives, peas, basil oil, and flowers.

Chef's Tip: *When choosing artichokes, always look for nice fat stems, an indicator of a large heart inside.*

Miso Soup and Hoisin Roasted Beef Meatballs

Forest Mushrooms, Serrano Chiles, Golden Pea Shoots

SERVES 6 / MAKES APPROXIMATELY 22 MEATBALLS

I've taken several trips to Japan over the years. I traveled around eating and experiencing the restaurants and culture, and I learned a great deal about misos. Each region of Japan had its own take on miso; some were dark and some were light. The soup in this recipe is a very clean, light miso. I added a California influence with fresh peas. The addition of mushrooms adds a special earthiness. The hot broth is brought to a boil just before serving, and when poured over the soup it cooks the raw peas and the bok choy naturally.

Suggested wine pairing: Off-Dry German Riesling

For the miso broth

3 tablespoons light olive oil
1 strip bacon, diced (optional)
½ cup sliced Spanish onion
2 green onions, roughly chopped
6 cloves garlic, roughly chopped
½-inch ginger cube, roughly chopped
18 shiitake mushroom stems (reserve
    mushroom caps and thinly slice)
1 teaspoon whole cumin
1 teaspoon whole coriander
1 teaspoon whole fennel seeds
¼ teaspoon chile flakes
6 cups chicken or vegetable stock (page 283
    or 288)
¼ cup soy sauce
¼ cup light miso paste

For the beef meatballs

1 tablespoon light olive oil, more for coating
    baking dish
1 Spanish onion, peeled and finely diced
3 tablespoons chopped garlic
3 tablespoons chopped ginger
1 (pound) ground beef
1 egg
¼ cup panko bread crumbs

3 tablespoons hoisin sauce
1 tablespoon hot sauce
2 tablespoons light soy sauce
1 teaspoon salt
1 teaspoon pepper

For the mushrooms

6 cups shiitake mushrooms, stems removed and
    reserved (substitute any mushroom varietal)
1 tablespoon light olive oil
1 teaspoon salt
Pinch of pepper

For the tofu

1 package (extra firm) tofu
2 tablespoons light soy sauce
2 tablespoons light olive oil

For garnish

3 baby bok choy
1 cup roughly chopped cilantro
1 cup roughly chopped green onions
1 cup fresh peas
Shiitake mushroom stems (reserved from above)
3 Serrano peppers, chopped
3 cups golden pea shoots or bean sprouts

FOR THE MISO BROTH

Heat olive oil and bacon in a small saucepot over medium heat, and cook for about 2 minutes.

Add onions, garlic, ginger, mushroom stems, cumin, coriander, fennel, and chile flakes, and cook, stirring frequently, for about 5 minutes.

Add stock, soy sauce, and miso paste. Bring to medium-high heat, then immediately reduce to low heat and simmer for 20 minutes.

Pass mixture through a fine-mesh sieve and reserve liquid in the small saucepot.

Just before serving, bring the miso broth to a boil.

FOR THE BEEF MEATBALLS

Preheat oven to 375°F.

Heat olive oil in sauté pan over medium heat. Add onion, garlic, and ginger, and cook until translucent, approximately 5 minutes. Remove from heat and set aside.

In a large mixing bowl, combine ground beef, egg, and bread crumbs with the cooked onion/garlic mixture. Add the hoisin, hot sauce, soy sauce, salt, and pepper. Mix with your hands and roll meat into 1-inch meatballs.

Coat a baking dish with light olive oil. Arrange meatballs in baking dish and cook for 15 minutes.

FOR THE MUSHROOMS

On a cutting board, slice the shiitake mushroom caps into thin strips.

Heat olive oil in a large sauté pan over medium-high heat. Add mushrooms, and cook until wilted, 3–5 minutes. Season with salt and pepper.

FOR THE TOFU

Rinse and drain tofu and slice into cubes. Add to a bowl and drizzle with soy sauce. Toss lightly and coat evenly.

Heat olive oil in a large nonstick sauté pan over medium heat. Add tofu and cook until caramelized, about 2½ minutes per side. Remove tofu from heat and set aside.

FOR GARNISH

Split bok choy in half and remove the base that holds the leaves together. Cut into thin strips.

In a small bowl, combine cilantro and green onions.

AT SERVICE

Add 2 meatballs to each soup bowl. Distribute the mushrooms, tofu, bok choy, and peas. Garnish with mushroom stems, peppers, pea shoots (or bean sprouts), and cilantro/green onion mixture. Ladle the miso broth into the bowl.

Chef's Tip: *To keep meatballs at a consistent size and ensure even cooking, use an ice-cream scoop when forming.*

Asparagus Soup and Crispy Peekytoe Crab Cake

Meyer Lemon Crème Fraîche, Asparagus-Mango Salad, Fennel Dusted Croutons

SERVES 6

Asparagus is a prominent spring vegetable that is earthy, subtly sweet, and widely available in California. Its subtle flavor is perfect as a soup base, and pairs flawlessly with delicately sweet crabmeat and the sugary and unique texture of mango. Just a hint of tart lemon is added to balance the flavors for a perfect finish.

Suggested wine pairing: Chablis

For the asparagus soup

2 tablespoons light olive oil
1 tablespoon butter
1 Spanish onion, peeled and sliced
1 leek, roughly chopped
½ fennel bulb, sliced
5 cloves garlic, roughly chopped
1 tablespoon salt
6 cups vegetable stock (page 288)
1 bay leaf
1 sprig thyme
12 pieces large asparagus, woody ends removed, sliced into small rounds
Small handful spinach
½ cup heavy cream

For the crab cakes

1 pound crabmeat
2 teaspoons finely diced pasilla pepper
2 teaspoons finely diced red bell pepper
1 teaspoon finely diced Spanish onion
1 tablespoon finely chopped chives
2 tablespoons mayonnaise (page 285)
1 cup, plus 2 tablespoons panko bread crumbs, divided
1 teaspoon lemon juice
Cayenne pepper, to taste
Salt, to taste
1 cup all-purpose flour
2 eggs, whisked

For the asparagus

12 pieces asparagus, blanched
Salt and pepper, to taste
House vinaigrette, for seasoning (page 285)
¼ cup chopped cilantro

For the mangos and mango sauce

3 mangos, peeled, pitted, and medium diced
1 lime, juiced
Pinch of cayenne pepper
Pinch of salt

For the Meyer lemon crème fraîche

½ cup crème fraîche
Zest from 1 Meyer lemon
¼ teaspoon salt

For the Meyer lemon aioli

Base aioli (page 281)
Zest from 1 Meyer lemon (2 teaspoons)

For the croutons

¼ loaf of a baguette, cut into ½-inch cubes
½ cup light olive oil
Ground toasted fennel, for sprinkling

FOR THE ASPARAGUS SOUP

Prepare an ice bath by nesting a medium bowl in a larger bowl that's partially filled with ice and water.

Heat olive oil and melt butter in a large saucepot over medium-high heat. Add onion, leek, fennel, garlic, and salt. Cover saucepot and cook the onions until translucent.

Add stock, bay leaf, and thyme. Bring to a boil, add asparagus, and boil for 1 minute.

Remove bay leaf and thyme, add spinach, and slowly stir in the cream. Add mixture to a blender and process until smooth. Strain through a fine-mesh sieve into ice bath-prepared bowl. Stir constantly until soup is completely chilled.

FOR THE CRAB CAKES

Place crabmeat in a cheesecloth and squeeze to release all moisture.

In a large mixing bowl, combine crabmeat, peppers, onion, chives, mayonnaise, 2 table-spoons bread crumbs, lemon juice, cayenne, and salt. Form mixture into 6 even and round crab cake balls.

Set up 3 mixing bowls. Place the flour in one, whisked eggs in another, and the remaining 1 cup of bread crumbs in the third.

Roll crabmeat ball in flour, dip into eggs, then roll in bread crumbs. Repeat for remaining crab cakes.

In a large pot or deep fryer, add enough cooking oil to completely submerge the crab cakes. Heat to 375°F. In batches, add the crab cakes to the hot oil. Cook crab cakes until crispy and light golden brown turning during frying if necessary. Remove the crab cakes onto a plate lined with paper towels.

FOR THE ASPARAGUS

Cut each asparagus spear into 3 even pieces and add to a shallow baking dish. Drizzle with salt and pepper, house vinaigrette, and cilantro.

FOR THE MANGOS AND MANGO SAUCE

Place 1 mango, 1 teaspoon lime juice, and salt in a blender. Process until smooth. Place chunks from the remaining 2 mangos in a small mixing bowl and drizzle with remaining lime juice, cayenne, and salt.

FOR THE MEYER LEMON CRÈME FRAÎCHE

In a small mixing bowl, combine crème fraîche with lemon zest and salt, and whip vigorously until creamy.

FOR THE MEYER LEMON AIOLI

In a small mixing bowl, combine base aioli with lemon zest.

FOR THE CROUTONS

Preheat oven to 325°F.

Add bread cubes to a bowl. Drizzle with olive oil and toss evenly until incorporated. Place cubes loosely on a baking sheet lined with parchment paper. Bake until golden brown and crunchy all the way through, approximately 15 minutes.

Remove bread cubes from the oven and immediately sprinkle with ground toasted fennel. Allow bread cubes to cool at room temperature on the baking sheet.

AT SERVICE

Bring soup to a rolling boil and blend with immersion blender. Ladle asparagus soup into small bowls. Add a dollop of the Meyer lemon crème fraîche and a sprinkle of croutons. Spoon the mango sauce onto the plate and top with asparagus and mangos. Add a crab cake to the top of the asparagus and mangos, and top crab cake with a dollop of aioli.

Chef's Tip: *When choosing a mango, look for skin that is tight and smooth, not wrinkled. The skin should be slightly firm and yield gently to pressure.*

Shiitake Mushroom and Udon Noodle Soup

Sugar Snap Peas, Tofu, Golden Pea Shoots, Sesame-Chile Oil

SERVES 6

I like to eat this soup by alternating with a spoon and chopsticks. It's a means of eating the noodles as well as tasting the flavors. Not a traditional miso soup, this soup has a refreshing salad component with layers of flavors and textural elements that creates a more substantial miso soup.

Suggested wine pairing: Austrian Grüner Veltliner

For the mushroom broth

2 tablespoons light olive oil
2 Spanish onions, peeled and sliced
1 bunch green onions, roughly chopped
2½ cups shiitake mushroom stems, finely chopped
  (reserve caps)
10 cloves garlic, peeled and roughly chopped
1 (1-inch) piece ginger, peeled and roughly chopped
½ teaspoon chile flakes
2 tablespoons cumin/coriander spice blend
  (page 288)
1 bay leaf
1 bunch cilantro (stems only), chopped
6 cups vegetable stock (page 288)
1 cup soup soy
2 cups dashi broth (page 284)
2 tablespoons white miso
1 (4-inch) piece kombu
1 teaspoon fish sauce
16 ounces extra-firm tofu, medium diced

For the sautéed mushroom caps

2 tablespoons light olive oil
2½ cups king oyster mushrooms, bases removed,
  stems peeled, and mushrooms sliced
2½ cups hon shimeji mushrooms, bases trimmed
2½ cups shiitake mushroom caps
Salt and pepper, to taste

For the udon noodles

2 (8-ounce) packages udon noodles

For the ginger vinaigrette and salad

1 tablespoon light olive oil
1 teaspoon chopped garlic
1 teaspoon chopped ginger
¼ cup seasoned rice wine vinegar
2 tablespoons light soy sauce
1 teaspoon chile sesame oil
¼ cup canola oil
2 cups pea shoots or bean sprouts
1 carton (2 cups) Daikon radish sprouts
2 cups snow peas, thinly sliced

FOR THE MUSHROOM BROTH

Heat olive oil in a large saucepot over high heat. Add onions, mushroom stems, and garlic, and cook until onions are translucent, about 3 minutes.

Add ginger, chile flakes, cumin/coriander, bay leaf, and cilantro stems, and cook until fragrant.

Add stock, soup soy, dashi broth, white miso, kombu, and fish sauce. Bring to a boil, reduce to low heat, and simmer for 20 minutes.

Strain through a fine-mesh sieve, add back to the saucepot, and warm over low heat.

Add the tofu and warm for 10 minutes.

FOR THE SAUTÉED MUSHROOM CAPS

Cut the reserved shiitake mushroom caps (from above recipe) into thin strips.

Heat olive oil in a large sauté pan over medium-high heat, add all mushrooms, and sauté until wilted, 3–5 minutes. Season with salt and pepper.

FOR THE UDON NOODLES

Cook the udon noodles according to label instructions.

FOR THE GINGER VINAIGRETTE AND SALAD

Heat olive oil in a small sauté pan over high heat. Add garlic and ginger, and sauté until just fragrant, about 2 minutes. Remove from heat and cool.

Combine mixture in a blender with vinegar and soy sauce. Process on high speed until smooth, then reduce speed to low and drizzle in oils.

In a large mixing bowl, combine pea shoots, radish sprouts, and snow peas. Drizzle with ginger vinaigrette and lightly toss to combine.

AT SERVICE

Distribute noodles evenly into six bowls. Add mushrooms and tofu and then ladle warm broth into the bowls. Distribute salad onto the edge of the bowls.

Chef's Tip: *Since there are several cold elements in this soup, bring the soup to a full boil so that the heat from the soup will cook the vegetables naturally.*

Morel Mushroom and Spring Onion Salad

Romaine Lettuce, Fava Beans, Smithfield Ham, Buttermilk Herb Dressing

SERVES 6

Morel mushrooms and fava beans are what I think about when I think about spring. I created this dish because of the saltiness of the ham and the creamy acidity of the dressing. The sweet little pops of fava bean and the earthiness of the mushrooms bring the spring season to a plate.

Suggested wine pairing: Puligny-Montrachet

For the mushrooms

4 tablespoons light olive oil
1 tablespoon butter
6 cups morel mushrooms, stems removed
Salt and pepper, to taste
2 tablespoons minced garlic
2 tablespoons shallots, finely chopped
¼ cup dry sherry
2 tablespoons red wine vinegar
1 tablespoon fines herbes (page 285)

For the spring onions

6 spring onions
4 tablespoons light olive oil
3 sprigs thyme
Salt and pepper, to taste

For the fava beans

2 cups shelled fava beans

For the romaine

3 romaine hearts

For the buttermilk dressing

½ cup buttermilk
1 cup sour cream
½ cup mayonnaise (page 285)

1 tablespoon Dijon mustard
1 teaspoon salt
½ teaspoon pepper
2 cloves garlic, finely minced
½ teaspoon sugar
2 tablespoons lemon juice
2 tablespoons finely chopped parsley
2 tablespoons finely chopped tarragon
2 tablespoons finely chopped basil
½ teaspoon thyme

For the Smithfield ham

6 large slices Smithfield ham (substitute your
    favorite ham)

FOR THE MUSHROOMS

Heat olive oil and melt butter in a large sauté pan over medium-high heat. Add mushrooms and season with salt and pepper.

Sauté mushrooms until slightly wilted, 3-4 minutes. Add the garlic and shallots and cook until fragrant, making sure the garlic and shallots are no longer raw, about 2 minutes. Remove from heat.

Add sherry and vinegar, and sprinkle with herbs. Reserve.

FOR THE SPRING ONIONS

Remove green tops and roots from the onions. (Keep the base of the onion that hold the layers together, leaving only the light green and white onion.) Cut the onions into quarters.

Heat olive oil in a large sauté pan over high heat. Add onions and thyme, sprinkle with salt and pepper, and cook the onions until slightly caramelized on all sides, about 5 minutes.

FOR THE FAVA BEANS

Bring salted water to a boil. Add fava beans and cook until tender, about 2 minutes. Drain beans and immediately immerse in a bowl of ice and water. Remove beans and remove the outer core from each bean.

Add mushrooms and fava beans to the pan of onions. Warm over medium heat, about 1 minute.

FOR THE ROMAINE

Remove any damaged leaves from the exterior of the heads of romaine. Split heads in half, keeping the core intact. Just before service, drizzle romaine wedges with buttermilk dressing.

FOR THE BUTTERMILK DRESSING

Combine all ingredients in a large mixing bowl and mix well.

AT SERVICE

Place one slice of ham in the center of each plate. Add a romaine wedge to the top, and top that with some of the morel, onion, and fava bean mixture.

Chef's Tip: *To thoroughly clean morel mushrooms, fill a large mixing bowl with lukewarm water. Working in small batches, place the mushrooms in the water and wash them vigorously by moving them around with your hands. Remove mushrooms to a large baking sheet lined with paper towels. You don't want the mushrooms to absorb too much water, so once they are cleaned, remove them quickly. This washing technique holds true for all mushrooms.*

Crispy Porcini, Risotto, and Asparagus Salad

Poached Egg, Tomato Jam, Truffle Aioli

SERVES 6

This salad contains so many different textures and temperatures. There's the flavor of the cold asparagus, warm risotto, and pop of salt from the Parmigiana Reggiano cheese and the prosciutto de Parma. The acidity from the tomatoes, the earthiness from the truffle, and the creaminess of the egg bring it all together.

Suggested wine pairing: Alsatian Pinot Blanc

For the asparagus

Salt, to taste
30 asparagus spears, ends trimmed
House vinaigrette, for seasoning (page 285)

For the tomato jam

6 medium heirloom tomatoes
4 tablespoons light olive oil
3 large shallots, finely minced
9 cloves garlic, finely minced
1 bay leaf
1 teaspoon red wine vinegar
Salt and pepper, to taste

For the crispy risotto arancini

4 cups mushroom stock (page 286)
4 tablespoons light olive oil
1 cup finely chopped Spanish onions
1 cup Arborio rice
1 tablespoon porcini powder
1 bay leaf
1 sprig thyme
Salt and pepper, to taste
½ cup dry white wine
¼ cup mascarpone cheese
¼ cup grated Parmigiana Reggiano
1 tablespoon fines herbes (page 285)
2 cups all-purpose flour
4 eggs, whisked
2 cups panko bread crumbs
Canola oil, for frying

For the truffle aioli

1 egg yolk
1 teaspoon fresh lemon juice
2 cloves garlic, mashed
1 teaspoon Dijon mustard
¾ cup light olive oil
¼ cup truffle oil
¼ cup finely minced truffles
Salt, to taste

For the truffle vinaigrette

¼ cup red wine vinegar
2 tablespoons water
1 teaspoon Dijon mustard
¾ cup light olive oil
1 tablespoon truffle oil
½ cup chopped truffles

For the garnish

6 eggs, poached
6 large thin Prosciutto de Parma slices, more
    if desired
1 small block Parmigiana Reggiano

FOR THE ASPARAGUS

Bring a saucepot of salted water to a boil. Place asparagus in the water for 1 minute, then remove to a bowl of ice and water.

Remove asparagus to a plate lined with paper towels to dry, then combine in a mixing bowl with vinaigrette and coat evenly.

FOR THE TOMATO JAM

Bring a large pot of salted water to a boil. Add tomatoes and blanch for 15 seconds. Using a slotted spoon, immediately remove tomatoes to a bowl of ice and water. Repeat method by adding tomatoes back to the same pot of boiling water for an additional 15 seconds and removing again to a bowl of ice and water. Remove tomatoes to a plate lined with paper towels, then peel, core, and finely dice them.

Heat olive oil in a saucepot over medium heat. Add shallots and garlic and cook until fragrant. Add tomatoes and bay leaf. Stir frequently and simmer on low heat until mixture is reduced to a tomato paste. Add vinegar and season with salt and pepper. Cool to room temperature.

FOR THE RISOTTO ARANCINI

In a saucepot over medium heat, warm the mushroom stock. Reserve.

Heat olive oil in a large saucepot over medium heat. Add onions and cook until translucent.

Add rice, coat with the hot oil, and, stirring constantly, cook for about 1 minute.

Stir in the porcini powder immediately followed by the warmed mushroom stock (added in thirds).

Add bay leaf, thyme, salt, and pepper. Cook risotto, stirring constantly, until all the liquid is absorbed.

Add wine and continue stirring until all liquid is absorbed again.

Remove from heat and stir in mascarpone, Parmigiana Reggiano, and herbes. Spread mixture onto a large sheet lined with parchment paper and cool to room temperature.

Set up 3 mixing bowls. Place flour in one, eggs in the second, and bread crumbs in the third.

Form risotto into 18 small, round balls. Roll each ball into flour then into eggs, then bread crumbs.

In a large pot or deep fryer, add enough cooking oil to completely submerge the food. Heat the oil to 375°F. In batches, add the risotto balls to the hot oil. Cook until crispy and light golden brown (turn the balls during frying if necessary).

Remove the balls onto a plate lined with paper towels, and season with salt and pepper.

FOR THE TRUFFLE AIOLI

In a mixing bowl, combine egg, lemon juice, garlic, and mustard, and whisk until foamy. Gradually add in the oils, truffles, and salt.

FOR THE TRUFFLE VINAIGRETTE

In a large mixing bowl, combine vinegar, water, and mustard. Whisk in oils and truffles.

AT SERVICE

Distribute 5 asparagus onto each plate. Add 3 tablespoons of the tomato jam around the asparagus. Place 1 fried risotto arancini on top of each tablespoon of jam. Place a dollop of aioli on top of each risotto ariancini. Place 1 slice of prosciutto onto asparagus. Place 1 poached egg onto the center of the plate. Shave Parmigiana Reggiano cheese over the salad, then drizzle with the aioli and vinaigrette.

Chef's Tip: *At Market I like to use fresh truffles when in season. If you have a hard time finding them, substitute mushroom duxelle (page 286).*

Sweet Pea Salad and Creamy Pepper Vinaigrette

Golden Pea Shoots, Chopped Dill, Manchego Cheese

SERVES 6

When pea vines are young, early in the season, I put this salad on my menu at Market. The first harvest of the super tender tips of the pea tendrils has an amazing sweet pea flavor. Even though this salad is so simple, it's one of my personal favorites and has a huge following.

Suggested wine pairing: Spanish Godello

For the creamy pepper vinaigrette

¼ cup mayonnaise (page 285)
¼ cup sour cream
¼ cup heavy cream
1 clove garlic, finely minced
1 teaspoon lemon juice
1 teaspoon coarse ground black pepper
1 tablespoon grated Parmigiana Reggiano

For the sweet pea salad

¼ cup lemon juice
1 cup light olive oil
½ teaspoon finely chopped garlic
1 teaspoon Dijon mustard
1 teaspoon lemon zest
Salt and pepper, to taste
3 cups sugar snap peas
12 cups fresh pea tendrils
2 cups golden pea shoots
½ cup roughly chopped dill
¼ cup sliced chives, sliced into ½-inch-long pieces

For the garnish

1 small block manchego cheese

FOR THE CREAMY PEPPER VINAIGRETTE

Combine all ingredients in a small mixing bowl and whisk until creamy.

FOR THE SWEET PEA SALAD

To make the lemon vinaigrette, combine lemon juice, olive oil, garlic, mustard, lemon zest, salt, and pepper in a large mixing bowl and whisk until thoroughly incorporated. Set aside.

Bring a small saucepot of salted water to a boil, add sugar snap peas, and blanch for 45 seconds.

Strain peas and place in a bowl of ice and water.

Remove peas and cut each pod in half at a 45-degree angle. Add peas to a small mixing bowl, drizzle with some of the lemon vinaigrette, and lightly toss.

In a large mixing bowl, combine pea tendrils, golden pea shoots, dill, and chives. Drizzle with the remaining lemon vinaigrette, season with salt and pepper, and lightly toss.

AT SERVICE

Distribute salad evenly onto each plate. Distribute the sugar snap peas on top and around the salad. Drizzle salad with the creamy pepper vinaigrette, and garnish with shaved slices of manchego.

Chef's Tip: Substitute your favorite hard cheese for this salad.

Barbecued Local Spot Prawn and Avocado Salad

Sweet Peas, Aleppo Pepper Oil, Belgian Endive

SERVES 6

The fresh avocado is really what makes this dish. The avocado adds a creaminess and smoothness and counterbalances some of the heat and spice from the Aleppo pepper oil. Warm shrimp and the texture from sweet peas make for a nice finish.

Suggested wine pairing: Albariño

For the shrimp

18 spot prawns (16/20), peeled and deveined
3 tablespoons agave syrup
5 tablespoons BBQ spice mix (page 281)

For the avocado salad

3 avocados
3 cups frisée lettuce, finely chopped
2 heads Belgian endive, finely chopped
3 Persian cucumbers, sliced
1½ cups peas
House vinaigrette, for drizzling (page 285)

For the Aleppo pepper oil

1 cup light olive oil
1 tablespoon crushed garlic
1 tablespoon paprika
½ teaspoon onion powder
1 teaspoon tomato paste
3 tablespoons Aleppo pepper flakes
½ teaspoon salt

FOR THE SHRIMP

In a large bowl combine shrimp with agave syrup and BBQ spice. Coat evenly, cover, and refrigerate for 1 hour.

Prepare a grill over medium-high heat and cook shrimp until done, about 2 minutes per side.

FOR THE AVOCADO SALAD

Peel avocados. Slice each in half and remove pits. Slice each half into 3 slices and set aside.

In a large bowl combine lettuces, cucumbers, and peas, drizzle with house vinaigrette, and lightly toss.

FOR THE ALEPPO PEPPER OIL

Combine all ingredients in a saucepot over medium-low heat, and simmer for 2–3 minutes.

Remove from heat and steep for 15 minutes.

Add to a blender and process until smooth.

AT SERVICE

Place 3 avocado pieces around the edges of each plate. Place the salad in the center of the plate, and place 3 shrimp on top of the salad. Drizzle Aleppo pepper oil around the plate.

Chef's Tip: *Substitute any type of shrimp for this recipe. My favorite way to cook the shrimp is over an outdoor mesquite grill.*

Grilled Spring Lamb Leg

Saffron Pearl Pasta, Watercress Salad, Pickled Onions

SERVES 6

Grilled spring lamb leg is always a hit at my restaurant, especially when paired with a tangy grain mustard vinaigrette.

Suggested wine pairing: Central Coast Viognier

For the saffron pearl pasta

2 cups uncooked pearl pasta
2 tablespoons light olive oil
2 pinches saffron threads
Salt and pepper, to taste
1½ cups assorted sliced olives
¼ chopped basil
House vinaigrette, to taste (page 285)

For the pickled onions

½ cup water
2 tablespoons granulated sugar
3 tablespoons white distilled vinegar
1 teaspoon chile flakes
3 spring onions cut into ¼-inch rounds

For the watercress salad

2 large bunches watercress
2 bulbs fennel, thinly sliced
House vinaigrette, to taste (page 285)
Salt and pepper, to taste

For the grain mustard vinaigrette

1 tablespoon whole grain mustard
1 tablespoon Dijon mustard
1 tablespoon pasteurized egg yolk
¼ cup red wine
2 tablespoons water
Salt and pepper, to taste
1 cup light olive oil

For the lamb leg

1½ pounds leg of lamb cut into long pieces
Light olive oil, for coating lamb
Salt and pepper, to taste

For the assorted summer squash

3 zucchini squash, cut into ¼-inch-thick slices
3 Goldbar squash, cut into ¼-inch-thick slices
3 tablespoons light olive oil
Salt and pepper, to taste

For the garnish

42 shelled fava beans
House vinaigrette, to taste
Salt and pepper, to taste

FOR THE SAFFRON PEARL PASTA

Bring a large pot of salted water to a boil, add the pasta, and cook until al dente per labeled instructions.

Strain the pasta in a colander and add to a large mixing bowl. Add olive oil and saffron (crush the saffron threads with fingertips to create a powder; this helps for a more even distribution) and lightly toss.

Season pasta with salt and pepper and remove to a sheet pan lined with parchment paper and refrigerate until cool (occasionally break up the pasta to prevent it from sticking together).

In a large mixing bowl, combine pasta with olives and basil. Season to taste with house vinaigrette and salt and pepper.

FOR THE PICKLED ONIONS

In a small saucepot over high heat, combine water, sugar, vinegar, and chile flakes. Bring to a boil, remove from heat, and let sit for about 15 minutes.

Place the onions in a small mixing bowl, strain the sugar/vinegar liquid over the onions, and chill in refrigerator for 1 hour.

Strain onions through a fine-mesh sieve and reserve.

FOR THE WATERCRESS SALAD

In a large mixing bowl, combine watercress, fennel, and pickled onions (from above) with house vinaigrette. Season with salt and pepper.

FOR THE GRAIN MUSTARD VINAIGRETTE

Combine all ingredients (except the oil) in a mixing bowl, and whisk thoroughly. In a small stream, add the olive oil, and vigorously whisk to emulsify. Set vinaigrette aside.

FOR THE LAMB LEG

Coat lamb with olive oil and season with salt and pepper. Prepare a grill over high heat (until almost smoking). Sear all sides of lamb to medium rare or desired doneness. Chill meat in refrigerator. When cool, cut into thin slices.

FOR THE ASSORTED SUMMER SQUASH

In a large mixing bowl, combine squash with olive oil, and season with salt and pepper.

Heat a large sauté pan over high heat, and cook the squash until caramelized on one side.

FOR THE GARNISH

Bring a small pot of salted water to a boil. Add fava beans and cook until tender, about 2 minutes.

Drain beans and immediately immerse in a bowl of ice and water.

Remove beans from ice water and remove the outer core from each bean.

In a small mixing bowl, combine fava beans with the house vinaigrette, and season with salt and pepper.

AT SERVICE

Place three heaping spoonfuls of pearl pasta on each plate. Place a few squash rounds onto each pile of pasta. Place a few slices of lamb to lean onto each pile of pasta and squash. Drizzle the mustard vinaigrette on the lamb. Distribute the salad onto the plate. Garnish with seven fava beans.

Chef's Tip: *Ask your local butcher to seam out the lamb leg and remove all the sinew and fat.*

Applewood-Smoked Trout and Crispy Potato Cake

Deviled Egg, Chive Crème Fraîche, Dill Oil, Watercress-Radish Salad, Duet of Caviar

SERVES 6

Some classics are hard to improve on, but here I've composed an old classic of crispy potatoes, smoked fish, and crème fraîche. I've slightly elevated this dish by adding a deviled egg and duet of caviar.

Suggested wine pairing: Vermentino

For the trout brine

1½ cups granulated sugar
½ cup salt
4 cups warm water
1 cup crushed ice
6 (5-ounce) boneless trout fillets, skin on
3 tablespoons light olive oil
Pepper, to taste

For the crème fraîche

1½ cups crème fraîche
1 teaspoon lemon juice
Lemon zest from one lemon (using a microplane or
    citrus zester, remove the zest and finely chop)
1 teaspoon salt
3 tablespoons finely chopped chives

For the salad

6 cups watercress (loosely packed)
6 large radishes, shaved thin
½ cup house vinaigrette (page 285)
Salt and pepper, to taste

For the dill oil

1 cup firmly packed dill
½ cup canola oil
Pinch of salt

For the deviled eggs

6 eggs
¼ cup mayonnaise (page 285)
1 teaspoon Dijon mustard
1 teaspoon lemon juice
¼ teaspoon cayenne
⅛ teaspoon salt
Smoked Spanish paprika, for garnish

For the potato rösti

2 russet potatoes
1 tablespoon cornstarch
2 teaspoons salt, more to taste
2 tablespoons fines herbs, finely chopped
    (page 285)
1 egg white
Light olive oil, for coating pan
Pepper, to taste

For the caviar

1 ounce paddlefish caviar
1 ounce trout roe caviar

FOR THE TROUT BRINE

Combine sugar, salt, and water in a large mixing bowl. Whisk until dissolved, then add the ice. Add fillets and brine for 45 minutes.

Remove fillets from the brine and place on a rack under refrigeration for approximately 24 hours until a sticky surface develops, then cold smoke (according to labeled instructions) for 30 minutes.

Remove from smoker and refrigerate.

Heat olive oil in a large nonstick sauté pan over medium-high heat. Sprinkle flesh side of fillets with a small amount of pepper. Add the fillets, flesh side down, to pan. Cook for about 2 minutes per side and remove to a plate lined with paper towels. Peel off skin and slice each fillet in half.

FOR THE CRÈME FRAÎCHE

In a mixing bowl, combine the crème fraîche, lemon juice, lemon zest, and salt. Whisk vigorously until thick and aerated. Fold in the chives. Refrigerate.

FOR THE SALAD

In a large mixing bowl, toss the watercress and radishes in vinaigrette until evenly coated. Season with salt and pepper.

FOR THE DILL OIL

Submerge dill in a small pot of boiling water; blanch for 30 seconds. Remove dill and squeeze in a cheesecloth, then place in a small bowl of ice and water for about 5 minutes. Remove from ice water and squeeze in cheesecloth again. Add dill, canola oil, and salt to a blender, and process until smooth. Chill in the refrigerator.

mixture in a piping bag and evenly disperse into the egg whites. Sprinkle with paprika to garnish.

FOR THE POTATO RÖSTI

Submerge potatoes in cold water (3–4 inches of water above the potatoes) and bring to a boil. Reduce heat to medium low and simmer potatoes for about 45 minutes or until just cooked through but still firm.

Remove potatoes and cool in the refrigerator for 1 hour. Peel the skins and grate the potatoes on the largest hole of a box grater.

Squeeze the grated potatoes in a tea towel to remove excess moisture, then add to a large mixing bowl. Using your hands, combine potatoes with cornstarch, salt, and fines herbes.

Add egg white and thoroughly combine.

Using a 3-inch diameter ring mold, form 6 cakes about 1 inch thick.

Heat olive oil (½ inch from the bottom) in a large sauté pan over medium heat. Add the potato cakes and fry until golden brown, about 3 minutes per side. Remove potato cakes to a plate lined with paper towels, and sprinkle with salt and pepper.

AT SERVICE

Place two trout halves in the center of each plate, and season with salt and pepper to taste. Distribute the salad onto the plate just above the fish. Place 1 potato rösti and 1 deviled egg onto each plate. Place a large dollop of crème fraîche onto each plate, and evenly distribute caviars on top of that. Drizzle dill oil around each plate.

Chef's Tip: *You can buy caviar at your local fishmonger, a specialty food market, or at a high-end grocery store.*

FOR THE DEVILED EGGS

Place eggs in a saucepot and cover with water, about an inch above the eggs. Bring to a strong boil, cover saucepot, turn off the heat, and let eggs sit for 11 minutes.

Remove eggs and place in a bowl of ice and water. Once cooled, crack eggshells and carefully peel under cool running water. Blot dry with paper towels.

Slice eggs in half lengthwise and remove yolks to a bowl (reserve the whites).

Mash the yolks into a paste using a fork. Add mayonnaise, mustard, lemon juice, cayenne, and salt;. Mix until thoroughly combined. Place

Duck Liver Pâté and Strawberry-Rhubarb Compote

Grilled Sourdough Wheat Toast, Strawberry-Fennel Salad

SERVES 6

This is a recipe that was handed down to me from my grandfather, who was an avid duck hunter. Having grown up in the Depression, he would always use all the parts of the duck. He started many a meal with this recipe. Here it's paired with a strawberry salad to lighten the richness of the liver and after all these years it still makes a great beginning to any meal.

Suggested wine pairing: Late Harvest Riesling

For the duck pâté

3 pounds duck liver
Cold milk
1 teaspoon salt
2 pounds plus 1 tablespoon duck fat
3 cloves garlic, peeled and crushed
2 shallots, peeled and coarsely chopped
1 cup heavy cream
3 unflavored gelatin sheets, soaked in cold water
    until they bloom
¼ cup top shelf brandy

For the strawberry-rhubarb compote

Zest of 1 orange
Zest of 1 lemon
6 stalks rhubarb, medium diced
2 pints strawberries, stemmed and quartered
¾ cup granulated sugar
¼ teaspoon vanilla extract

For the anise syrup (Makes ½ cup)

2 cups granulated sugar
2 cups water
1 tablespoon toasted ground fennel (page 287)
6 star anise

For the strawberry fennel salad

18 strawberries, sliced in ¼-inch-thick rounds
½ cup house vinaigrette (page 285), divided
3 cups watercress (loosely packed), large stems
    removed
Salt and pepper, to taste
1 cup shaved fennel

For the griddle sourdough-wheat toast

1 loaf sourdough-wheat bread, cut into ½-inch-thick
    slices
Soft butter, for brushing bread
Salt and pepper, to taste

FOR THE DUCK PÂTÉ

In a large bowl, soak duck liver in milk and refrigerate for two hours. Rinse under cold water, then place on a dish lined with paper towels. Pat dry and season with salt.

Melt 2 pounds of duck fat in a large sauté pan over medium-high heat. Add duck liver and cook for 2 minutes. Set aside.

Melt remaining 1 tablespoon of duck fat in a sauté pan over medium heat. Add garlic and shallots and cook until fragrant. Add cream and bring to a boil, then remove from heat.

Combine duck and cream mixture in a blender with gelatin and brandy. Process until smooth.

Place pâté in a 3 × 5 × 9-inch terrine or loaf pan lined with plastic wrap. Cover and refrigerate for at least 1½ hours.

Just before serving, remove pâté from loaf pan and slice into squares. (You can keep the pâté covered in the refrigerator for up to 4 days.)

FOR THE STRAWBERRY-RHUBARB COMPOTE

Preheat oven to 325°F.

In a small bowl, combine orange and lemon zests.

In a large mixing bowl, combine rhubarb and strawberries. Add zest, sugar, and vanilla, and lightly toss.

Place fruit mixture on a baking sheet lined with a nonstick baking mat. Roast the fruit mixture, periodically tossing, until tender. Remove fruit from oven and cool at room temperature.

FOR THE ANISE SYRUP

In a saucepot over medium heat, combine sugar and water, then add fennel and star anise. Simmer and reduce mixture to half its volume.

Add to a blender and pulse 4 or 5 times, then strain mixture through a fine-mesh sieve. Cool to room temperature and reserve.

FOR THE STRAWBERRY FENNEL SALAD

In a mixing bowl, combine the strawberries in a bowl with some of the vinaigrette, and season with salt and pepper.

In another mixing bowl, combine the watercress and fennel with some of the vinaigrette, season with salt and pepper, and lightly toss.

FOR THE GRIDDLE SOURDOUGH-WHEAT TOAST

Brush both sides of bread with butter and season with salt and pepper.

Heat a stovetop grill pan over high heat, add bread, and toast both sides until deep golden brown and crunchy.

AT SERVICE

Stack and arrange the strawberries across each plate. Lay the watercress and fennel over the top of the berries. Place 1 square of duck pate on the plate, add the rhubarb compote over the top, and place some of the sourdough-wheat toast slices to the side.

Chef's Tip: *Using a sheet pan lined with a nonstick baking sheet helps the strawberries dry more quickly. It distributes the heat evenly so the fruit is less apt to burn.*

Artichoke and Goat Cheese Tart

Shaved Chorizo, Sweet Red Peppers, Kalamata and Picholine Olives

SERVES 6

The creamy goat cheese further complements the brininess and acidity of the olives and braised artichokes in this dish. The richness of the flaky crust of the tart pastry and the spiciness and pops of heat from the chorizo make this the perfect spring plate.

Suggested wine pairing: Rueda Verdejo

For the tart dough

1½ cups all-purpose flour, more for dusting
1 cup cold butter
½ teaspoon salt
½ cup cold water

For the salad

3 red bell peppers
Light olive oil, as needed
Salt and pepper, as needed
3 cups frisée lettuce
House vinaigrette, for drizzling (page 285)
6 whole artichokes

For the goat cheese filling

2 tablespoons light olive oil
3 large leeks, white part only, small diced
2 cups goat cheese
Salt, to taste

For the garnish

¾ cup sliced kalamata olives
¾ cup sliced picholine olives
48 thin slices of dry chorizo, or your favorite
    cured meat
48 shaved slices from a block of Parmigiana
    Reggiano
Micro arugula, for garnish

FOR THE TART DOUGH

In a large mixing bowl (from a stand mixer), add flour, butter, and salt. With your hands, break up the butter so that the pieces are no larger than small peas.

Place the bowl on stand mixer with paddle attachment in place. Add water and process at low speed until a dough forms.

Remove the dough to a floured covered surface and knead for 2 minutes. Wrap the dough in plastic wrap and refrigerate for 1 hour.

Place dough on a floured surface, roll flat, and cut out circles with a 5-inch circular cookie cutter. Mold dough into 3 ¼-inch tart molds. Place tart molds onto a large baking sheet lined with parchment paper and refrigerate for 30 minutes.

Preheat oven to 350°F.

Place a small piece of parchment paper onto each tart mold and weigh down with tart weights or a handful of dry beans.

Bake until light golden brown, 25–30 minutes. Once cooled, remove tarts from molds.

FOR THE SALAD

Preheat oven to 450°F.

Coat peppers with olive oil and season with salt and pepper. Place peppers on a baking sheet and roast in oven until completely wrinkled and charred, 30–40 minutes, turning them twice during roasting.

Place peppers in a mixing bowl, cover with plastic wrap, and let rest for 5 minutes.

Peel peppers, remove stems and seeds, and cut into ½-inch pieces.

In a large mixing bowl, combine peppers with lettuce, and drizzle with house vinaigrette. Toss until evenly coated.

Add artichokes to a large saucepot with a couple inches of water at the bottom; cover, bring to a boil, then reduce heat to medium low. Cook artichokes until the outer leaves can be easily pulled off, 40–45 minutes.

Remove the leaves and chokes and dice the hearts, storing leaves in a covered container in the refrigerator to enjoy later.

FOR THE GOAT CHEESE FILLING

Heat olive oil in a large sauté pan over medium-low heat. Add leeks and cook until translucent, about 5 minutes.

Add goat cheese to a large mixing bowl in a stand mixer with paddle attachment in place.

Process until smooth and creamy. Add leeks to the goat cheese, season with salt, and process until thoroughly incorporated.

Fill tart molds with goat cheese filling.

Just before serving, preheat oven to 350°F. Place tarts on a baking sheet, and warm for 5–10 minutes.

AT SERVICE

Place warmed goat cheese tart in the center of each plate. Distribute frisée and peppers around the tart. Evenly distribute the artichoke hearts, olives, chorizo, and Parmigiana Reggiano slices on top of the frisée and peppers. Garnish with micro arugula.

Chef's Tip: *Refrigerating the tarts before baking keeps the dough from shrinking and pulling back from the edges of the tart mold.*

Chef's Tip: *Use a vegetable peeler to get shavings from a block of Parmigiana Reggiano.*

Sandabs Salad with Braised Baby Artichokes

Tomato Relish, Basil Remoulade

SERVES 6

These little sandabs show up during springtime. As a kid I would go out on the fishing boats and, while the other fishermen were catching sandabs and throwing them back into the water, I would recatch them and keep them for myself. I really like the sweet and delicate meat. For this recipe, I pair it with a few of my favorite spring ingredients.

Suggested wine pairing: Alsatian Gewurztraminer

For the sandabs

6 sandabs
Salt and pepper, for seasoning
8 tablespoons butter, divided
1 lemon

For the basil remoulade

2 cups (packed) basil leaves
1 clove garlic
1 cup light olive oil
1 egg yolk
1 tablespoon lemon juice
3 tablespoons capers, rinsed and dried
2 tablespoons finely minced red onion

For the frisée salad

6 cups frisée lettuce, stems removed
1 cup lemon vinaigrette (page 285)
1 tablespoon fines herbes (page 285)

For the artichokes

12 baby artichokes
6 tablespoons light olive oil
6 cloves garlic, peeled
1 (3-inch) sprig rosemary
2 sprigs thyme
1 bay leaf
1 teaspoon whole black peppercorns
1 teaspoon red chile flakes
2 cups dry white wine
1 cup vegetable stock (page 288)

For the tomato relish

12 Roma tomatoes
4 tablespoons light olive oil
2 tablespoons minced garlic
2 tablespoons minced shallots
2 tablespoons red wine vinegar
Salt and pepper, to taste

FOR THE SANDABS

Season both sides of sandabs with salt and pepper.

Preheat two large sauté pans over medium-high heat. Melt 4 tablespoons of butter in each pan. Add 3 sandabs to each pan, and cook for about 1½ minutes on each side. Squeeze juice of half a lemon over each filet. Remove from pan.

FOR THE BASIL REMOULADE

Submerge basil in boiling water for 3 minutes. Using a slotted spoon, remove basil and place in a bowl of ice and water.

Remove basil to a cheesecloth and squeeze out excess moisture.

In a blender combine basil with garlic and olive oil, and process until smooth.

In a mixing bowl, whisk together egg yolk and lemon.

Whisk in the basil mixture to emulsify.

Add capers and red onion, and combine thoroughly.

FOR THE FRISÉE SALAD

In a large mixing bowl, combine the frisée with some of the lemon vinaigrette to coat. Sprinkle with fines herbes.

FOR THE ARTICHOKES

Remove outer fibrous leaves from the artichokes by pulling down firmly to snap off. Using a vegetable peeler, peel off the fiber from the stems. Cut about a ½ inch off the top of each artichoke (tops should be flat). Cut artichokes in half lengthwise.

Prepare an ice bath by nesting a medium bowl in a larger bowl that's partially filled with ice and water.

In a saucepot over medium heat, add olive oil, garlic, rosemary, thyme, bay leaf, peppercorns, and chile flakes, and sauté until fragrant.

Add artichokes, coat with the oil and herbs, and cook for about 1 minute.

Add wine and vegetable stock, cover saucepot, reduce heat to low, and cook artichokes until tender. To check for doneness, insert a knife into the artichokes. When knife inserts easily, remove entire mixture to the medium bowl over the ice bath and chill.

Remove artichokes from the braising liquid, cut in quarters, and lightly dress with lemon vinaigrette.

FOR THE TOMATO RELISH

Bring a large pot of salted water to a boil. Add the tomatoes and blanch for 15 seconds. Using a slotted spoon, immediately remove tomatoes to a bowl of ice and water. Repeat method by adding tomatoes back to the same pot of boiling water for an additional 15 seconds, than removing them, again, to the bowl of ice and water. Remove tomatoes to a plate lined with paper towels, and peel, core, and finely dice them.

Heat olive oil in a sauté pan over low heat. Add garlic and shallots and cook until soft, about 5 minutes. Remove pan from heat and cool.

In a large mixing bowl, combine tomatoes with the cooked garlic and shallot mixture. Add vinegar and toss to combine. Season with salt and pepper.

AT SERVICE

Evenly distribute the frisée into the center of each plate. Interweave some of the artichoke quarters into the frisée. Placed seared fish on top. Place the tomato relish on and around the fish. Place a dollop of basil remoulade on top of fish.

Chef's Tip: *Baby artichokes are available year-round, but you'll find them in greater supply during the spring months of March, April, and May. Choose artichokes that are firm and heavy for their size. They are very easy to prepare and their flavor is the same as that of the big artichokes.*

Hickory-Smoked Bison Tenderloin Carpaccio and Spot Prawn "Surf & Turf"

Shaved Asparagus-Seaweed Salad, Ginger-Miso Vinaigrette

SERVES 6

Bison is a very lean cut of meat, making for a great carpaccio. For this dish, I like to pair bison with a sweet spot prawn, while adding an Asian twist with an asparagus-seaweed salad and ginger-miso vinaigrette.

Suggested wine pairing: Cru Beaujolais

For the smoked bison tenderloin

12–14 ounces bison tenderloin
2 tablespoons Chinese five-spice powder
3 tablespoons light olive oil, for coating
Salt and pepper, to taste

For the miso vinaigrette

¼ cup white miso
2 tablespoons rice wine vinegar
1 clove garlic, chopped
1 teaspoon ginger juice (fresh ginger grated, then squeezed by hand into a bowl)
1 teaspoon sesame oil

For the asparagus-seaweed salad

3 pieces large asparagus
2 Japanese cucumbers
1 small Daikon radish
1½ cups seaweed
2 tablespoons seasoned rice wine vinegar

For the spot prawn marinade

1 large bunch chopped cilantro
4 tablespoons seasoned rice wine vinegar
4 tablespoons light olive oil, plus more for coating prawns
2 cloves garlic, peeled and finely chopped
12 spot prawns, peeled, tail on, head attached
Salt and pepper, to taste

For garnish

Spicy sesame seed oil, to taste
Maldon sea salt
1 pack enoki mushrooms

FOR THE SMOKED BISON TENDERLOIN

Using paper towels, dry the tenderloin of excess moisture. Place meat on a rack on a sheet pan in the refrigerator for 1–2 hours to allow meat to dry slightly.

Remove tenderloin from the refrigerator, rub with Chinese five-spice powder, and season with salt and pepper.

Heat a large sauté pan over high heat. Coat the tenderloin with olive oil. Place in the pan and sear on all sides, about 10 seconds each side.

Place tenderloin on a baking sheet lined with parchment paper and freeze until solid, 2–3 hours.

Using an electric slicer or sharp knife, slice the tenderloin across the grain into 18 ¼-inch-thick slices.

FOR THE MISO VINAIGRETTE

Add all ingredients to a blender and process until smooth.

FOR THE ASPARAGUS-SEAWEED SALAD

Using a mandoline, shave the asparagus, cucumbers, and radish (on a bias) very thin. Combine in a bowl and drizzle with the miso vinaigrette.

In a small mixing bowl, combine seaweed and vinegar, and toss lightly.

FOR THE SPOT PRAWN MARINADE

Combine cilantro, vinegar, 4 tablespoons olive oil, and garlic in a blender, and process until smooth to make a marinade.

Place prawns in a large bowl, cover with marinade and evenly coat. Cover with plastic wrap, place in the refrigerator to marinate for 1–2 hours.

Submerge 6 wooden skewers in hot tap water, then place in the refrigerator for several hours (this will keep the skewers from burning on the grill).

Prepare a grill over high heat. Coat the prawns with olive oil and season with salt and pepper. Skewer the prawns (2 per skewer) and grill until cooked, about 1 minute per side.

AT SERVICE

Layer 3 bison tenderloin slices onto each plate. Place a small pile of seaweed salad to the left side of the tenderloins. Distribute the salad onto the upper half of tenderloins. Lean 2 spot prawns on the seaweed salad. Garnish with sesame seed oil, salt, and enoki mushrooms.

Chef's Tip: *Although once difficult to find, seaweed is now easily accessible at specialty markets. Although many varieties are preseasoned, I prefer to buy an unseasoned variety and dress it myself.*

Chef's Tip: *The bison could also be prepared using a smoker according to labeled instructions. I suggest cold smoking the meat using hickory or mesquite chips for about 1 hour.*

Cornish Game Hen à l'Orange

Purple Peruvian Potatoes, Wild Blackberry Jus, Sautéed Escarole

SERVES 6

Everyone loves fowl paired with an orange glaze. This is a dish I never hesitate to pull out of my repertoire because my guests absolutely love it. There are few things better than a caramelized citrus glaze as in this perfectly cooked chicken with à l'orange sauce.

Suggested wine pairing: Willamette Valley Pinot Noir

For the game hen

3 medium rock Cornish game hens
2 tablespoons Dijon mustard
Salt and pepper, to taste
2 tablespoons fines herbes (page 285)

For the potatoes

24 small purple Peruvian potatoes
Salt, to taste
¼ cup plus 2 tablespoons light olive oil
1 large Spanish onion, peeled and sliced
2 tablespoons fines herbes (page 285)
Pepper, to taste

For the sautéed escarole

2 tablespoons light olive oil
2 teaspoons finely chopped garlic
2 bunches escarole, roughly chopped
½ teaspoon salt

For the sauce à l'orange

3 tablespoons light olive oil
½ cup sliced shallots
1 teaspoon whole peppercorns
1 bay leaf
1 sprig thyme
1 teaspoon coriander

1 stick cinnamon
2 star anise
3 cloves
1 cup sherry vinegar
½ cup triple sec
½ cup Grand Marnier
4 cups fresh squeezed orange juice

For the wild blackberry jus

3 hen carcasses
Light olive oil, for coating hen carcasses
2 cups sliced Spanish onions
1 cup carrots
1 cup celery
2 bay leaves
1 tablespoon peppercorns
2 sprigs thyme
1 bunch parsley stems
1 tablespoon coriander
1 (750-mililiter) bottle Syrah wine
8 cups brown chicken stock (page 282)
2 cups blackberries

For the kumquats

12 kumquats, seeds removed and sliced into rounds
Simple syrup (page 286)

FOR THE GAME HEN

Remove the legs and breasts from the hens, leaving the wings on the breasts. Reserve the game hen bones for the sauce.

Take all the breasts, remove the wing tips, and "French" the remaining wing bone (remove all meat, skin, and connective tissue from the bone).

Take the legs and, using a boning knife, remove the thighbone, being careful not to cut through the skin side. After the thighbones have been removed, French the remaining "drumstick" so about 2 inches of bone are exposed and clean.

Spread Dijon mustard in the thigh cavity from which you removed the bone, and season with a small amount of salt and pepper. Finish with some of fine herbs.

Using butcher twine, tie the thigh into a cylinder shape pulling the skin on each side so that it meets and fully wraps the thigh in skin.

Reserve the butchered breasts and legs.

FOR THE POTATOES

Place the potatoes in a large saucepot and cover with water (about 3 inches above the potatoes).

Season the water with salt, and stir it in so it dissolves. Taste the water, it should taste like a well-seasoned soup. Bring to a boil, reduce heat to medium low, and simmer potatoes until fork tender, but not falling apart, 15–20 minutes.

Remove potatoes from water, place in a large mixing bowl, and cool to room temperature. Slice the potatoes into ¼-inch-round pieces.

Heat 2 tablespoons olive oil in a large sauté pan over high heat. Add onions and cook until caramelized and slightly wilted. Remove onions to a dish.

Heat ¼ cup olive oil in the same pan over high heat. Add potatoes, lower heat just slightly, and cook until crispy on all sides. Drain off any excess oil then add the onions back to the pan, and sprinkle with herbs and season with salt and pepper.

FOR THE SAUTÉED ESCAROLE

Heat olive oil in a large sauté pan over medium heat. Add garlic and sauté until just fragrant.

Add escarole and salt, toss lightly, and cook until just wilted.

FOR THE SAUCE À L'ORANGE

Heat olive oil in a large saucepot over medium heat. Add shallots, peppercorns, bay leaf, thyme, coriander, cinnamon, star anise, and cloves. Cook, stirring often, until shallots are translucent, 10–15 minutes.

Add vinegar, triple sec, and Grand Marnier, and cook over medium heat until reduced by half its volume.

Add orange juice and continue to reduce to a syrup consistency.

FOR THE WILD BLACKBERRY JUS

Preheat oven to 375°F.

Cut hen carcasses into 4 pieces each (for a total of 12 pieces), and coat with oil. Add carcasses to a baking dish and roast for 1 hour, tossing occasionally.

Remove carcasses from oven and set aside.

Pour out some of the fat from the baking dish and add onions, carrots, and celery. Roast in oven for 30 minutes.

In a large stockpot, add the hen carcasses, roasted vegetables, bay leaves, peppercorns, thyme, parsley, coriander, and wine. Bring to a boil then reduce heat to medium low. Reduce liquid to ¼ of its original volume.

Add stock and reduce liquid to a sauce consistency. Strain liquid through a fine-mesh sieve into a large mixing bowl and gently stir in blackberries. Strain liquid again through a fine-mesh sieve and reserve blackberries.

FOR THE KUMQUATS

Bring simple syrup to a boil in a small saucepan. Pour over sliced kumquats. Reserve.

AT SERVICE

Place 2 mounds of escarole on each plate and top with potatoes and onions. Top each potato mound with one game hen leg and one game hen breast. Spoon sauce à l'orange and blackberry jus around the plates. Garnish with kumquats and blackberries.

Chef's Tip: *Substitute any sweet onion in this recipe.*

Cabrilla Grouper and Peekytoe Crab

Fennel Puree, Grilled Asparagus, Tarragon Butter

SERVES 6

While fishing in Mexico over the years, I've caught many types of grouper. However, my favorite is a smaller cabrilla grouper. Although many grouper vary in consistency throughout, the cabrilla is consistent in texture from head to tail. It's very mild tasting and makes a nice canvas for the asparagus and citrus.

Suggested wine pairing: Austrian Grüner Veltliner

For the cabrilla grouper

6 (5-ounce) cabrilla grouper fillets
Salt and pepper, to taste
6 tablespoons oil, divided

For the tarragon butter

3 egg yolks
1 cup melted butter
1 tablespoon lemon juice
3 tablespoons chopped tarragon
Salt, to taste

For the blood orange reduction

1 cup fresh-squeezed blood orange juice
1 stick cinnamon
2 star anise
3 cardamom pods
1 tablespoon coriander
2 (½-inch) slices fresh ginger

For the grilled asparagus

24 asparagus spears
Light olive oil, for drizzling
Salt and pepper, to taste

For the fennel puree

1 cup medium peeled and diced potatoes
Salt, to taste
4 tablespoons light olive oil
2 bulbs fennel, sliced
½ teaspoon toasted ground fennel seed (page 287)

1 leek, roughly chopped
½ Spanish onion, peeled and sliced
1 bay leaf
2 tablespoons butter
½ cup heavy cream

For the sautéed sweet pea tendrils

2 tablespoons light olive oil
2 teaspoons finely chopped garlic
2 bunches sweet pea tendrils, roughly chopped
    (reserve some fresh for garnish)
½ teaspoon salt

For the garnish

½ pound picked crabmeat
36 blood orange segments

FOR THE CABRILLA GROUPER

Preheat oven to 350°F.

Season fish on both sides with salt and pepper.

Heat 3 tablespoons of olive oil in a large sauté pan over high heat. Add 3 fillets to the pan and reduce heat to medium high. Sear fillets until lightly golden brown, 2–3 minutes per side. Remove fillets to a large baking dish. Add 3 tablespoons of oil to the sauté pan and repeat searing process for remaining fish fillets.

Place seared fillets in a baking dish, and bake until cooked through.

FOR THE TARRAGON BUTTER

In a stainless steel mixing bowl over simmering hot water, add egg yolks, then immediately add butter in a thin stream, whisking constantly until sauce is thickened.

Add lemon juice, tarragon, and salt.

FOR THE BLOOD ORANGE REDUCTION

Combine all ingredients in a saucepot, and bring to a boil. Reduce to low heat and simmer until the sauce is thickened and coats the back of a spoon.

FOR THE FENNEL PUREE

In a small saucepot of salted boiling water, cook potatoes until very soft, then strain and set aside.

Heat olive oil in a large sauté pan over medium heat. Add fennel, ground fennel seed, leek, onion, and bay leaf. Cover sauté pan and cook onions until translucent.

Add potatoes, butter, and cream. Bring to a boil and then remove from heat.

Remove bay leaf, add mixture to a blender, and process until smooth.

FOR THE SAUTÉED SWEET PEA TENDRILS

Heat oil in a large sauté pan over medium heat. Add garlic and cook until just fragrant.

Add pea tendrils and season with salt. Lightly toss to coat evenly with oil, and cook until wilted.

AT SERVICE

Place pea tendrils in the center of each plate with fennel puree to the side. Place one grouper fillet on top of pea tendrils, and top grouper with asparagus, crabmeat, and tarragon butter. Garnish with six blood orange segments.

Chef's Tip: *The peak season for blood oranges is March through May. The flesh and juice of a blood orange is (as its name implies) blood red. When picking them out, look for small to medium oranges with a smooth or pitted skin that sometimes has a reddish hue.*

Chef's Tip: *When catching fish, pack your catch in crushed ice immediately. Shortly after, cut the belly open and remove the guts.*

FOR THE GRILLED ASPARAGUS

Prepare a grill over high heat.

Place asparagus on a baking sheet, drizzle with olive oil, season with salt and pepper, and grill for 1 minute per side.

Shrimp-Crusted Alaskan Halibut

Bok Choy, Shaved Radish Salad, Spring Peas, Truffled Ponzu

SERVES 6

This dish is one of my all-time favorites at Market restaurant. I've developed it over the years. The mild flaky halibut partners perfectly with the flavorful shrimp mousse and sesame seeds.

Suggested wine pairing: Russian River Valley Chardonnay

For the halibut

6 (5-ounce) halibut fillets, about 1½ inches thick
7 tablespoons light olive oil, divided
1 teaspoon minced garlic
1 teaspoon minced ginger
2 scallions, finely chopped
½ pound raw shrimp, peeled, deveined, and roughly chopped
1 egg, whisked
1 teaspoon light soy sauce
2 teaspoons hot sauce
6 tablespoons heavy cream
1 cup sesame seeds

For the bok choy

3 tablespoons light olive oil, divided
6 heads baby bok choy, cut in half
2 teaspoons finely minced garlic, divided

For the spring peas

Salt, for seasoning
1 cup shelled English peas

For the truffled ponzu sauce

1 cup tsuyu sauce
4 tablespoons seasoned rice vinegar
3 tablespoons lemon juice
¾ cup cold truffle butter, diced

For the radish salad

8 assorted radishes
6 sugar snap peas
Seasoned rice vinegar, to taste
Sesame oil, to taste

FOR THE HALIBUT

Place halibut fillets on a large baking sheet lined with paper towels to thoroughly dry.

Heat 3 tablespoons of olive oil in a small sauté pan over low heat. Add garlic, ginger, and scallions, and cook until fragrant and soft, about 3 minutes. Chill in refrigerator.

In a food processor, combine the ginger/garlic/scallion mixture with shrimp, egg, soy sauce, and hot sauce. Pulse until fully incorporated but still a little chunky.

Add cream, and pulse until fully incorporated, being careful not to overprocess (you want the shrimp to have a little texture and you don't want the cream to turn to butter).

Spread a layer of shrimp about ¼-inch thick on one side of each halibut. Place the shrimp-crusted fillet on a sheet pan, shrimp side up, until ready to cook.

Spread some sesame seeds onto each halibut portion (shrimp side), pressing down so they adhere properly.

Heat 4 tablespoons of olive oil in a large sauté pan or cast-iron skillet over medium heat. Add the halibut (shrimp side) to the pan. Cook just long enough to brown the sesame seeds. Carefully flip over and cook to desired doneness, about 3–5 minutes.

FOR THE BOK CHOY

Heat olive oil in a large sauté pan over medium-high heat. Add the bok choy and sauté until tender. Add garlic and cook for a few seconds more.

FOR THE SPRING PEAS

Blanch peas in a pot of boiling salted water for about 20-30 seconds. Remove to a bowl of ice and water. Drain and reserve.

FOR THE TRUFFLED PONZU SAUCE

Combine all ingredients, with the exception of the butter, in a small saucepot, and bring to a simmer over medium heat.

Add the butter and immersion blend until slightly frothy.

FOR THE RADISH SALAD

Using a mandoline or sharp knife, shave the radishes and sugarsnap peas very thin. Combine in a small mixing bowl with vinegar and sesame oil.

AT SERVICE

Ladle the ponzu sauce into large soup bowls. Add one piece of halibut (sesame side up) to the center of each. Arrange the bok choy and peas around the halibut. Garnish with the radish salad.

Seared Day Boat Scallops and Forest Mushroom Tortellini

Sweet Pea Emulsion, Ginger-Carrot Puree, Chermoula, Pea Tendril Sauté

SERVES 6 / YIELDS 1½ POUNDS PASTA DOUGH

While this recipe requires numerous steps, the preparation comes together quite easily. Seared day boat scallops are topped with a chermoula marinade, which is found in many Moroccan dishes. Rustic homemade mushroom tortellini topped with truffle cream offers a delicate yet powerful balance.

Suggested wine pairing: Greek Assyrtiko

For the tortellini mushroom filling

3 tablespoons light olive oil
8 cups shiitake mushroom caps, small diced
    (reserve mushroom stems)
½ teaspoon salt
3 shallots, finely chopped
8 cloves garlic, finely chopped
3 tablespoons mascarpone cheese
2 teaspoons fines herbes (page 285)
2 tablespoons grated Parmigiana Reggiano
1 teaspoon lemon zest

For the pasta dough

3½ cups all-purpose flour, more if needed
5 large eggs, divided
¼ cup light olive oil
10 tablespoons very cold water, divided,
    plus more as needed
Salt, to taste

For the truffle cream

3 tablespoons light olive oil
1 Spanish onion, peeled and sliced
1 tablespoon chopped garlic
Reserved shiitake mushrooms stems, finely chopped
1 teaspoon porcini powder
3 cups heavy cream
2 tablespoons high-quality truffles (may substitute
    1 teaspoon truffle oil)
1 tablespoon sherry

For the chermoula marinade

2 red bell peppers
2 yellow bell peppers
4 tablespoons light olive oil, divided
Salt and pepper, to taste
½ cup small diced Spanish onions
2 teaspoons minced garlic
Pinch of saffron
1 teaspoon cumin/coriander spice (page 283)
½ teaspoon paprika
1 teaspoon tomato paste
1 tablespoon champagne vinegar

For the sweet pea emulsion

3 cups fresh peas
¼ cup butter
½ teaspoon salt

For the ginger-carrot puree

3 cups carrots, cut into ½-inch pieces
5 cups vegetable stock (page 288)
2 large slices of ginger
½ teaspoon salt
1 bay leaf
¼ cup butter

Seared Day Boat Scallops and Forest Mushroom Tortellini   183

For the sautéed sweet pea tendrils

2 tablespoons light olive oil

2 teaspoons finely chopped garlic

2 bunches sweet pea tendrils, roughly chopped,
    reserve some fresh for garnish

½ teaspoon salt

For the pan-seared sea scallops

3 tablespoons light olive oil

18 fresh sea scallops (size U/10), patted dry with
    paper towels

Salt and pepper, to taste

For the garnish

Salt, to taste

1 cup shelled fava beans

½ cup fresh pea tendrils

FOR THE TORTELLINI MUSHROOM FILLING

Heat olive oil, mushrooms, and salt over medium-low heat. Cook mushrooms until dry, about 30 minutes. Add shallots and garlic, and continue cooking for 10 minutes more. Remove from heat and arrange loosely on a baking sheet to cool to room temperature.

Combine mushrooms in a large mixing bowl with mascarpone, fines herbes, Parmigiana Reggiano, and lemon zest, and incorporate thoroughly.

FOR THE PASTA DOUGH

Add flour to a mixing bowl in a stand mixer with dough hook attachment in place. Add 3 eggs, olive oil, and 8 tablespoons of water. Process until a soft dough forms, 1–2 minutes. Turn the dough out onto a lightly floured surface and knead by hand for 1 minute until smooth, soft, and stretchy. Wrap dough in plastic wrap and allow it to rest at room temperature for 30 minutes.

If rolling pasta dough by hand, cut the dough into quarters and, using a rolling pin, roll out the dough until ⅛–1/16 inch thick. If using a pasta-rolling machine, cut the dough into quarters, press flat, and run each piece of pasta dough several times through the machine, adjusting the setting each time, until the pasta is ⅛–1/16 inch thick.

In a small bowl, create an egg wash by whisking together the remaining 2 eggs and 2 tablespoons of water.

Cut the pasta sheet into rounds using a 3-inch-round cutter, spacing the rounds as close together as possible.

Place 1 teaspoon of mushroom filling in the middle of each round of pasta. With a pastry brush, moisten edges of pasta with egg wash. Fold the dough over to form a half moon, then draw the two corners together to form a rounded bonnet shape. Continue until pasta and filling are finished. Place tortellinis on a sheet pan lined with parchment paper dusted with flour.

Bring a large pot of salted water to a boil. Drop tortellini in boiling water and cook until floating. Drain in a colander.

FOR THE TRUFFLE CREAM

In a saucepot, combine olive oil, onion, garlic, and mushrooms over medium heat, and cook for 10–15 minutes. Add porcini powder and incorporate. Add cream and reduce the mixture by half its volume. It should have a thick sauce consistency after 15–20 minutes.

Strain mixture through a fine-mesh sieve into a large mixing bowl, and add butter and sherry and immersion blend until creamy.

FOR THE CHERMOULA MARINADE

Preheat oven to 450°F.

Coat peppers with 2 tablespoons olive oil and season with salt and pepper. Place on a baking sheet and roast in oven until completely wrinkled and charred, turning them twice during roasting, 30–40 minutes.

Place peppers in a mixing bowl, cover them with plastic wrap, and let them rest for 5 minutes. Peel peppers, remove stems and seeds, and cut into ½-inch pieces.

Heat remaining 2 tablespoons olive oil in a saucepot over medium heat. Add onions and garlic, and sauté until onions are translucent. Add peppers, saffron, cumin/coriander, paprika, tomato paste, and vinegar. Stirring often, simmer mixture on low heat for 15–20 minutes.

FOR THE SWEET PEA EMULSION

Bring a saucepot of water to a boil. Add peas, cook for about 1 minute, and strain.

Combine peas in a blender with butter and salt, and process until smooth. Reserve.

FOR THE GINGER-CARROT PUREE

In a small saucepot, combine carrots with stock, ginger, salt, and bay leaf. Bring to a boil then reduce heat to medium high, cooking carrots until soft, 25–30 minutes.

Remove carrots to a bowl, reserving cooking liquid, and discard bay leaf and ginger.

Combine carrots in a blender with butter and enough of the remaining liquid so that carrots will blend easily. Process until smooth.

FOR THE SAUTÉED SWEET PEA TENDRILS

Heat olive oil in a large sauté pan over medium heat. Add garlic and sauté until just fragrant. Add pea tendrils and salt, lightly toss, coating evenly with oil, and cook until wilted.

FOR THE PAN-SEARED SEA SCALLOPS

Heat olive oil in a large sauté pan over high heat. Add scallops and cook until browned on each side, about 2 minutes per side.

FOR THE GARNISH

Bring a small pot of salted water to a boil. Add fava beans and cook until tender, about 2 minutes. Drain beans and immediately immerse in a bowl of ice and water. Remove beans from ice water and remove the outer core from each bean.

AT SERVICE

Place the sweet pea emulsion on one side of each plate. Using the back of a spoon, smear some of the emulsion across the plate. Place the ginger-carrot puree next to the sweet pea emulsion, smearing puree across the plate in the same manner. Place the sautéed sweet pea tendrils in 3 small mounds on each plate. Place 1 scallop onto each mound. Scatter 3 tortellinis onto each plate between and around the scallops. Top scallops with chermoula. Spoon truffle cream on top of tortellinis and garnish with fresh sweet pea tendrils. Garnish each plate with fava beans and pea tendrils.

Chef's Tip: *I have a method I like to use at Market to clean scallops. To remove any grit or sand, I dunk individual scallops in a bowl of ice water. Using my fingers, I remove grit and sand, and also feel for any attached shell. With a sharp knife, I shave off the small thin layer that holds onto the shell. I then remove scallops to a large baking sheet lined with paper towels until ready to use.*

Jidori Chicken and Chicken Potpie

Assorted Mushroom Stuffing, Savoy Spinach, Fava Beans, Sweet Pea Tendrils

SERVES 6

This is a non-traditional potpie prepared à la minute. Chicken breasts are filled with stuffing made with assorted springtime mushrooms, and thighs are prepared to be super moist and tender. Fully shelled fava beans are not only tender, but they are emerald green in color, making for a nice garnish along with fresh sweet pea tendrils that are a common sight in springtime farmers' markets or Asian markets.

Suggested wine pairing: Burgundian Pinot Noir

For the chicken potpie velouté

3 tablespoons butter
3 cloves garlic, roughly chopped
½ Spanish onion, peeled and roughly chopped
½ leek, roughly chopped
1 stalk celery, finely chopped
Pinch of chile flakes
2 tablespoons all-purpose flour
4 cups cold brown chicken stock (page 282)
2 stems fresh parsley
1 sprig fresh thyme
6 each black peppercorns
1 bay leaf
Salt and pepper, to taste

For the chicken thighs

6 chicken thighs
Light olive oil, for seasoning
Salt and pepper, for seasoning

For the chicken potpie filling

2 potatoes, peeled, medium diced
Salt, to taste
2 tablespoons light olive oil
½ Spanish onion, peeled, medium diced
2 carrots, peeled, medium diced
2 stalks celery, medium diced
Pepper, to taste
1 tablespoon crushed garlic
3 cups chicken velouté (page 283)
1 teaspoon fresh tarragon, finely chopped
1 tablespoon fresh parsley, finely chopped

For the mushroom stuffing

2 tablespoons butter
¼ cup minced shallots
6 cups sliced, assorted wild mushrooms
1 tablespoon minced garlic
¼ cup dry sherry
1 teaspoon salt
½ teaspoon pepper
¼ cup mascarpone cheese
¼ cup grated Parmigiana Reggiano
1 tablespoon fines herbes (page 285)
1 teaspoon truffle oil
¼ cup bread crumbs

For the chicken breast

3 (8-ounce) organic boneless chicken breasts
Salt and pepper, for seasoning
3 tablespoons light olive oil
6 cloves garlic
1 sprig rosemary
¼ cup diced cold butter

For the puff pastry

1 egg
1 tablespoon water
1 (6 x 6-inch) square puff pastry
Salt and pepper, for seasoning
1 tablespoon fresh chopped thyme

For the Savoy spinach

2 tablespoons light olive oil
2 teaspoons finely chopped garlic
2 bunches Savoy spinach, roughly chopped
½ teaspoon salt

For the garnish

1 cup shelled fava beans
Handful of fresh sweet pea tendrils

For the grain mustard sauce

¼ cup diced cold butter, plus 1 tablespoon butter, divided
1 teaspoon finely chopped garlic
1 teaspoon finely chopped shallots
1 cup brown chicken stock (page 282)
2 tablespoons whole grain mustard
1 teaspoon lemon juice
1 teaspoon fines herbes (page 285)
Salt and pepper, to taste

FOR THE CHICKEN POTPIE VELOUTÉ

Melt butter in a saucepan over medium-high heat. Add garlic, onion, leek, celery, and chile flakes. Sauté, stirring frequently, until onions are translucent, about 15 minutes. Add flour and stir well to combine. Cook over medium-low heat until a pale or blond roux forms, about 12 minutes.

Add 2 cups of stock to the pan and whisk vigorously to work out any lumps. Add remaining stock, bring to a full boil, then lower heat to a simmer.

Add parsley, thyme, peppercorns, and bay leaf. Continue to simmer, until a good flavor and consistency develop, about 30 minutes.

Strain the sauce through a fine-mesh sieve and season with salt and pepper.

FOR THE CHICKEN THIGHS

Preheat oven to 350°F.

Rub chicken thighs with oil and season both sides with salt and pepper. Place thighs, skin side up, in a baking dish and roast until cooked through, 25–30 minutes. Remove thighs from oven. When thighs cool, dice into large bite-size pieces.

FOR THE CHICKEN POTPIE FILLING

Add potatoes to a small pot filled with cold water and salt. Bring to a boil then reduce heat to low and simmer potatoes until tender, about 20 minutes. Strain potatoes in a colander and place on a plate lined with paper towels.

Heat olive oil in a large saucepot over high heat. Add onions, carrots, and celery, and sauté over medium-high heat until tender, 10–15 minutes. Season with salt, pepper, and garlic.

Add the potatoes, chicken thigh meat, and velouté. Lower to medium heat and simmer for 5 minutes.

Add tarragon and parsley. Ladle the filling evenly into six 6-ounce ramekins.

FOR THE MUSHROOM STUFFING

Melt butter in a sauté pan over medium-high heat. Add shallots and cook for 5-6 minutes. Add mushrooms and sauté until almost dry. Add garlic and sherry, and season with salt and pepper. Cook mushrooms until the sherry has evaporated and the mushrooms are almost dry.

Add mushrooms to a large mixing bowl and cool slightly. Add mascarpone, Parmigiana Reggiano, fines herbes, truffle oil, and bread crumbs. Spread the stuffing onto a baking sheet, and place in the refrigerator until chilled.

FOR THE CHICKEN BREAST

Preheat oven to 375°F.

Cut a pocket in each chicken breast (from the wing end), and season the chicken with salt and pepper. Place a portion of the mushroom stuffing into each chicken breast, stuffing loosely into pocket.

Heat olive oil in an ovenproof sauté pan over high heat. Add chicken breasts, skin side down, and sear until golden brown.

Flip the breast over, and add garlic, rosemary, and butter. Continuously baste the chicken with butter mixture, and cook for 3–4 minutes.

Place chicken in the oven and roast until cooked through.

Slice each breast into 6 pieces.

FOR THE PUFF PASTRY

Preheat oven to 400°F.

Cut puff pastry into 1-inch squares.

In a small bowl, whisk the egg with water. Brush egg wash on the top of the puff pastry squares and sprinkle with salt, pepper, and thyme.

Place parchment paper on a large baking sheet and coat it with nonstick cooking spray. Evenly distribute the puff pastry squares onto the parchment paper. Spray another piece of parchment paper (of equal size) with nonstick cooking spray and place it (cooking spray side down) on top of the puff pastry squares. Place another baking sheet (of equal size) on top of the baking sheet with the parchment paper on top of the puff pastry squares. (This method will keep the puff pastry from rising too high).

Bake puff pastry in oven for 10 minutes, then reduce heat to 325°F. Remove top sheet pan and

parchment paper covering the puff pastry and continue cooking puff pastry until crispy and golden brown.

FOR THE SAVOY SPINACH

Heat olive oil in a large sauté pan over medium heat. Add garlic and sauté until just fragrant. Add spinach and salt, lightly toss to coat spinach evenly with oil, and cook until wilted.

FOR THE GARNISH

Bring a small pot of salted water to a boil. Add fava beans and cook until tender, about 2 minutes. Remove fava beans and add to a bowl of ice and water to cool for 3–5 minutes (this stops the cooking from the blanching and makes them easier to peel). Remove fava beans from water, and remove the outer cover from each bean.

FOR THE GRAIN MUSTARD SAUCE

Melt 1 tablespoon of butter in a sauté pan over medium-high heat. Add garlic and shallots, and sauté until fragrant. Add stock, bring to a boil, and whisk in ¼ cup cold butter, mustard, lemon juice, fines herbes, and salt and pepper. Reduce to a sauce consistency over medium-low heat.

AT SERVICE

Mound spinach onto the front of each plate. Place 3 stuffed chicken breast pieces on top of the spinach, then spoon the mustard sauce over the chicken breasts. Place chicken potpie ramekin on the plate, and garnish with puff pastry squares, fava beans, and pea tendrils.

Chef's Tip: *You can purchase 2 (5-6 pound) whole organic chickens for this recipe. Brown the bones from the whole chickens for both the potpie velouté and the grain mustard sauce.*

Miso-Glazed Black Cod with Sugar Snap Peas and Golden Pea Shoots

Soba Noodles, Five-Spice Broth, Shaved Radishes

SERVES 6

I was introduced to misos and fell in love with them during my travels to Japan. My memories of Japan and a love of their delicious Japanese cuisine led me to experiment and play around with different styles and tastes. In this recipe, two worlds collide with an early spring harvest of crispy snap peas and golden pea shoots paired with the richness and texture of miso black cod in a rich savory broth.

Suggested wine pairing: Loire Valley Sauvignon Blanc

For the miso-glazed cod

1 cup sake
½ cup red miso paste
¼ cup mirin
⅔ cup granulated sugar
6 (5-ounce) portions black cod

For the five-spice broth

3 tablespoons canola oil
1 strip bacon, finely diced (optional)
6 cloves garlic, roughly chopped
½ cup Spanish onion, peeled and sliced
2 green onions, roughly chopped
1 (½-inch) ginger cube, roughly chopped
18 shiitake mushroom stems, sliced about a ¼-inch
    thick (reserve mushroom caps and thinly slice)
1 teaspoon whole cumin
1 teaspoon whole coriander
1 teaspoon whole fennel seed
¼ teaspoon chile flakes
1 stick cinnamon
2 star anise
4 cups chicken or vegetable broth (page 283
    or 288)
¼ cup soy sauce
1 tablespoon fish sauce
¼ cup seasoned rice wine vinegar
4 whole cloves

For the soba noodles

1 (16-ounce) package of dried or fresh soba noodles
Canola oil, for coating noodles

For the mushroom caps

1 tablespoon light olive oil
18 mushroom caps (reserved from above)

For the garnish

3 cups snap peas, sliced in half
1 package golden pea shoots or daikon radish
    sprouts (optional)
1 bunch red radishes, sliced

FOR THE MISO-GLAZED COD

In a blender, combine sake, miso, mirin, and sugar, and process for 2 minutes.

Place cod in a large bowl. Add miso glaze and thoroughly coat. Cover bowl with plastic wrap and refrigerate for 12 hours or up to 2 days.

When ready to cook, preheat oven to broil.

Arrange cod in a large baking dish or sheet pan with a half-inch space between portions. Place on rack in oven about 6 inches from heating element. Checking every 5 minutes, broil cod until golden brown and caramelized, 10–15 minutes. If the fish starts to get dark and caramelized, but still needs time to cook, reposition oven rack farther away from the heating element and allow cod to continue cooking until done.

FOR THE FIVE-SPICE BROTH

Heat oil in a small saucepot over medium heat. Add bacon and cook for 2 minutes.

Add garlic, onions, ginger, mushroom stems, cumin, coriander, fennel, chile flakes, cinnamon, and star anise. Stirring frequently, cook for 5 minutes.

Add broth, soy sauce, fish sauce, and vinegar. Simmer over medium-high heat, reduce to low heat, and simmer for 20 minutes. Pass through a fine-mesh sieve and add back to the saucepot.

Just before serving, bring broth to a boil.

FOR THE SOBA NOODLES

Place soba noodles in a pot of boiling water and cook until desired doneness, approximately 5 minutes for dry noodles and 2 minutes for fresh noodles. Strain noodles in a colander and place in a large mixing bowl. Coat noodles with a very small amount of canola oil (just enough to keep the noodles from sticking together).

FOR THE MUSHROOM CAPS

Heat olive oil in a sauté pan over medium-high heat. Add mushroom caps and sauté until wilted, 3-5 minutes.

AT SERVICE

Add soba noodles to each bowl. Add mushroom caps and snap peas, then ladle the five-spice broth into the bowls until just covering the noodles. Top with miso-glazed cod, and garnish with snap peas, pea shoots, and radishes.

Chef's Tip: *When I select snap peas at a farmers' market, I always taste one first. When the snap peas are sweet and crunchy, you know you've found a good batch.*

Cabernet Braised Beef Short Ribs

Spring Peas, Baby Carrots, Truffled Potato Pavé

SERVES 6

Coming out of winter I see flashes of above-ground vegetables. This is the time of year where chefs are chomping at the bit to use a different product because the winter months can drag on too long. When I think of spring, I can't help but think about the lively first harvest of sweet tender peas and baby carrots. By incorporating these bountiful vegetables into our dishes, this playful rendition on Mom's old-fashioned stew or pot roast is a comforting and rustic dish brought to life with signs of a warm summer to come.

Suggested wine pairing: Napa Valley Cabernet

For the ribs

18 beef short ribs, deboned
Salt and pepper to taste
2 tablespoons light olive oil
2 slices bacon, chopped
2 yellow onions, peeled and chopped
1 large carrot, chopped
1 rib celery, chopped
8 cups demi-glace (page 284)
1 (750 mililiter) bottle cabernet wine
2 bay leaves
¼ bunch fresh thyme, chopped
¼ bunch fresh parsley, chopped

For the truffled potato pavé

2 tablespoons butter
2 tablespoons all-purpose flour
4 cups of heavy cream
2 teaspoons salt
½ cup Monterey Jack cheese
½ cup Gouda cheese
½ cup truffle Gouda cheese
2½ pounds russet potatoes, cut in ¼-inch slices
Mushroom duxelle (page 286)
1 cup breadcrumbs

For the spinach

2 tablespoons light olive oil, divided
1 tablespoon butter, divided
1 teaspoon chopped garlic, divided
8 cups fresh baby spinach, rinsed
Pinch of salt and pepper

For the roasted carrots

54 baby carrots, peeled, tops removed
¼ cup light olive oil
Salt and pepper, to taste

For the peas

1 tablespoon butter
2 tablespoons water
2 cups fresh peas
Salt and pepper, to taste

FOR THE RIBS

Preheat the oven to 275°F.

Season ribs with salt and pepper. Heat olive oil in a large saucepot over high heat, and sear ribs until golden brown on all sides. Add the bacon halfway through the searing process and cook until the fat of the bacon is released.

Remove ribs from the pan and add onions, carrots, and celery. Cook onions until translucent.

Add the demi-glace, wine, bay leaves, thyme, and parsley, and season with salt and pepper.

Simmer the sauce over medium-low heat, uncovered, until it's reduced by half its volume, about 20 minutes.

Add ribs to a large baking dish, cover with sauce, and bake for 4 hours. Remove from oven and place ribs on a large platter.

Strain remaining sauce through a fine-mesh sieve and pour back into its original saucepot. Simmer, uncover, over medium heat until it's

reduced to a heavy syrup consistency. Add the ribs back to the saucepot.

FOR THE TRUFFLED POTATO PAVÉ

Preheat the oven to 375°F.

Melt butter in a small saucepot over medium heat. Add flour, and whisk until incorporated. Add cream and salt, bring to a boil, and whisk vigorously until hot and bubbly, about 3 minutes. Reduce heat to low, and simmer for 5 minutes. Remove béchamel from heat and cool slightly.

In a large bowl, combine cheeses.

In a large mixing bowl, combine potatoes with béchamel. Arrange the potatoes in a single layer in a 13 × 9-inch baking pan. Pour some of the béchamel over the top layer and top with ⅓ of the cheese mixture. Repeat steps for a total of 3 layers. Top the final layer of potatoes with the mushroom duxelle.

Bake potatoes until fork tender, about 45 minutes. Garnish with breadcrumbs, Set aside.

FOR THE SPINACH

Heat olive oil in a large sauté pan over medium heat. Add ½ tablespoon butter and ½ teaspoon garlic. As soon as the garlic starts to sizzle, add half of the spinach. Season with salt and pepper and cook spinach until wilted, 1–2 minutes.

Holding the spinach in place with a pair of tongs, drain out the liquid from the pan and place spinach on a plate lined with paper towels. Using the same pan repeat this process for the remaining half of the butter, garlic, and spinach. Set aside.

FOR THE ROASTED CARROTS

Preheat oven to 400°F.

In a large mixing bowl, combine carrots with olive oil and season with salt and pepper. Arrange carrots on a large baking sheet, and cook for 5–10 minutes. Flip carrots over and cook for an additional 5–10 minutes.

FOR THE PEAS

Heat butter and water in a small sauté pan over medium heat. When water starts to steam, add peas and cook for 15 seconds. Season with salt and pepper.

AT SERVICE

Place 3 small mounds of spinach on each plate. Place 1 short rib on top of each pile of spinach. Garnish short ribs with some of the carrots and peas. Cut potatoes into 6 squares or circles using a circular ring mold. Place 1 potato pavé onto each plate.

Chef's Tip: *When sautéing any type of green such as spinach, escarole, or swiss chard, initially use less salt because there's a natural amount of salt that occurs in the vegetable. Adjust seasoning to taste after the greens are fully cooked.*

Warm Beignets with Strawberries

Rhubarb Gelee, Shiso Syrup, Yuzu Vanilla Ice Cream

SERVES 6-8

This dessert is a play off of a jelly doughnut, but a bit lighter, not as sweet, and with some Asian-inspired flavors. The beignets are surprisingly easy to put together and highly addictive on their own. Rather than combining the strawberries and rhubarb, I separate them into different preparations so they can both have their own unique texture. Both shiso and yuzu can be found at most Asian markets.

Suggested wine pairing: Moscato d'Asti

For the beignets

½ cup plus 2 tablespoons milk
4 tablespoons butter
⅔ cup bread flour
½ teaspoon kosher salt
½ teaspoon granulated sugar
2 eggs
½ teaspoon vanilla paste

For the macerated strawberries

1 pint fresh strawberries, rinsed, dried, and stems removed
2 teaspoons granulated sugar

For the poached rhubarb:

1 (14-inch) thin stalk of rhubarb
1 cup granulated sugar
1 cup water
½ vanilla bean, scraped
Tiny pinch kosher salt

For the rhubarb gelee

1 teaspoon powdered gelatin
1 tablespoon orange juice
½ cup water
¼ cup granulated sugar
2 cups rhubarb, chopped into 1-inch pieces
Zest of ¼ orange
Tiny pinch of kosher salt

For the shiso syrup

¼ cup granulated sugar
2 tablespoons water
5 shiso leaves

For the yuzu vanilla ice cream

1½ cups heavy cream
1¼ cups milk
½ cup plus 3 tablespoons granulated sugar
1 vanilla bean pod, scraped
Pinch of kosher salt
8 egg yolks
3 tablespoons yuzu juice

FOR THE BEIGNETS

In a small saucepan, combine milk and butter, and bring to a boil over medium heat. All at once, add flour, salt, and sugar, and stir with a wooden spoon until mixture forms a ball. Continue to cook for 1 minute.

Remove and transfer mixture to an electric mixer with paddle attachment in place. Mix on low speed for 30 seconds to slightly cool down the mixture.

In a separate bowl, break up the eggs, then add them into the flour-milk mixture in 4 stages, on medium speed, scraping down the bowl after each addition.

Add vanilla paste, and mix for 30 seconds.

Transfer to a piping bag with a ¾-inch round piping tip and hold at room temperature until ready to fry (may hold for up to 2 hours).

FOR THE MACERATED STRAWBERRIES

Cut strawberries into ½-inch cubes. In a small mixing bowl, combine strawberries with sugar and lightly toss.

Cover bowl with plastic wrap and chill in the refrigerator for 30 minutes.

FOR THE POACHED RHUBARB

Clean and slice rhubarb on a slight bias about ¼-inch thick. In a small saucepan, combine sugar, water, vanilla bean, and salt. Bring to a boil. Add rhubarb and remove from heat. Cover saucepan and let mixture poach for 30 minutes. Chill until ready to use.

FOR THE RHUBARB GELEE

In a small bowl, combine gelatin and orange juice, and set it aside to soften.

In a saucepot, combine water and sugar and bring to a simmer over medium-low heat. Add rhubarb, orange zest, and salt. Bring mixture back to a simmer over medium-low heat. Cover saucepot with a lid and continue to simmer mixture for 15 minutes.

Remove mixture from heat and allow it to rest for 15 minutes. Strain the mixture through a fine-mesh sieve, being careful not to press any solids through (you want a clear pink liquid).

Stir in gelatin until it melts.

Cover rhubarb with plastic wrap and chill until fully set, about 4 hours.

FOR THE SHISO SYRUP

In a small saucepan, combine sugar and water, and bring to a boil. Remove from heat to cool.

In a separate pan, bring a small pot of water to a boil. Add shiso leaves and quickly blanch for 5 seconds.

Remove leaves and rinse in cold water. Towel dry leaves and roughly chop.

Combine leaves with sugar syrup, add to a blender, and process until syrup is green, about 20 seconds.

Cover and chill.

FOR THE YUZU VANILLA ICE CREAM

Prepare an ice bath by nesting a medium bowl in a larger bowl that's partially filled with ice and water.

In a medium saucepot, combine cream, milk, sugar, vanilla bean (seeds and pod), and salt. Bring just to boiling point and then reduce heat to scald. Cover and let steep for 30 minutes, then bring back to a scald.

In a mixing bowl, whisk the egg yolks and gradually add some of the cream mixture while continually whisking. Scrape the yolk mixture into the pan with remaining cream mixture and cook on low heat, stirring with a wooden spoon until mixture slightly thickens and coats the back of a spoon.

Quickly remove from heat and strain ice cream base through a fine-mesh sieve into the chilled ice bath bowl. Stir mixture gently until fully chilled. Once chilled, stir in yuzu juice and transfer mixture to the refrigerator. Cover and let rest overnight.

Freeze the ice cream base in ice-cream maker according to labeled instructions.

AT SERVICE

Heat a deep fryer to 335°F.

Dip the ends of a pair of scissors in oil. Pipe beignet batter into oil, using the scissors to cut them into 1-inch pieces. Allow plenty of room in oil for beignets to puff. Fry for 3–4 minutes, moving them around often to brown evenly.

Remove beignets with a slotted spoon and drain on a plate lined with paper towels. Continue to fry beignets from the remaining batter.

Dust beignets with powdered sugar.

Place strawberries, poached rhubarb, rhubarb gelee, and a small amount of shiso syrup on each plate with yuzu ice cream. Serve some of the beignets on top of macerated strawberries or in a separate bowl.

Chef's Tip: *Substitute the shiso leaves with 10 large mint leaves.*

Chef's Tip: *If you can't find yuzu juice, use lemon, lime, or passion fruit juice for a similar variation.*

Coconut Cream Tartlet

Chocolate Rum Sorbet, Vanilla-Roasted Pineapple, Marcona Almonds

SERVES 6

Pastry chefs can find spring a bit challenging since there aren't as many seasonal fruits available in this season as there are in winter. We are somewhat in-between seasons trying to be as creative as possible while we wait in anticipation for the abundant summer crops of berries, melons, and stone fruit varietals. This is the time I reach for the stand-by tropical fruits, such as pineapple, to add a fruit element to a dish like this one. It was first inspired by the flavors of an Almond Joy and was reworked into this composed plated dessert.

Suggested wine pairing: Vendange Tardive Gewurztraminer

For the phyllo shell

2 tablespoons melted butter, plus additional for ramekins
1 tablespoon granulated sugar
Pinch kosher salt
4 (13 x 18-inch) sheets phyllo dough

For the coconut pastry cream

1 cup shredded sweetened coconut
¼ cup granulated sugar
1 tablespoon plus 1½ teaspoons cornstarch
⅛ teaspoon kosher salt
4 egg yolks
1¼ cup milk
½ vanilla bean, scraped (seeds only)
1 tablespoon butter

For the whipped crème fraîche

¼ cup crème fraîche
¼ cup heavy cream
2 teaspoons granulated sugar

For the chocolate sorbet

2½ cups water
¾ cup plus 2 tablespoons granulated sugar
¾ cup cocoa powder
¼ cup milk powder
Pinch kosher salt
¾ cup chocolate (70 percent chocolate)

2 teaspoons instant espresso powder
3 tablespoons dark rum
½ teaspoon vanilla

For the vanilla roasted pineapple

1½ cups pineapple, cut into ½-inch cubes
2 teaspoons brown sugar
½ vanilla bean, scraped
Tiny pinch kosher salt

For the garnish:

½ cup Marcona almonds

FOR THE PHYLLO SHELL

Preheat oven to 350°F.

Lightly brush melted butter into six 6-ounce ramekins and set aside.

In a small mixing bowl, combine sugar and salt.

Lightly brush 1 sheet of phyllo dough evenly with melted butter. Sprinkle 2 teaspoons sugar mixture over buttered phyllo and place second sheet on top. Repeat this process for the third sheet and cover with fourth sheet. Place a clean dry towel on top and firmly roll out to flatten layers.

Remove towel and cut prepared phyllo into six 6-inch squares. Brush the tops with melted butter and press into prepared ramekins.

Bake shell until golden brown and crisp, 12–15 minutes. Cool to room temperature and store in airtight container.

FOR THE COCONUT PASTRY CREAM

Preheat oven to 325°F.

Place coconut on a baking sheet and lightly toast, about 10 minutes.

Sift sugar, cornstarch, and salt together. Whisk the egg yolks in well for 30 seconds. Set aside.

In a small saucepot, bring the milk and vanilla just to the boiling point and then reduce heat to scald. While whisking egg yolk mixture, slowly start to incorporate ¼ of the hot milk in a steady stream. Combine all together in saucepot and cook over medium-low heat, constantly whisking bottom and sides of pan until mixture thickens and is at a boil when not whisking. Continue to cook for another 30 seconds while constantly whisking.

Remove and stir in butter until melted and incorporated.

Fold in coconut, cover with plastic wrap, and chill in the refrigerator for at least 2 hours.

FOR THE WHIPPED CRÈME FRAÎCHE

In a small mixing bowl, combine all ingredients, and whip until soft peaks form. Chill in the refrigerator.

FOR THE CHOCOLATE SORBET

In a medium stainless steel pan, combine water, sugar, cocoa powder, milk powder, and salt, and bring to a boil. Whisk for 1 minute (continuing to boil).

Remove from heat and immersion blend while adding chocolate and espresso powder. Chill for 4 hours in the refrigerator.

Add rum and vanilla, and freeze in an ice cream machine according to labeled instructions.

FOR THE VANILLA ROASTED PINEAPPLE

Heat oven to 350°F.

Combine all ingredients in a medium stainless pan over medium heat, and sauté until lightly caramelized, about 5 minutes.

Cover with aluminum foil and place in oven for 15 minutes.

Remove vanilla pod and cool to room temperature, then transfer to refrigerator to cool.

FOR THE MARCONA ALMONDS

Preheat oven to 350°F.

Place almonds on a baking sheet and roast for 8-10 minutes until nuts are light brown and fragrant. Once cool, roughly chop.

AT SERVICE

Right before serving, spoon coconut pastry cream into phyllo cups, and top with whipped crème fraîche, Marcona almonds, and sweetened shredded coconut. Serve with a scoop of chocolate rum sorbet and roasted pineapple.

Chef's Tip: *Phyllo cups can be made a couple of days ahead of time and kept in an airtight container at room temperature. Pastry cream can be made 2 days ahead and kept cold in the refrigerator until needed.*

Crispy Tapioca Pudding

Green Tea Ice Cream, Passion Fruit Caramel, Mango, Lychee

SERVES 9

Being executive pastry chef at The Mandarin Oriental Hotel in San Francisco for a number of years, I became very influenced by Asian culture and cuisine. I often played around with familiar classic dessert preparations by adding twists that represented the hotel's theme and origin. Since the menu at Market often reflects some influences from the East, I was pleased to add this dessert with fond memories of my days in San Francisco. It's a glimpse of where I was, and where I am now, as a pastry chef.

Suggested wine pairing: Late Harvest Viognier

For the tapioca pudding

Unflavored oil, for coating pan
½ cup small pearl tapioca (not instant)
3 cups whole milk
1 vanilla bean pod, scraped
¼ teaspoon salt
½ cup granulated sugar
2 eggs, whites and yolks separated
½ cup all-purpose flour
2 more eggs, whisked well
1 cup panko bread crumbs

For the green tea ice cream

1½ cups whole milk
1½ cups heavy cream
½ cup plus 3 tablespoons granulated sugar
½ vanilla bean, scraped
Pinch kosher salt
8 egg yolks
2 tablespoons green tea powder

For the passion fruit caramel sauce

⅔ cup granulated sugar
¼ cup water, divided
2 tablespoons butter
3 tablespoons passion fruit puree or fresh juice
Kosher salt, to taste

For the garnish

2 mangos, peeled, pitted, and diced
3 lychee, peeled, pitted, and sliced

FOR THE TAPIOCA PUDDING

Lightly coat the bottom and sides of a 9 × 5-inch pan with oil and line with plastic wrap.

In a 1½-quart saucepot, combine tapioca, milk, and vanilla bean pod over medium-high heat and stir until boiling. Turn heat down to lowest possible setting and simmer for 5 minutes, uncovered, while gradually adding in ¼ cup plus 2 tablespoons of the sugar.

In a small bowl, whisk egg yolks. Mix in approximately ¼ of the hot tapioca very slowly to the egg mixture while gently whisking. Return egg yolk mixture to the saucepot with tapioca, slowly bring mixture to barely a boil, stirring constantly. Reduce heat and stir several minutes at a low simmer, stirring constantly until a nice thick pudding consistency is reached, about 5 minutes. Remove vanilla bean pod.

In a small mixing bowl, whisk egg whites and remaining 2 tablespoons of sugar to a medium peak. Gently fold into pudding and pour into prepared pan. Cover directly with plastic wrap and cool to room temperature. Place in freezer for 4 hours (to overnight).

Remove the pudding from the freezer and cut into 1½-inch squares, then place back in freezer.

Set up 3 mixing bowls. Place flour in one, whisked eggs in the second, and bread crumbs in the third.

Place each frozen square in flour to coat lightly and evenly, next drop in egg mixture to coat, then drop into bread crumbs, pressing lightly, allowing it to stick to all sides. Once all pieces are breaded, place them back in freezer.

In a deep fryer heated to 350°F, fry tapioca puddings until outside is golden and center of pudding is slightly warm when pierced with a knife, 5–7 minutes.

FOR THE GREEN TEA ICE CREAM

Prepare an ice bath by nesting a medium bowl in a larger bowl partially filled with ice and water.

Combine milk, cream, sugar, vanilla bean, and salt in a medium saucepan, bring just to a boiling point, and then reduce heat to scald. Remove from heat and cover for 30 minutes, then scald again.

In a large mixing bowl, whisk the egg yolks and gradually add some of the vanilla-infused cream mixture while continually whisking. Scrape the yolk mixture into pan with remaining cream and cook on low heat, stirring with a wooden spoon, until mixture slightly thickens and coats the back of the spoon.

Quickly remove from heat and mix in green tea powder with an immersion blender.

Strain the ice cream base through a fine-mesh sieve into chilled ice bath bowl. Stir gently until fully chilled.

Transfer to refrigerator to rest overnight. Freeze the ice cream base in ice-cream maker according to labeled instructions.

FOR THE PASSION FRUIT CARAMEL SAUCE

In a small saucepot, dissolve sugar and 3 tablespoons of water and bring to a boil. Continue boiling without stirring until the sugar starts to turn a light-medium amber color.

Carefully stir in butter, followed by the passion fruit juice and remaining 1 tablespoon of water. Season with salt.

When the mixture comes back to a boil, remove and cool to room temperature.

AT SERVICE

Spread some passion fruit caramel on each plate. Place 2 fried crispy tapioca puddings on top followed by green tea ice cream. Sprinkle with diced mango and sliced lychee.

Chef's Tip: *Small tapioca pearls, lychee, Matcha powder, and panko bread crumbs can be purchased at most specialty Asian markets. If you can't find passion fruit puree, juice one or two passion fruits and strain through a fine-mesh sieve to yield 3 tablespoons of liquid.*

Chef's Tip: *The tapioca pudding can be made 2 weeks in advance as long as it is kept wrapped well in the freezer.*

Warm S'mores Tart

Brown Sugar Marshmallow, Espresso Bailey's Ice Cream, Smoked Sea Salt

SERVES 10

Rather than having straight melted chocolate on a graham cracker, I created a filling with a smooth, warm, melted ganache under an almost soufflé-like texture with a creamy brown sugar toasted marshmallow cream. Throw in a small scoop of espresso Bailey's ice cream for a cool finish, and you have one of the most requested desserts we've had since its inception.

Suggested wine pairing: Malmsey Madeira

For the tart crust

½ cup butter, room temperature
2 tablespoons honey
¼ cup plus 1 tablespoon dark brown sugar
½ teaspoon kosher salt
½ teaspoon vanilla extract
1 cup all-purpose flour
¼ cup whole-wheat flour
½ teaspoon cinnamon

For the chocolate ganache

¼ cup high-quality chocolate (58 percent cocoa), chopped
¼ cup heavy cream

For the tart filling

5 tablespoons butter
½ cup high-quality chocolate (70 percent cocoa)
2 eggs, room temperature
3 tablespoons granulated sugar
Pinch kosher salt
1 tablespoon cake flour

For the espresso Bailey's ice cream

1½ cups heavy cream
1¼ cup milk
½ cup plus 3 tablespoons granulated sugar
Pinch kosher salt
8 egg yolks
2 tablespoons instant espresso
3 tablespoons Bailey's Irish Cream liqueur

For the brown sugar marshmallow cream

¼ cup egg whites
¼ cup granulated sugar
¼ cup dark brown sugar
¼ teaspoon cream of tarter
Pinch kosher salt

For the chocolate plate paint

¼ cup granulated sugar
¼ cup water
3 tablespoons cocoa powder
Pinch kosher salt

For the cocoa tuile

1½ tablespoons butter, softened
¾ cup powdered sugar, sifted
Pinch kosher salt
2 tablespoons all-purpose flour
1½ tablespoons cocoa powder
2½ tablespoons water

For the garnish

½ teaspoon smoked sea salt

FOR THE TART CRUST

Preheat oven to 350°F.

In an electric mixer with paddle attachment in place, cream together the butter, honey, brown sugar, salt, and vanilla on medium speed for 5 minutes, scraping sides down twice until light and smooth.

Sift flours and cinnamon together, and add to cream mixture on low speed (in two stages) until just combined.

Cover in plastic wrap and chill in refrigerator for at least 1 hour.

Compress dough on a lightly floured flat work surface a few times to soften. Roll dough out to an even ⅛ inch. Cut circles out large enough to fit into ten 4 × ¾-inch tart molds, and gently press dough on the bottom and sides evenly. Trim any excess dough from top and place filled molds in the refrigerator for 20 minutes.

Dock the dough by pressing a fork into the bottom a few times to prevent dough from puffing during baking.

Bake for 12–15 minutes until evenly golden brown, then cool to room temperature.

FOR THE CHOCOLATE GANACHE

Place chopped chocolate in a small mixing bowl.

In a small saucepot bring the cream just to a boiling point and then reduce heat to scald. Pour hot cream over chocolate. Let it sit for 1 minute, then gently stir until chocolate is melted and ganache is smooth.

Pour ganache into the bottoms of baked tart shells and chill in freezer.

FOR THE TART FILLING

Melt butter and chocolate together in a double boiler, and cool to just slightly warm.

In an electric mixer with whisk attachment in place, whip the eggs, sugar, and salt on high speed to full volume, about 5 minutes.

Gently fold chocolate mixture into egg mixture until incorporated.

Fold sifted flour into chocolate egg mixture.

Remove tart shells from freezer and pour filling to the top of each. Place in refrigerator until ready to bake and serve.

FOR THE ESPRESSO BAILEY'S ICE CREAM

Prepare an ice bath by nesting a medium bowl in a larger bowl partially filled with ice and water.

In a medium saucepot, combine cream, milk, sugar, and salt, and bring just to a boiling point, then reduce heat to scald.

In a large mixing bowl, whisk together the egg yolks. Gradually add some of the cream mixture while continually whisking. Scrape the yolk mixture into pan with remaining cream mixture and cook on low heat while stirring with a wooden spoon until mixture slightly thickens and coats the back of the spoon.

Quickly remove from heat and strain ice cream base through a fine-mesh sieve into chilled ice bath bowl.

Add espresso and immersion blend until incorporated. Stir gently until fully chilled.

Stir in Bailey's liqueur, cover, and transfer to refrigerator to rest overnight.

Freeze ice cream base in ice-cream maker according to the labeled instructions.

FOR THE BROWN SUGAR MARSHMALLOW CREAM

Whisk all ingredients together in a metal bowl and place over a double boiler. Continue to gently whisk until mixture reaches 165°F. Transfer to an electric mixer with whisk attachment in place and whip until room temperature. Transfer to a piping bag with a ½-inch straight tip.

FOR THE CHOCOLATE PLATE PAINT

In a small stainless steal pan, combine all ingredients and bring to a boil, stirring often. Continue to boil and reduce mixture until it is a thick sauce consistency when dripped onto a tilted, cool plate. Chill until ready to use.

FOR THE COCOA TUILE

Preheat oven to 325°F.

Combine butter, powdered sugar, and salt together in a medium bowl with a wooden spoon until light and fluffy. Sift the flour and cocoa powder into bowl. Add water and stir until well combined.

Spread thinly, and evenly on a flat baking sheet lined with a nonstick mat, and bake for 12–15 minutes until tuile is bubbling.

Remove from oven and let cool until crispy. Break up into 10 roughly 2-inch pieces. Store in airtight container until ready to serve.

AT SERVICE

Preheat oven to 350°F.

Bake tarts for 12–15 minutes until filling starts to puff slightly. Remove from oven and pipe brown sugar marshmallow cream on top. Wave a blowtorch across tops to toast marshmallow cream slightly and sprinkle with smoked sea salt. Drizzle chocolate paint on plates and place tart, along with espresso Bailey's ice cream and cocoa tuile, on each. Serve immediately.

Chef's Tip: *These tarts can be made ahead of time and kept unbaked and frozen. Just defrost them for 2 hours in a refrigerator until ready to bake.*

SUMMER

Summer is the star of the show. The seasonal color palate is wide open at this time of year. It's all about the stone fruits, heirloom tomatoes, sweet corn, cherries, green beans, melons, and so much more. I love this season because I hardly ever have to repeat ingredients to make new dishes, making my menu so diverse. I think you will truly appreciate my recipes for Local Stone Fruit and Saint Angel Triple Cream Cheese Tart or Oysters on the Half Shell and Spiced Tomato Granita.

Bing Cherry Smash

SERVES 2

8 ripe Bing cherries
3 ounces bourbon
1 ounce lime juice
1 ounce orgeat syrup (page 286)
1 ounce simple syrup (page 286)
Splash of club soda

Muddle 6 cherries and bourbon with ice. Add orgeat syrup, simple syrup, and lime juice. Shake and strain drink into 2 tall glasses filled with fresh ice. Splash club soda in each glass. Garnish with 1 cherry each.

Tomato Tini

SERVES 2

3 ounces basil-infused vodka (page 281)
3 ounces tomato water (page 287)
¼ ounce lemon juice
6 drops basil oil
6 heirloom cherry tomatoes (skins removed)
4 small basil leaves

Shake vodka, tomato water, and lemon juice together. Shake and strain into 2 chilled martini glasses.

Garnish each with 3 drops basil oil and skewer of skinless tomatoes and basil.

Gingered Fennel Soup and Vietnamese Meatballs

Pineapple, Savoy Spinach, Sesame-Chile Oil, Nori Goma

SERVES 6

I wanted to create a unique soup, something in season but non-traditional. One summer day my chef came back from the famers' market with beautiful fennel. I felt I had done every soup, until this one. I thought outside the box and this soup came together.

Suggested Wine Pairing: Chenin Blanc

For the soup

4 tablespoons light olive oil
1 Spanish onion, peeled and sliced
3 scallions (white part only), sliced
1 small leek (white part only), chopped
1 small fennel bulb, sliced
¼ cup small diced russet potato
10 cloves garlic, minced
1 (1-inch) piece ginger, peeled and minced
1 sachet (see recipe below)
1 tablespoon salt
5 cups vegetable stock (page 288)
½ cup heavy cream

For the sachet

1 teaspoon whole peppercorns
1 tablespoon cumin
1 tablespoon coriander
1 bunch cilantro stems (reserve leaves for garnish)
1 (2-inch) piece lemongrass, roughly chopped
1 teaspoon chile flakes

For the meatballs

2 tablespoons light olive oil, more for coating pan
4 cloves garlic, minced
1 tablespoon minced ginger
3 scallions, chopped (reserve tops for garnish)
1 pound shrimp, peeled and deveined (ground or finely chopped)

1 pound ground pork shoulder
½ egg (white and yolk mixed, use half, discard other half)
¼ cup panko bread crumbs
2 teaspoons brown sugar
1 tablespoon low-sodium soy sauce
½ teaspoon fish sauce
2 teaspoons hot sauce
1 teaspoon cumin/coriander spice blend (page 283)

For the meatball glaze

3 tablespoons light olive oil
½ cup sweet chile glaze (page 287)
3 tablespoons nori goma (sesame seeds)

For the Savoy spinach

3 tablespoons light olive oil
1 tablespoon minced garlic
6 cups Savoy spinach
Pinch salt

For the garnish

1 cup fresh pineapple, diced
Reserved cilantro leaves, finely chopped
Reserved scallion tops, finely chopped

FOR THE SOUP

Heat olive oil in a large saucepot over medium heat. Add onion, scallions, leek, fennel, potato, garlic, ginger, sachet and salt. Cover and cook until onions are translucent.

Remove cover, add stock, and bring to a boil. Reduce heat to medium low and simmer for 15–20 minutes, then remove from heat.

Remove sachet and add cream.

Add mixture to a blender, process until smooth, then pass through a fine-mesh sieve. Just before serving, return soup to its original saucepot, warm over low heat, and immersion blend.

FOR THE SACHET

Preheat oven to 325°F. Cut a double layer of cheesecloth into a 1 × 1-foot square. Place peppercorns, cumin, and coriander on a small baking sheet, and toast in oven until 2 shades darker, about 15 minutes. Using a mortar and pestle, smash slightly but do not powder the spices. Combine with cilantro stems, lemongrass, and chile flakes into the center of the cloth and tie the top tight with butcher twine to form a small package.

FOR THE MEATBALLS

Heat 2 tablespoons of olive oil in a sauté pan over medium-low heat. Add garlic, ginger, and scallions and cook until fragrant, 1–2 minutes. Remove and cool.

Preheat oven to 350°F.

In a large mixing bowl, combine garlic/ginger/scallion mixture with remaining ingredients. Using your hands, mix until thoroughly incorporated. Form into 18 meatballs.

Coat a baking sheet with olive oil, and arrange meatballs on the pan. Cook until done, 20–25 minutes. Remove and cool to room temperature.

FOR THE MEATBALL GLAZE

Heat olive oil in a large nonstick pan over high heat. Add meatballs and brown. Add sweet chile glaze, and toss to coat the meatballs evenly. Once fully glazed, top meatballs with nori goma.

FOR THE SAVOY SPINACH

Heat olive oil in a large sauté pan over medium-high heat, and add garlic and spinach. Toss, season with salt, and cook spinach until slightly wilted, 1–2 minutes.

AT SERVICE

Ladle the soup evenly into 6 bowls. Add 3 meatballs to each, and distribute the spinach and pineapple. Drizzle with sesame-chile oil and garnish with the cilantro and scallions.

Chef's Tip: *For the meatballs, substitute ground beef, chicken, or turkey.*

Cherokee Purple Heirloom Tomato Gazpacho and Avocado Sorbet

SERVES 6

Nothing tastes better on a sizzling hot day than a cold gazpacho soup. Heirloom tomatoes offer a heightened sweetness and a rich, mellow taste. Surprise your guests with this special version topped with fresh farmers' market vegetables and a creamy frozen avocado sorbet.

Suggested Wine Pairing: Albariño

For the gazpacho

4 tablespoons light olive oil
1 Spanish onion, peeled and sliced
1 leek, chopped
8 cloves garlic, peeled and roughly chopped
1 teaspoon Aleppo chile flakes
1 tablespoon salt
Herb sachet (page 285)
4 cups Cherokee purple heirloom tomatoes, cored and roughly chopped
2 cups vegetable stock (page 288)

For the diced vegetables

2 cucumbers, peeled, seeded, and small diced
3 red bell peppers, cored, seeded, and small diced
¼ red onion, peeled, and small diced
30 assorted heirloom cherry tomatoes, halved
2 avocados, peeled, pitted and diced
Lemon juice, to taste
Salt, to taste

For the avocado sorbet

2 avocados, peeled and pitted
4 tablespoons lemon juice
2 tablespoons lime juice
1 cup vegetable stock (page 288)
1 teaspoon salt

For the garnish

6 radishes, thinly sliced
Extra-virgin olive oil, for drizzling
Small handful of micro basil (substitute fresh chopped basil)

FOR THE GAZPACHO

Heat olive oil in a saucepot over medium heat. Add onion, leek, garlic, chile flakes, salt, and sachet, and combine. Cover saucepot and cook until onions are translucent, about 15 minutes.

Add tomatoes and stock. Bring to a boil, reduce heat to low, and simmer, uncovered, for 20 minutes.

Remove from heat. Remove sachet. Pass mixture through a fine-mesh sieve, add liquid to a blender with 1 cup of the remaining solids (from the sieve), and process until smooth. Refrigerate mixture until cool.

FOR THE DICED VEGETABLES

In a large mixing bowl, toss together the cucumbers, peppers, onions, and tomatoes. Sprinkle with lemon juice and salt.

In a small mixing bowl, combine avocados with lemon juice and salt.

FOR THE AVOCADO SORBET

Add all ingredients to a blender, and process until smooth. Place in an ice-cream machine and follow labeled instructions.

AT SERVICE

Ladle chilled broth into each shallow bowl, leaving room for diced vegetables. Distribute the diced vegetables into each bowl. Distribute some of the avocado into each bowl. Using a small ice cream scoop, spoon sorbet into the middle of each bowl. Garnish with radishes, olive oil, and micro basil.

Chef's Tip: *Heirloom tomatoes are considered soft tomatoes with a limited shelf life. They can be found in all colors and varieties at farmers' markets, natural food stores, and high-end supermarkets with more extensive produce sections.*

Golden Jubilee Heirloom Tomato Soup and Sweet Corn Rock Shrimp Fritters

Bacon Froth, Smoked Paprika Aioli, Chiffonade of Basil

SERVES 6

Things don't get much simpler than this heirloom tomato soup with a pleasing fresh flavor. When served hot, the sweet corn rock shrimp fritters will form a golden, crisp crust, leaving the inside moist.

Suggested Wine Pairing: Torrontes

For the soup

8 cups roughly chopped Golden Jubilee heirloom tomatoes (substitute your favorite heirloom tomato)
1 Spanish onion, peeled and thinly sliced
1 leek (white part only), roughly chopped
1 cup sliced fennel
4 tablespoons light olive oil
1 teaspoon salt
4 cups vegetable stock (page 288)
2 tablespoons roughly chopped garlic
Herb sachet (page 285)

For the fritters

1½ cups all-purpose flour
½ teaspoon cumin/coriander spice blend (page 283)
¼ teaspoon cayenne pepper
¼ teaspoon paprika
½ teaspoon salt
½ teaspoon baking powder
2 eggs
¾ cup of your favorite beer
2 cups corn kernels
4 scallions, chopped
2 jalapeños, seeded and finely chopped
¼ cup chopped cilantro
2 cups of cooked rock shrimp (may substitute any shrimp)
3 cups panko bread crumbs
Salt and pepper, to taste

For the bacon froth

¼ cup chopped bacon
1 teaspoon chopped garlic
1 cup vegetable stock (page 288)
1 tablespoon whole milk
Salt, to taste
½ teaspoon lecithin

For the smoked paprika aioli

Base aioli (page 281)
¼ teaspoon smoked paprika

For the chiffonade of basil

Small handful of fresh basil, cut into long, thin strips

FOR THE SOUP

Preheat oven to 325°F.

In a large mixing bowl, combine tomatoes, onion, leek, fennel, olive oil, and salt, and arrange on large baking sheet. Roast vegetables, turning often, until soft, 45–60 minutes.

Remove vegetables from heat and place in a large saucepot. Add stock, garlic, and sachet, and bring to a boil. Reduce to a simmer over medium-low heat and cook for 25–30 minutes.

Remove soup from heat. Remove sachet, add soup to a blender, and process until smooth. Strain soup through a fine-mesh sieve back into the same pot.

Just before serving, warm over low heat, and immersion blend.

FOR THE FRITTERS

In a large mixing bowl, combine flour, cumin/coriander spice blend, cayenne, paprika, salt, and baking powder. Whisk in the eggs, and combine until smooth.

Add beer, and whisk until smooth.

Add corn, scallions, jalapeños, cilantro, and shrimp. Combine.

Add bread crumbs to a large bowl. With your hands, form the fritters into desired shaped balls and roll in the bread crumbs.

Heat a deep fryer to 350°F. Drop fritters into hot oil and deep fry until golden brown and puffy. Turn if necessary for even color. Remove fritters from fryer and place on a plate lined with paper towels. Season with salt and pepper.

FOR THE BACON FROTH

Heat bacon and garlic in a saucepot over medium heat. Sauté bacon until slightly rendered. Add stock and bring to a boil, then reduce heat to medium low and simmer for 10–15 minutes.

Strain mixture into a large cup and skim fat off the surface. Add milk, salt, and lecithin. Immediately process with an immersion blender until foamy.

FOR THE SMOKED PAPRIKA AIOLI

Add smoked paprika to base aioli recipe and stir until blended.

AT SERVICE

Ladle soup into 6 small soup bowls. Garnish with bacon froth and chopped basil. Evenly distribute fritters into small bowls lined with parchment paper. Put a heaping tablespoon of aioli on the center of each of 6 plates. Place one small soup bowl on one end of each plate and one bowl of fritters on the opposite end.

Chef's Tip: *You can buy lecithin in the dietary section of your local health food store.*

Sweet Pepper and Cauliflower Soup

Chermoula, Sautéed Eggplant, Basil Pesto, Goat Cheese

SERVES 6

This fresh summer soup offers a taste of the Mediterranean. The combination of sweet peppers and cauliflower give it excellent depth for an exciting flavor. Basil pesto and goat cheese fall along the lines of a standard pairing. The chermoula is the wild card to the palate.

Suggested Wine Pairing: Sauvignon Blanc

For the soup

2 tablespoons light olive oil
1 tablespoon butter
1 Spanish onion, peeled and sliced
2 leeks, roughly chopped
2 yellow bell peppers, cored, seeded, and sliced
½ cup sliced fennel
6 cloves garlic, minced
1 tablespoon salt
7 cups vegetable stock (page 288)
½ head cauliflower, roughly chopped
Herb sachet (page 285), with 3 sprigs of thyme
    added
1 cup heavy cream

For the chermoula marinade

2 red bell peppers
2 yellow bell peppers
¼ cup light olive oil, plus extra for coating peppers
Salt and pepper, to taste
½ cup small diced Spanish onion
2 teaspoons minced garlic
Pinch of saffron
1 teaspoon cumin/coriander spice blend (page 283)
½ teaspoon paprika
1 teaspoon tomato paste
1 tablespoon champagne vinegar

For the sautéed eggplant

5 tablespoons light olive oil
1 medium eggplant, peeled and cut into ½-inch
    cubes
Salt and pepper, to taste

For the basil pesto

2 cups fresh basil leaves
1 clove garlic
1 cup light olive oil
¼ cup grated Parmigiana Reggiano
1 teaspoon salt

For the garnish

1 cup fresh goat cheese

FOR THE SOUP

In a large saucepot over medium heat, combine olive oil, butter, onion, leeks, peppers, fennel, garlic, and salt. Cover saucepot and cook until the onions are translucent, 15–20 minutes.

Add stock, cauliflower, and herb sachet. Bring to a boil, then reduce heat to medium low and cook cauliflower until very soft, about 15 minutes.

Add cream, bring mixture to a boil, then immediately remove from heat.

Remove sachet and add mixture to a blender and process until smooth. Strain the mixture through a fine-mesh sieve. Just before serving, return soup to its original saucepot, warm over low heat, and immersion blend.

FOR THE CHERMOULA

Preheat oven to 450°F.

Coat peppers with olive oil, salt, and pepper. Place on a large baking sheet and roast in oven until completely wrinkled and charred, turning them twice during the roasting process, 30-40 minutes.

Remove peppers to large mixing bowl, cover with plastic wrap, and let rest for 5 minutes. Peel peppers and remove the core and seeds. Cut peppers into ½-inch pieces.

Heat ¼ cup of olive oil in a saucepot over medium heat. Add onions and garlic, and sauté until onions are translucent.

Add roasted peppers, saffron, cumin/coriander spice blend, paprika, tomato paste, and vinegar. Stirring often, simmer mixture on low heat for 15-20 minutes.

FOR THE SAUTÉED EGGPLANT

Heat olive oil in a large skillet over medium-high heat. Add eggplant and cook until soft. Season with salt and pepper.

FOR THE BASIL PESTO

Submerge basil in boiling water for 3 minutes. Remove basil using a slotted spoon and place in a bowl of ice water. After fully chilled, squeeze out all excess water from the basil and place in a blender with garlic, olive oil, Parmigiana Reggiano, and salt. Process until smooth, approximately 3 minutes.

AT SERVICE

Ladle the soup into bowls. Distribute the chermoula and sautéed eggplant evenly between the soup bowls. Garnish each soup with a few dollops of goat cheese and some of the basil pesto.

Chef's Tip: *Drizzling a small amount of red wine vinegar or white balsamic adds acidity to this soup, lending another layer of complexity and flavor, and brightening it up even more.*

Local Stone Fruit and Saint Angel Triple Cream Cheese Tart

Bing Cherry Chutney, Watercress, Shaved Fennel, Champagne Vinaigrette

SERVES 6

This is a perfect summer dish. The stone fruit variety coupled with their different sugar and acidity levels and textures makes for the perfect pairing with the creaminess of the Saint Angel cheese and the pistachio crust.

Suggested Wine Pairing: Off-Dry Riesling

For the salad

2 peaches, pitted and cut into ½-inch wedges, about 3 inches in length
2 Santa Rosa plums, pitted and cut into ½-inch wedges, about 3 inches in length
2 apricots, pitted and cut into ½-inch wedges, about 3 inches in length
2 nectarines, pitted and cut into ½-inch wedges, about 3 inches in length
Champagne vinaigrette (recipe below)
Salt and pepper to taste
4 cups watercress, thick stems removed
2 cups shaved fennel

For the champagne vinaigrette

4 teaspoons Dijon mustard
½ cup champagne vinegar
2 tablespoons minced shallots
1 teaspoon salt
Pinch of freshly ground black pepper
1½ cups extra-virgin olive oil
2 tablespoons fines herbes (page 285)

For the cherry chutney

1 pound fresh Bing cherries, pitted
½ cup cider vinegar
¼ cup champagne vinegar
⅛ cup granulated sugar
⅛ cup brown sugar
1 tablespoon minced ginger
1 teaspoon ground coriander
1 stick cinnamon
½ teaspoon salt

For the pistachio tart

1½ cups cake flour, sifted
¼ cup pistachios
2 sticks soft butter
¼ cup granulated sugar
½ teaspoon vanilla extract
1 egg, whisked

For the Saint Angel triple cream cheese

18 ounces triple cream cheese (substitute a similar triple cream, such as brie)

FOR THE SALAD

Just before serving, arrange all the fruit on a sheet pan (keeping like fruit next to each other). Drizzle some of the vinaigrette onto each pile of fruit (use your fingers to distribute evenly onto the fruit). Sprinkle with a little salt and pepper.

In a mixing bowl, combine the watercress and fennel with some of the champagne vinaigrette, and lightly toss to combine.

FOR THE CHAMPAGNE VINAIGRETTE

In a mixing bowl, combine mustard, vinegar, shallots, salt, and pepper, and whisk until combined. In a slow stream, add olive oil, whisking rapidly to emulsify. Add the fines herbes, and incorporate thoroughly.

FOR THE CHERRY CHUTNEY

In a large saucepot, combine all ingredients and bring to a simmer over medium-high heat, then reduce heat to medium-low. Cover and simmer until thick, stirring occasionally, about 45 minutes. Remove cinnamon stick, and cool to room temperature.

FOR THE PISTACHIO TART

In a food processor, add half the flour and all the pistachios. Process until fine and well incorporated, about 1 minute. Add to a large mixing bowl with remaining flour and mix well.

In an electric mixer with paddle attachment in place, combine the butter, sugar, and vanilla. Beat on medium speed until smooth (and light and white in color), scraping down the sides often. Slowly add egg, and mix until incorporated. Reduce speed to low, add flour mixture, and mix just until blended. Remove dough, wrap tightly in plastic wrap, and refrigerate for at least 1 hour.

Preheat oven to 375°F.

On a lightly floured surface, roll out the dough to about ¼-inch in thickness. Cut into 5½-inch rounds. Lay the dough rounds into the 3¼-inch tart molds, forming to the bottom and the sides. Trim excess dough to conform to the molds. Chill molds in refrigerator for about 15 minutes. Place 6 × 6-inch pieces of parchment paper over the top, forming to the dough. Top parchment with pie weights, pressing gently to ensure dough is held firmly in place.

Bake tarts for 10-15 minutes. To test and see if the crust is ready, pull up a corner of the parchment paper. Crust should be set to the mold. Remove tarts from oven. Remove pie weights and parchment paper. Return crusts to oven and continue to bake until golden brown, 5-10 minutes.

Remove from oven and cool slightly to room temperature. Remove tarts from molds and place on a rack to cool.

FOR THE SAINT ANGEL TRIPLE CREAM CHEESE

Remove as much of the rind as possible, being careful not to discard the cheese (you will have about 12 ounces).

Add the rindless brie to a mixer with paddle attachment in place, and run the mixer on medium-high speed until the cheese is well whipped and soft, about 10 minutes. Remove from mixer and place in a piping bag.

Just prior to serving, pipe about 2 ounces of cheese into the bottom of each tart in a circular pattern, completely covering the bottom of each tart shell. Warm in a 375°F oven for 3-5 minutes.

AT SERVICE

Remove from the oven and place one tart just off center to the right on each plate. Build the salad to the left of the tart. Place an assortment of sliced stone fruit in a single layer down the plate, and top with a small amount of watercress and fennel. On top of this, place more slices of fruit in a single layer. Top that with more watercress and fennel, until you have a layered salad. Top the triple cream tart with a heaping spoonful of cherry chutney. Following a circular motion, spoon a little of the vinaigrette around the salad and tart.

Chef's Tip: *Substitute watercress with your favorite in-season lettuce.*

Chef's Tip: *When available, fresh tart cherries are a great substitute.*

Chargrilled Calamari and Haricots Verts Salad

Marinated Eggplant, Goldbar Squash, Lima Beans, Sweet Pepper-Tomato Emulsion, Fennel Vinaigrette

SERVES 6

My friends and I liked to jig for squid off the coast of La Jolla where I grew up. We'd barbeque, grill, and marinate whatever fish we had available to us. This dish is inspired by my super fresh catches and paired with summer vegetables.

Suggested Wine Pairing: Austrian Grüner Veltliner

For the calamari

½ cup plus 3 tablespoons light olive oil

6 cloves garlic, roughly chopped

1 shallot, sliced

2 tablespoons Aleppo chile flakes

1 teaspoon fennel seed

2 tablespoons tomato paste

4 tablespoons red wine vinegar

1 teaspoon salt

1½ pounds cleaned squid (about 3 pounds whole squid, cut into tubes and tentacles)

For the fennel vinaigrette

1½ cups extra-virgin olive oil, plus 4 tablespoons for sautéeing

1 fennel bulb, small diced (fronds, chopped)

1 tablespoon finely minced garlic

1 tablespoon finely minced shallots

4 teaspoons Dijon mustard

½ cup champagne vinegar

1 teaspoon salt

Pinch of freshly ground black pepper

For the sweet pepper–tomato emulsion

2 tablespoons light olive oil

1 red bell pepper, seeded and sliced

¼ cup red onion, sliced

1 small Serrano chile, chopped

4 cloves garlic, peeled and chopped

¼ cup fennel, sliced

¼ teaspoon Aleppo pepper flakes

1 small bay leaf

1 pinch dry oregano

¼ teaspoon salt

1 sprig thyme

1 cup chopped Roma tomatoes

¼ cup sourdough bread, diced

⅓ cup extra virgin olive oil

1 tablespoon egg yolk

Salt and pepper, to taste

For the eggplant

3 small Japanese eggplant, peeled and cut into ¼-inch rounds

Add ¼ cup olive oil to ingredients per recipe

Salt and pepper, to taste

Fennel vinaigrette, for seasoning (see recipe)

For the haricots verts

6 handfuls (around 96 pieces), cleaned haricots verts

Fennel vinaigrette, for seasoning (see recipe above)

Salt and pepper, to taste

For the cherry tomatoes

18 assorted heirloom cherry tomatoes, halved

Fennel vinaigrette (see recipe above)

Salt and pepper, to taste

For the Goldbar squash

2 small Goldbar squash

Fennel vinaigrette, for seasoning (see recipe)

FOR THE CALAMARI

Heat 3 tablespoons olive oil in a small saucepot over medium heat. Add garlic and shallot, and cook until fragrant, about 3 minutes. Add chile flakes and fennel, and cook for about 30 seconds. Add tomato paste, and cook for 1 minute. Remove from heat and add vinegar and salt. Chill in refrigerator.

Butterfly the calamari tubes by cutting them lengthwise along one side (it should resemble a flat triangle). Using a sharp knife, with the interior of the tube facing up, lightly score the meat, cutting a crisscross pattern (use the weight of your knife and be sure not to cut completely through the meat).

Add the calamari tubes to a large mixing bowl, and drizzle with some of the marinade. Using your hands, mix thoroughly so that all the meat is fully coated.

Marinate, covered, for 2 hours in the refrigerator. Repeat this step with the tentacles in a separate mixing bowl, then marinate those for 2 hours in the refrigerator as well.

Prepare a grill over high heat. Grill the calamari tubes for about 30 seconds per side. (Time will vary depending on the thickness of the calamari. It is done when it starts to whiten and is no longer transparent. The marinade should be slightly caramelized). Repeat this step with the tentacles.

Cut the calamari tubes into small squares, about 1 inch. Cut the calamari tentacles in half.

FOR THE FENNEL VINAIGRETTE

Heat 4 tablespoons olive oil over medium heat. Add diced fennel bulb and cook until slightly softened, 3-4 minutes. Add garlic and shallots and cook until fragrant and soft, about 5 minutes. Remove from heat and chill in refrigerator.

In a mixing bowl, whisk together mustard, vinegar, salt, and pepper. Slowly stream in the remaining 1½ cups olive oil, whisking rapidly to emulsify. Once emulsified, stir in the cooked fennel, garlic, and shallots. Add the fennel fronds just before serving to retain color.

FOR THE SWEET PEPPER-TOMATO EMULSION

Heat olive oil in a saucepot over medium-high heat. Add the bell pepper, onions, Serrano chile, garlic, fennel, Aleppo pepper flakes, bay leaf, oregano, salt, and thyme, and cook until very soft, about 10 minutes. Add tomatoes and bread, and continue cooking for about 20 minutes or until slightly thickened.

Remove from heat, place in a blender, and process until smooth. Chill in refrigerator.

Place in a small mixing bowl, and, using a hand blender on a high setting, add the egg yolk and blend until totally incorporated. Slowly drizzle in extra-virgin olive oil, keeping the blender set to high, and blend until emulsified. Season with salt and pepper.

FOR THE EGGPLANT

Arrange eggplant on a baking sheet and coat generously with olive oil on both sides. Season both sides with salt and pepper.

Prepare a grill over high heat. Grill eggplant until tender and grill marks are visible, about 2 minutes per side. Place a few drops of the fennel vinaigrette onto each eggplant round, and distribute evenly with your finger.

FOR THE HARICOTS VERTS

Bring a large pot of salted water to a boil. Add the haricots verts and blanch for 2–3 minutes. Remove and place in a bowl of ice and water. Remove to a baking sheet lined with paper towels.

In a mixing bowl, combine the haricots verts with enough fennel vinaigrette to coat. Season with salt and pepper.

FOR THE CHERRY TOMATOES

In a mixing bowl, coat tomatoes with some of the fennel vinaigrette, then season with salt and pepper.

FOR THE GOLDBAR SQUASH

Using a mandoline or other slicing device, slice the squash very thin, about 1/16-inch thick (it needs to be thin and pliable).

Place a small amount of vinaigrette in a mixing bowl. Drag the thinly shaved squash through the vinaigrette until coated, one piece at a time. Wrap it around your finger to create a small cylinder (the vinaigrette will allow the squash to stick to itself).

AT SERVICE

On one end of a rectangular plate, place a heaping spoonful of the sweet pepper–tomato emulsion. Using the back of the spoon or small offset spatula, pull the emulsion down the plate so that it coats evenly across to the other side of the plate. Place the haricots verts on top of the emulsion in a crisscross fashion down the length of the plate. Place a few eggplant rounds on the hericots verts. Distribute the cherry tomatoes sporadically over the haricots verts and eggplant. Top the salad with some of the calamari squares and tentacles. Using a slotted spoon, remove some of the diced fennel from the remaining vinaigrette and garnish over the top of the salad. Finish by placing squash cylinders over the top.

Chef's Tip: *Talk to your local fishmonger about what times of the year fresh squid is available. There's no substitute for the texture and flavor of fresh squid when pulled from the ocean.*

Curried Melon and Fried Chicken Oyster Salad

Pickled Corn, Red Onion, Creamy Feta, Cilantro

SERVES 6

Chicken "oyster meat" is the most flavorful and tender part of the bird. It's located just above the thigh, is small, and is often overlooked. Once you've tried one, you'll understand why it's the best part of the chicken.

Suggested Wine Pairing: Loire Valley Chenin Blanc

For the curried melon

18 cubes red watermelon, cut into 1-inch squares
18 cubes honeydew melon, cut into 1-inch squares
1 tablespoon chopped cilantro
1 tablespoon chopped mint
½ cup sliced red onion

For the pickled corn

½ cup water
2 tablespoons granulated sugar
3 tablespoons white distilled vinegar
1 teaspoon chile flakes
1 cup sweet corn kernels (cut from the cob)

For the curry vinaigrette

3 tablespoons light olive oil
2 teaspoons finely minced garlic
2 teaspoons finely minced ginger
2 tablespoons finely minced green onion
1 teaspoon minced lemongrass
1 teaspoon yellow curry powder
1 teaspoon paprika
¼ teaspoon turmeric
¼ teaspoon salt
¼ cup orange juice
¼ cup apple cider vinegar
1½ teaspoons honey
¼ cup light olive oil

For the creamy feta

2 tablespoons heavy cream
1 tablespoon sour cream
¼ cup buttermilk
½ teaspoon lemon juice
¼ teaspoon salt
¼ teaspoon cayenne pepper
1 cup feta cheese, crumbled

For the fried chicken oysters

18 pieces chicken oysters (skin on, cleaned of any
   bone or excess fat)
4 cups buttermilk
2 cups all-purpose flour
4 teaspoons smoked paprika
2 teaspoons cayenne pepper
2 teaspoons poultry seasoning
2 teaspoons onion powder
2 teaspoons garlic powder
2 teaspoons dry mustard powder
2 teaspoons salt

FOR THE CURRIED MELON

Combine all ingredients in a large mixing bowl. Arrange on a baking sheet and drizzle with curry vinaigrette (see recipe below).

FOR THE PICKLED CORN

In a small saucepot over high heat, combine water, sugar, vinegar, and chile flakes. Bring to a boil, remove from heat, and let sit for about 15 minutes.

Place the corn in a small mixing bowl, strain the sugar/vinegar liquid over the corn, and chill in refrigerator for 1 hour. Strain and reserve.

FOR THE CURRY VINAIGRETTE

Heat olive oil in a small saucepot over medium heat. Add garlic, ginger, onions, and lemongrass, and cook until fragrant and a little soft, about 1 minute.

Reduce heat to low and add curry powder, paprika, turmeric, and salt. Cook until fragrant, about 30 seconds (being careful not to burn).

Add orange juice, vinegar, and honey, and simmer for 5 minutes over medium-low heat.

Strain through a fine-mesh sieve lined with a double layer of cheesecloth (don't force the liquid; just allow it to strain through on its own for about 20 minutes, then give it a couple light presses with the back of a spoon or ladle).

Add liquid to a mixing bowl and emulsify by vigorously whisking in the olive oil. Chill in refrigerator.

FOR THE CREAMY FETA

In a small mixing bowl, whisk together all ingredients (except for feta), then gently fold in feta.

FOR THE FRIED CHICKEN OYSTERS

Add the chicken to a mixing bowl. Add the buttermilk and incorporate until chicken is evenly coated. Cover bowl with plastic wrap and refrigerate for at least 1 hour.

Preheat a deep fryer to 375°F.

In a large mixing bowl, combine flour with paprika, cayenne, poultry seasoning, onion powder, garlic powder, mustard powder, and salt.

Remove the chicken from the buttermilk (shaking off excess), and coat all sides with seasoned flour. Carefully drop chicken into the deep fryer and fry until crispy and golden brown, 2–3 minutes.

AT SERVICE

Stacking the melon, arrange 3 red cubes of watermelon and 3 green cubes of honeydew in the center of each plate. Distribute the cilantro and mint onto the watermelon stacks. Spoon creamy feta onto the watermelon. Sprinkle corn over each salad and garnish with sliced red onions. Place three pieces of chicken around the salad.

Chef's Tip: *Your local butcher can provide you with "chicken oysters."*

BLT Salad and Brioche Grilled Cheese

Braised Bacon, Creamy Basil Dressing, Heirloom Tomatoes, Avocado

SERVES 6

This dish encompasses all my favorite ingredients on one plate.

Suggested Wine Pairing: Dry Furmint

For the braised bacon

¼ cup light olive oil
18 strips thick-cut bacon, cut in half (or substitute
   standard bacon)

For the creamy basil dressing

3 cups basil (leaves only, firmly packed)
1 clove garlic
1 teaspoon finely chopped Serrano chile
¼ cup grated Parmigiana Reggiano
Pinch of salt
Light olive oil, as needed
2 cups mayonnaise (page 285)
1 tablespoon Dijon mustard
1 tablespoon lemon juice
Salt and pepper, to taste

For the grilled cheese sandwiches

¼ cup butter (room temperature)
10 slices brioche
Salt and pepper, to taste
6 (¼-inch-thick) slices Raclette cheese

For the salad

3 heads romaine lettuce
3 avocados, peeled, pitted, and halved
24 assorted heirloom cherry tomatoes, halved
6 medium assorted heirloom tomatoes, cored and
   sliced in rounds and wedges
1 cup house vinaigrette (page 285)
Salt and pepper, to taste

For the garnish

MIcro or chopped basil

FOR THE BRAISED BACON

Preheat oven to 325°F.

Heat olive oil in a large ovenproof sauté pan over medium heat. Add bacon and cook for 15 seconds per side (bacon should be sizzling). Remove pan from heat and cover with tin foil. Place pan in the oven and cook bacon for 30 minutes.

FOR THE CREAMY BASIL DRESSING

Heat a small saucepot of water over high heat. Blanch basil leaves for 1 minute and remove to a bowl of ice and water. Place basil in a cheesecloth, squeeze out excess water, and roughly chop.

Combine basil with garlic, chile, Parmigiana Reggiano, and salt in a blender with just enough olive oil to cover the basil, and process until a very green oil is produced, about 2 minutes.

In a large mixing bowl, combine basil mixture with mayonnaise, mustard, lemon juice, and salt. Whisk until fully incorporated. Refrigerate until ready to use.

FOR THE GRILLED CHEESE SANDWICHES

Spread butter on one side of each bread slice, and sprinkle with salt and pepper. Layer the cheese between two slices of bread, making sure the buttered side is on the outside of each sandwich.

Heat a large skillet over medium heat. Cook the sandwiches, pressing them occasionally with a

spatula, until the cheese melts and the bread is golden, 3–4 minutes per side.

Make two cuts diagonally to create 4 wedges out of each sandwich (20 wedges total) and remove crusts.

FOR THE SALAD

Split the romaine heads in half from top to bottom, leaving the core at the base of the lettuce intact. Drizzle romaine with creamy basil dressing and fan open each wedge.

Slice each avocado half into 3 slices each (18 slices total).

Carefully arrange all the tomatoes and avocados separately on a large baking sheet, drizzle with house vinaigrette, and season with salt and pepper.

AT SERVICE

Place one romaine wedge in the center of each plate. Distribute tomatoes, avocado, bacon, and three wedges of grilled cheese around each wedge. Garnish with basil.

Chef's Tip: *Raclette is a semi-firm, cow's milk cheese, most commonly used for melting. Feel free to substitute your favorite melting cheese for the grilled cheese sandwiches.*

Oysters on the Half Shell and Spiced Tomato Granita

Fresh Horseradish, "Drunken" Heirloom Tomatoes

SERVES 6

This super-refreshing starter plate gets things rolling, and is perfect to enjoy while sitting out on the patio on a warm summer's day.

Suggested Wine Pairing: Chablis

For the oysters

36 cold-water oysters (about 3-inches long, shucked and void of all shell fragments)
1 (4-inch) piece of fresh horseradish (microplane-grated)

For the vodka-soaked tomatoes

3 large heirloom tomatoes
½ cup vodka

For the tomato water

4 pounds vine-ripened golden heirloom tomatoes (approximately 10 medium tomatoes)
1½ tablespoons salt
2 teaspoons Old Bay Seasoning
2 teaspoons ground celery seeds
1 tablespoon chile flakes
¼ cup lemon juice
Salt, to taste (optional)

For the garnish

6 small white paper napkins
24 cups crushed ice
1 cup assorted flower petals
Freshly grated horseradish, to taste

FOR THE VODKA-SOAKED TOMATOES

Prepare a large bowl with ice and water to make an ice bath.

Bring a medium pot of water to a boil. Add tomatoes and blanch for 3 seconds then remove with a hand strainer to the ice bath.

Allow the water in the pot to come back to a full boil and repeat this process (blanching tomatoes for a total of three times into the boiling water).

Remove the tomato skins, core, and seeds, and chop into a small dice. In a small mixing bowl, combine tomatoes and vodka, and marinate for 15–20 minutes.

FOR THE TOMATO WATER

Roughly chop tomatoes into large pieces and add to a large mixing bowl. Add salt, Old Bay Seasoning, celery seeds, and chile flakes. Working in batches, add tomatoes to a food processor, pulse until just broken down (do not overprocess), and place back into large mixing bowl.

Line a large bowl with an 18 × 18-inch cheesecloth. Pour tomato mixture into the cheesecloth, and, using butcher twine, tie the ends of the cheesecloth together to form a semi-loose sack. Suspend the cloth over a bowl so the tomato juices (aka water) can flow into the catch

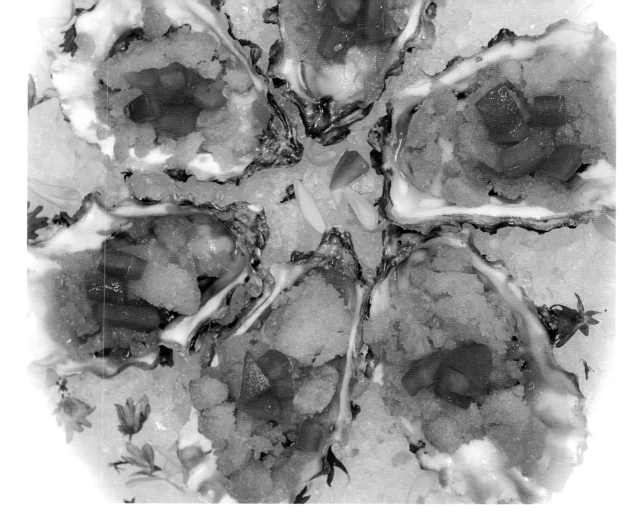

bowl (do not squeeze the cheesecloth because this will cloud the tomato water). Allow sack to hang refrigerated overnight or a minimum of 8 hours (maximum 48 hours).

Discard cheesecloth and tomato pulp. Add lemon juice and adjust seasoning with salt.

Pour the tomato water into a baking dish, and place dish in freezer. Every 15 minutes, scrape the mixture with a fork. At the end of 1 hour or so you should have a very white, flaky, light ice. Place this ice in a smaller container and continue to store in the freezer. Fluff the ice once again with a fork just before using.

AT SERVICE

Place one paper napkin in the center of each bowl. Distribute crushed ice into each bowl and flatten it. Sprinkling flower petals on top of the ice. Arrange 6 shucked oysters also on top of the ice. Top each oyster with horseradish and 1 tablespoon of tomato water granita. Top each oyster with 3 vodka-soaked heirloom tomatoes. Serve immediately.

Chef's Tip: *You can tell which coast oysters are from by looking at them: West Coast oysters have a wavy shell, while East Coast have flat shells.*

Flash-Seared King Salmon Cake

Macadamia Crust, Mango and Shaved-Radish Salad, Yuzu Sabayon

SERVES 6

I often take river-fishing trips in Alaska with four of my buddies. On one trip, we wanted to pack lightly, so the only things we brought with us were chopsticks, soy sauce, wasabi, and one little dipping dish to share. When we were hungry, we'd take the salmon we'd just caught, lay it on a wooden log, and cut sashimi out of it. We'd dip it in soy sauce and wasabi. The freshness and quality of the salmon were so amazing and the simplicity of what we were doing inspired super fresh salmon creations like this one.

Suggested Wine Pairing: California Chardonnay

For the salmon cake

2 tablespoons light olive oil, plus more for
   coating pan
2 tablespoons finely chopped ginger
2 tablespoons finely chopped garlic
1 pound of salmon, diced
1 teaspoon salt
1 egg, whisked well
1 tablespoon water
¾ cup chopped macadamia nuts
¼ cup panko bread crumbs

For the mango salad

4 tablespoons seasoned rice wine vinegar
2 tablespoons fish sauce
1 tablespoon chopped ginger
1 tablespoon lime juice
2 tablespoons water
1 jalapeño pepper, seeds removed and chopped
1 teaspoon sesame oil
3 tablespoons canola oil
2 mangos, peeled and sliced (about ¼-inch thick)
3 radishes, thinly sliced
1 tablespoon chopped mint
1 tablespoon chopped Thai basil
1 tablespoon chopped cilantro

For the yuzu sabayon

¼ cup heavy cream
4 tablespoons sour cream
4 tablespoons mayonnaise (page 285)

2 tablespoons yuzu (or lemon juice)
½ teaspoon cayenne
Salt, to taste

For the ponzu

1 cup seasoned rice wine vinegar
1 cup tsuyu (soup soy)

For the garnish

Nori goma (sesame seeds), for sprinkling
Small handful of Asian micro greens, for sprinkling
   (optional)
Sesame chile oil, for drizzling

FOR THE SALMON CAKE

Heat 2 tablespoons of olive oil in a small sauté pan over low heat. Add ginger and garlic and sauté until fragrant, about 1 minute. Remove from heat and set aside to cool.

Set up 3 mixing bowls. Combine the salmon and salt with the ginger/garlic mixture in one; egg and water, well combined, in another; and the macadamia nuts and breadcrumbs in the third.

Evenly divide salmon mixture into 6 ring molds, firmly packing the salmon into each ring mold using the back of a spoon. Brush top of salmon cakes with a generous amount of egg wash. Evenly divide the nut mixture by sprinkling over the tops of salmon cakes. Gently press the nut mixture down so it adheres to the egg wash.

Generously coat a large nonstick skillet pan to medium-high heat. Working in batches of three, carefully flip salmon molds (nut side down) onto the pan (ring mold stays on while cooking). With a spoon, gently press down on the salmon cake so the nut mixture is touching the skillet. Cook salmon until seared, about 2 minutes.

Using an oven mitt and a spatula tucked underneath each salmon mold, carefully remove the salmon from the pan and flip onto a large plate with the nut mixture facing on top.

FOR THE MANGO SALAD

Place wine vinegar, fish sauce, ginger, lime juice, water, pepper, sesame oil, and canola oil in blender, and process until smooth, about 2 minutes. Set vinaigrette aside.

In a small mixing bowl, combine mango with some of the vinaigrette, and coat evenly.

In a small mixing bowl, combine radishes with mint, basil, cilantro, and some of the vinaigrette, and toss gently.

FOR THE YUZU SABAYON

Place cream in a small mixing bowl and beat vigorously with a hand mixer until stiff peaks form. Whisk in sour cream, mayonnaise, yuzu, and cayenne. Season with salt.

FOR THE PONZU

In a small mixing bowl, combine the vinegar and soup soy. Reserve.

AT SERVICE

Distribute the salmon cakes into flat-bottom bowls (position cakes in the center). Carefully lift the ring mold off the salmon. Arrange some of the mango in a layered fashion to the side of salmon cakes. Place radish mixture between layers and on top of salmon cakes. Place a dollop of sabayon on top of each salmon cake. Drizzle the ponzu around the salmon cakes. Garnish salmon cakes with desired amount of nori goma and micro greens. Bead a few drops of sesame chile oil onto the ponzu.

Chef's Tip: *Best to buy in season, wild salmon can usually be obtained from your local fish market.*

Yellowtail Tartare and Dungeness Crab

Bok Choy-Apple Salad, Wasabi Tobiko, Avocado, Sesame-Nori Crackers

SERVES 6 / MAKES 12 CRACKERS

Often times when our cooks and I go on spear-fishing adventures, we'll catch a large yellowtail from the local waters. We bring it back to the restaurant, prepare it in a variety of ways, and eat it for lunch. We create anything from fresh ceviche to fish tacos or tartare with toasted bread, sliced avocado, and hot sauce. This dish is inspired by our love for the fresh yellowtail harvested in summertime.

Suggested Wine Pairing: Austrian Grüner Veltliner

For the tartare

1½ pounds yellowtail tuna (substitute any tuna)
2 tablespoons lemon oil
Salt and pepper, to taste

For the spicy pepper vinaigrette:

2 tablespoons light olive oil
1 red bell pepper, finely diced
1 tablespoon chopped fresh ginger
3 scallions, finely chopped
1 cup seasoned rice wine vinegar
½ cup green hot sauce
½ cup white soy sauce (may substitute light soy sauce)
½ cup lime juice

For the bok choy-apple salad

2 baby bok choy
2 apples, peeled and cut into thin strips
½ cup chopped cilantro
Spicy pepper vinaigrette (see above), for drizzling

For the crackers

1 cup all-purpose flour
½ tablespoon cumin
½ tablespoon coriander
½ teaspoon salt
¼ cup hot water
1 teaspoon light olive oil
1 egg
1 tablespoon water

2 tablespoons sesame seeds
Sea salt, to taste

For the yuzu mayonnaise

1 cup mayonnaise (page 285)
2 tablespoons yuzu juice (substitute lemon juice)
Pinch of salt

For the garnish

1½ cups Dungeness crabmeat
3 tablespoons yuzu mayonnaise
3 avocados, peeled, pitted, cut in half, and sliced into strips lengthwise
6 teaspoons wasabi tobiko
2 tablespoons sesame seeds

FOR THE TARTARE

Dice tuna into small cubes, place in a mixing bowl, and add lemon oil. Season with salt and pepper, and cover with plastic wrap and refrigerate.

FOR THE SPICY PEPPER VINAIGRETTE:

Heat olive oil in a pan over medium heat. Add peppers, ginger, and scallions, and sauté until tender, about 3 minutes. Add remaining ingredients and reduce mixture by half over low heat, about 5 minutes. Remove from heat and chill in the refrigerator.

FOR THE BOK CHOY-APPLE SALAD

Split the bok choy in half and remove the base that holds the leaves together. Cut it into thin strips. In a large mixing bowl, combine bok choy with apples and cilantro, drizzle with spicy pepper vinaigrette, and toss gently.

FOR THE CRACKERS

Preheat oven to 350°F.

In a large mixing bowl, combine flour, cumin, coriander, and salt. Add hot water and olive oil, and incorporate. Once the dough is cool enough to handle, transfer to a floured surface and knead to a smooth consistency, about 5 minutes, then place dough in refrigerator for 1 hour.

Create an egg wash by whisking egg and water together in a mixing bowl.

Using a rolling pin, roll the dough until very thin so that it fits the back of a large baking sheet. Cut dough into 12 triangular shapes. Brush egg wash over triangles, and sprinkle with sesame seeds and sea salt.

Place in oven and bake until golden brown, 10–15 minutes.

FOR THE YUZU MAYONNAISE

In a small mixing bowl, combine mayonnaise, yuzu, and a pinch of salt. Stir until fully incorporated.

FOR THE GARNISH

In a large mixing bowl, combine crabmeat with yuzu mayonnaise.

AT SERVICE

Distribute tartare in small mounds onto each plate. Fan the avocado slices over the tartare, followed with a topping of some of the crabmeat. Add a dollop of the yuzu mayonnaise and wasabi tobiko. Drizzle spicy pepper vinaigrette around each plate. Place some bok choy–apple salad onto each plate along with 2 crackers on the side. Garnish with sesame seeds.

Chef's Tip: *For the crackers, use a pasta attachment on a stand mixer to get the dough very thin.*

Crispy Tempura Soft-Shell Crab and Summer Melon

Thai Chile Aioli, Ginger–Fish Sauce Vinaigrette

SERVES 6

The tastes in Asian cuisine range from sweet and salty to sour and bitter. This dish encompasses all of those with the crispiness of the tempura and tenderness of the crab. This is a super light dish and a great way to start a meal as an appetizer. It also makes the perfect entree on a warm summer night.

Suggested Wine Pairing: Spanish Godello

For the melons

2 medium melons of your choice (best to choose different colors)

For the ginger–fish sauce vinaigrette

1 cup plus 3 tablespoons light olive oil
1 jalapeño pepper, seeded and chopped
1 Serrano pepper, chopped
2 tablespoons chopped garlic
2 tablespoons chopped ginger
6 scallions, roughly chopped
1 cup seasoned rice wine vinegar
¼ cup granulated sugar
¼ cup water
½ cup fish sauce
¼ cup light soy sauce
1 tablespoon fresh squeezed lime juice
1 tablespoon chile oil

For the Thai chile aioli

1 egg yolk
2 cloves garlic, crushed
3 teaspoons unseasoned rice wine vinegar
1 cup light olive oil
Salt and pepper, to taste
1 teaspoon lemon juice
1 tablespoon hot sauce

For the soft-shell crabs

1 cup all-purpose flour
1 cup cornstarch
1 tablespoon baking powder
¼ teaspoon salt
1½ cups soda water
2 tablespoons vodka
1 tablespoon finely chopped chives
Canola oil, for frying
6 medium soft-shell crabs, precleaned and cut in half

For the herb garnish

2 tablespoon roughly chopped fresh Thai basil
2 tablespoons roughly chopped fresh mint
2 tablespoons finely chopped fresh cilantro

FOR THE MELONS

Peel melons and remove seeds. Cut into wedges about ¼-inch thick.

FOR THE GINGER–FISH SAUCE VINAIGRETTE

Heat 3 tablespoons of olive oil in a sauté pan over medium heat. Add peppers, garlic, ginger, and scallions, and cook for 5 minutes. Spread mixture onto a plate and refrigerate until chilled.

In a blender, combine above mixture with vinegar, sugar, water, fish sauce, soy sauce, and lime juice. Process on high speed until smooth, then set the blender to low speed and drizzle in remaining 1 cup of olive oil and chile oil.

FOR THE THAI CHILE AIOLI

In a mixing bowl, combine egg yolk, garlic, and vinegar. Whisk thoroughly until slightly foamy.

Gradually add olive oil in a thin stream, constantly whisking until mixture is thickened.

Incorporate salt and pepper, lemon juice, and hot sauce. Store aioli in the refrigerator in a covered container until ready to use.

FOR THE SOFT-SHELL CRABS

In a mixing bowl, combine flour, cornstarch, baking powder, and salt. Add water and vodka; gently whisk until just incorporated. Set aside.

Heat oil in a deep fryer to 350°F.

Dip each crab into the tempura batter and drop carefully into hot oil. Deep fry crabs until golden brown and puffy. Turn if necessary for even color.

FOR THE HERB GARNISH

In a small mixing bowl, combine basil, mint, and cilantro.

AT SERVICE

Lay the melon out on a sheet pan and drizzle with vinaigrette, generously coating each piece. Arrange the melons by overlapping, interlacing 6 on each plate in a circular pattern. Sprinkle the herbs over the melon. Place two halves of crab on the plate (interlocked together) on top of melon salad. Drizzle the plate with some of the vinaigrette, followed by desired amount of aioli. Top with a sprinkling of more herbs.

Chef's Tip: *I like to use small French or honeydew melons*

Corn Meal–Crusted Scallops and Sweet Corn Risotto

Herb-Roasted Tomatoes, Shellfish Emulsion, Porcini Mushrooms

SERVES 6

The beginning harvest of mussels for the summer season makes me think of the subtle notes of saffron that complement this dish so nicely. The sweetness of the scallops and the corn also pair really well in this unique presentation. Serve this delicious small plate with a light summer wine while relaxing on the patio after a day at the beach.

Suggested Wine Pairing: Vermentino

For the tomatoes

4 plum tomatoes, each tomato cut into
    three ½-inch rounds
¼ cup light olive oil
Salt and pepper, to taste
3 cloves garlic, peeled and thinly sliced
2 sprigs thyme

For the shellfish emulsion

1 tablespoon light olive oil
5 cloves garlic, peeled and chopped
1 large shallot, finely chopped
2 cups white wine (chardonnay)
¼ teaspoon saffron
2 black peppercorns
2 sprigs thyme
2 sprigs parsley
1 bay leaf
24 mussels, rinsed until cold water
6 tablespoons butter, cubed
Salt and pepper, to taste

For the scallops

1 egg
1 tablespoon water
1 cup finely ground yellow corn meal
1 tablespoon finely chopped parsley
12 large sea scallops (size/U8)
Salt and pepper, to taste
1 tablespoon light olive oil

For the sweet corn risotto

4 tablespoons butter, divided
½ Spanish onion, finely chopped
1 cup Arborio rice
4 cups vegetable stock, hot (page 288)
1½ cups fresh corn kernels
¼ cup grated Parmigiana Reggiano
3 tablespoons mascarpone
2 tablespoons fines herbes (page 285)
Salt and pepper, to taste

For the porcini mushrooms

4 tablespoons light olive oil
18 small porcini mushrooms, cut in half
1 tablespoon chopped garlic
Salt and pepper, to taste

FOR THE TOMATOES

Preheat oven to 225°F.

Place the tomatoes on a baking sheet. Drizzle with olive oil and season with salt and pepper. Add garlic and thyme, and place in oven for 2 hours.

Remove from oven and set aside.

FOR THE SHELLFISH EMULSION

Heat olive oil in a large saucepan over medium heat. Add garlic and shallots, and cook until translucent.

Add wine, saffron, peppercorns, thyme, parsley, and bay leaf. Bring to a boil. Add mussels and cook until the mussels just open. Strain sauce and mussels through a fine-mesh sieve and reserve liquid.

Add butter and immersion blend until frothy. Season with salt and pepper.

FOR THE SCALLOPS

In a bowl, whisk egg and water to create an egg wash.

In a mixing bowl, combine corn meal and parsley.

Season scallops with salt and pepper and dip one end into egg wash, then into corn meal and parsley mix.

Heat olive oil in a small sauté pan over medium-high heat. Place scallops onto the pan, corn meal side down. Cook until golden brown, about 2 minutes on each side.

FOR THE SWEET CORN RISOTTO

Add 2 tablespoons of butter and onions to a saucepot. Over medum heat, cook the onions until translucent. Add rice and cook stirring constantly until the rice is lightly toasted. Using 3 cups of stock, add 1 cup of stock at a time, cooking rice until liquid is absorbed and the rice is al dente. Add corn and continue cooking until corn is warmed through. Add Parmigiana Reggiano, mascarpone, and remaining butter and adjust to a creamy, but somewhat loose, consistency by using the remaining 1 cup of the vegetable stock as needed. Add fines herbes and season with salt and pepper.

FOR THE PORCINI MUSHROOMS

Heat a sauté pan over high heat. Add oil and mushrooms; sauté, stirring often, for about 2 minutes. Add garlic, season with salt and pepper, and sauté for another 2 minutes.

AT SERVICE

Spoon creamy corn risotto into the center of a bowl. Add 2 tomato rounds on top of the risotto. Arrange 2 scallops on the tomato rounds and garnish with 6 mushroom halves Spoon shellfish emulsion around the risotto and top each scallop with a little bit of the shellfish emulsion froth.

Chef's Tip: *Fresh scallops smell sweet like the ocean and should not smell fishy. They should have a slightly opaque pearl color.*

Beer-Battered Anaheim Peppers With Lobster

Avocado Salad, Lemon Crème Fraîche, Cilantro

SERVES 6

Where I grew up, close to the border, Mexican taco shops were abundant and something I have been frequenting for years. One of my favorite dishes has always been the chile relleno, traditionally made with an egg-white batter that's not super crispy. Here, I elevate this dish with a beer batter and large chunks of lobster.

Suggested Wine Pairing: Sauvignon Blanc

For the lobster

¼ cup butter
1 pound cooked lobster tail meat, cut into
    large chunks
Salt and pepper, to taste

For the sauce

2 red tomatoes
2 tomatillos
2 jalapeño peppers
1 tablespoon light olive oil
½ Spanish onion, peeled and chopped
4 cloves garlic, peeled and chopped
2 tablespoons cumin/coriander spice blend
    (page 283)
½ cup chicken stock (page 283)
Salt and pepper, to taste

For the filling

2 tablespoons butter
½ Spanish onion, peeled and chopped
2 cloves garlic, peeled and finely chopped
½ green pepper, seeded and chopped
½ cup corn
1 cup vegetable stock (page 288)
¼ cup white corn grits
½ teaspoon cayenne pepper
Salt and pepper, to taste
1 tablespoon mascarpone cheese
½ cup white cheddar cheese, grated
2 tablespoons chopped cilantro

For the batter

1 cup all-purpose flour
1 cup cornstarch
1 tablespoon baking powder
1 egg
2 cups beer
¼ bunch chives, chopped

For the avocado salad

2 avocados, peeled, pitted, and diced
3 tablespoons chopped cilantro
Juice of 1 lime
Salt and pepper, to taste

For the Anaheim peppers

2 tablespoons light olive oil
6 Anaheim peppers
3 lobster tails, boiled, shelled, and sliced
Cornstarch, for coating peppers

For the garnish

1 cup cherry tomatoes, halved
Handful of micro cilantro, finely chopped
1 cup crème fraîche
Zest of 1 lemon (or lime)

FOR THE LOBSTER

Melt butter over low heat in a sauté pan. Add lobster and warm slightly. Season with salt and pepper.

FOR THE SAUCE

Prepare a grill over high heat. Add tomatoes, tomatillos, and jalapeños, and grill until charred on all sides.

Chop tomatoes and tomatillos.

Chop jalapeños and remove seeds.

Heat olive oil in a medium saucepot over medium-high heat. Add onions and garlic, and sauté until onions are translucent. Add cumin/coriander and tomatoes, tomatillos, jalapeños, and stock. Season with salt and pepper.

Transfer mixture to a blender and puree, then pass it through a fine-mesh sieve. Keep warm.

FOR THE FILLING

Melt butter in a large ovenproof sauté pan over medium-low heat. Add onion, garlic, pepper, and corn, and cook until onions are translucent.

Add stock and bring to a boil.

Whisk in grits, add cayenne, and season with salt and pepper. Bring back to boil, stirring constantly.

Cover and place in oven for 30 minutes.

Remove from oven and stir in mascarpone, cheddar cheese, and cilantro.

FOR THE BATTER

In a small mixing bowl, combine flour, cornstarch, and baking powder. Make a well in the center of the dry ingredients, and add egg and beer. Mix until combined and add chives. The batter should be the consistency of a heavy cream. Set aside, keeping cool.

FOR THE AVOCADO SALAD

In a small mixing bowl, combine ingredients and mix well. Set aside.

FOR THE ANAHEIM PEPPERS

Preheat oven to 400°F.

In a small mixing bowl, toss peppers with olive oil, and season with salt and pepper.

Arrange peppers on a small sheet pan and roast until skins are blistered. Place back in the mixing bowl, cover tightly with plastic wrap, and allow to steam for 5 minutes. Remove the skin and seeds.

Preheat a deep fryer and oven to 350°F.

Fill each pepper halfway with the filling and lobster. Coat peppers with cornstarch and dip into batter. Fry until golden brown and transfer to oven to finish cooking. Remove from oven and serve.

FOR THE GARNISH

In a small mixing bowl, combine crème fraîche with lemon zest, and whisk until creamy.

AT SERVICE

Place sauce in the center of each plate. Place a pepper on top of sauce and garnish with lobster, tomatoes, cilantro, lemon crème fraîche, and avocado salad.

Chef's Tip: *Substitute a mild pepper such as a poblano pepper for the Anaheim pepper. Other names for Anaheim peppers are California green chile, long green pepper, and chile verde.*

Pan-Seared Skate Wing and Chilled Soba Noodle Salad

Uni Vinaigrette, Charred Shishito Peppers,
Haricots Verts–Oyster Mushroom Stir-Fry, Gingered Tomatoes

SERVES 6

Growing up eating the local uni from the Catalina Islands, I never realized what an international delicacy it was until I traveled to Japan and went to the world's largest fish market. It was in the uni room that I spotted the best uni from my hometown waters right there on the center table, elevated above the rest!

Suggested Wine Pairing: Alsatian Gewurztraminer

For the skate wings

12 (3-ounce) skate wings, cleaned
Salt and pepper, to taste
3 cups all-purpose flour
8 tablespoons light olive oil, divided

For the ginger marinated tomatoes

3 tablespoons olive oil
1 tablespoon minced garlic
1 tablespoon minced ginger
¼ cup scallions (green and white parts), chopped
6 large Roma tomatoes
¼ cup rice wine vinegar
½ cup finely chopped toasted pistachios
1 tablespoon soy sauce
Salt and pepper, to taste (optional)

For the haricots verts–oyster mushroom stir-fry

6 tablespoons light olive oil, divided
6 small handfuls haricots verts, cleaned
3 tablespoons sweet Thai chili sauce (a staple in any Asian section of a grocery store)
1 tablespoon toasted sesame seeds
6 cups oyster mushrooms, cleaned and separated
1 tablespoon minced garlic
1 tablespoon minced ginger

For the charred Shishito peppers

30 Shishito peppers
2 tablespoons light olive oil
1 teaspoon salt
½ teaspoon ground black pepper

For the uni vinaigrette

¼ cup light olive oil
1 tablespoon minced garlic
1 tablespoon minced ginger
¼ cup chopped scallions (green and white part)
6 fresh uni tongues
3 tablespoons rice wine vinegar
2 tablespoons white soy sauce

For the salad

4 cups fresh buckwheat soba noodles
Canola oil, for coating noodles
1 cup tatsoi spinach, finely sliced
2 red jalapeños, seeded and finely sliced

For the uni

12 fresh uni tongues
Juice of ½ a lemon

FOR THE SKATE WINGS

Season skate wings with salt and pepper, then dredge in flour, coating both sides evenly.

Evenly divide olive oil between two large sauté pans (4 tablespoons per pan) and heat over medium-high heat. Sauté skate wings until cooked through, 2–3 minutes per side. Remove to a large baking sheet lined with paper towels.

FOR THE GINGER MARINATED TOMATOES

Heat olive oil in a small sauté pan over medium-low heat. Add garlic, ginger, and scallions and, stirring often, sauté until fragrant and soft, about 2 minutes.

Remove from heat, add to a small bowl, and refrigerate until chilled.

Using a tomato shark knife or small melon baller, remove the brown stem end from the tomatoes. Bring a large pot of salted water to a boil, add tomatoes, and blanch for 15 seconds. Using a slotted spoon, immediately remove tomatoes to a large bowl of ice and water. Repeat method by adding tomatoes back to the same pot of boiling water for an additional 15 seconds and removing again to a bowl of ice and water.

Remove tomatoes to a plate lined with paper towels. Remove tomato skins and cut in half widthwise. Gently but firmly squeeze out the tomato seeds and excess juices. Place the tomatoes on a cutting board and small dice.

Combine tomatoes in a mixing bowl with garlic/ginger/scallion mixture, vinegar, pistachios, and soy sauce. Season with salt and pepper.

FOR THE HARICOTS VERTS–OYSTER MUSHROOM STIR-FRY

Heat a large sauté pan over high heat. Add 3 tablespoons olive oil. Add haricots verts and allow to blister, 15–20 seconds. Add chile glaze, toss to coat, and continue to cook for another 30 seconds (beans should be cooked, but still crunchy). Sprinkle with sesame seeds and remove from heat.

Heat 3 tablespoons of olive oil in a large sauté pan over high heat. Add mushrooms and cook until caramelized, about 2 minutes. Add garlic and ginger, toss to combine, and cook for an additional minute. Remove from heat and reserve.

Just before plating, combine the haricots verts with the mushrooms in a large mixing bowl and toss to combine.

FOR THE CHARRED SHISHITO PEPPERS

In a mixing bowl, combine peppers with olive oil, salt, and pepper.

Heat a large sauté pan over high heat. In small batches, add peppers in a single layer and, tossing often, cook until well charred on all sides. Remove from heat and reserve.

FOR THE UNI VINAIGRETTE

Heat olive oil in a small saucepot over medium-low heat. Add garlic, ginger, and scallions and, stirring often, sauté until fragrant and soft, about 2 minutes.

Remove mixture from heat, add to a small bowl, and chill in refrigerator. Combine mixture in a blender with uni tongues, vinegar, and soy sauce. Process until smooth.

FOR THE SALAD

In a large pot of salted water, boil the noodles until done, about 6 minutes. Strain noodles in a colander, and add to a bowl of ice and water.

Remove noodles to a plate lined with paper towels and coat with a small amount of canola oil. Chill in refrigerator.

In a large mixing bowl, combine noodles, tatsoi, and jalapeños. Toss to combine.

AT SERVICE

Using a large dinner fork, spin the noodles around the fork to create a tight bundle, making sure to incorporate the vegetables as you spin. Place a small bundle of noodles onto the right side of each plate. Top bundles with the vegetables left over in the mixing bowl. Drizzle a little more vinaigrette around the noodles and top with 2 tongues of fresh uni. Distribute 2 small mounds of the haricots verts and oyster mushroom stir-fry on the left side of each plate. Place 1 skate wing on top of each pile of stir-fry. Drizzle each skate wing with lemon juice, and top with ginger-marinated tomatoes.

Chef's Tip: *When purchasing uni, look for bright vibrancy and no damage. Look for tongues that are big, fat, and plump.*

Yakutata Alaskan King Salmon and Tamale Roulade

Creamed Corn, Tomatillo Salsa, Cilantro-Mango

SERVES 6

In southern California there's an abundance of really fresh Mexican ingredients around us. Using fresh masa in this recipe creates a really light filling for the roulade.

Suggested Wine Pairing: California Viognier

For the salmon

6 (5-ounce) fillets wild king salmon
Salt and pepper, for seasoning
Sumac spice, for seasoning
6 tablespoons light olive oil, divided

For the tomatillo salsa

4 tablespoons light olive oil
1 Spanish onion, finely chopped
½ bunch green onions, roughly chopped
6 cloves garlic, finely chopped
10 tomatillos, finely chopped
1 bay leaf
1 jalapeño (remove half the seeds), chopped
½ bunch cilantro, roughly chopped
1 tablespoon cumin/coriander spice blend
    (page 283)
2 teaspoons salt
½ cup vegetable stock
2 teaspoons white distilled vinegar

For the tamale roulade

4 pasilla peppers
2 tablespoons light olive oil
Salt and pepper, for seasoning

For the masa

3 tablespoons light olive oil
1 red bell pepper, finely chopped
1 cup fresh corn kernels cut from the cob
Salt, to taste
2 teaspoons cumin/coriander spice blend
    (page 283)
1 teaspoon chile powder

3 cups fresh prepared masa (available at your local
    Mexican market)
1 bunch scallions, sliced

For the roulade

All-purpose flour, for coating
3 tablespoons light olive oil

For the mango

2 mangos, peeled, medium diced
1 tablespoon lime juice
2 tablespoons chopped cilantro
Salt, to taste

For the creamed corn

6 cups corn
1 cup whole milk
4 tablespoons butter, divided
Salt and pepper, to taste

For the garnish

Handful of fresh cilantro sprigs

FOR THE SALMON

Preheat oven to 350°F.

Season the salmon on both sides with salt and pepper. Season the presentation side of the salmon with sumac spice.

Heat 3 tablespoons of olive oil in a large sauté pan over high heat. Add 3 pieces of salmon to the pan and reduce heat to medium high. Sear salmon until lightly golden brown, 2–3 minutes per side.

Remove salmon to a large baking dish. Add 3 tablespoons of oil to the sauté pan and repeat searing process for the remaining 3 pieces of salmon. Remove salmon to a baking dish and cook to desired doneness.

FOR THE TOMATILLO SALSA

Heat olive oil in a saucepot over medium heat, and add onions, garlic, tomatillos, bay leaf, jalapeño, cilantro, cumin/coriander, and salt. Cover the saucepot and, stirring often, cook the vegetables until very soft and falling apart, 20–30 minutes.

Remove cover, add stock and vinegar, and cook until the mixture has a sauce consistency, about 10 minutes. Remove bay leaf, add mixture to a blender, and pulse a few times.

FOR THE TAMALE ROULADE

Preheat oven to 450°F.

Arrange peppers on a baking sheet, coat with oil, and season with salt and pepper. Roast peppers in oven until skins start to blister and peppers soften slightly, 15–20 minutes.

Remove peppers from oven, transfer to a mixing bowl, and cover with plastic wrap for about 10 minutes (this will allow the skins to be easily peeled).

Using a paring knife make a single cut from the stem end of the pepper to the bottom. Remove all seeds, ribs, and top. This should leave you with one flat sheet of pepper. Repeat with the other 3 peppers.

On a flat work surface, place 1½ feet of foil with a slightly shorter piece of plastic wrap on top of it. Working from the torn edge closest to you, lay the peppers across so that there is a wide sheet of peppers stretching from one side to the other, leaving about 3 inches on each side with nothing on it. Let this stay on the work surface while prepping the masa.

FOR THE MASA

Heat olive oil in a sauté pan over medium-high heat. Add pepper, corn, and salt, and sauté for 2 minutes. Add cumin/coriander blend and chile powder, and remove from heat.

In a large mixing bowl, combine masa, tamale roulade, and scallions. Incorporate thoroughly.

Place a steam basket in a medium pot of simmering water. Line the steam basket with a double layer of cheesecloth and spoon in the masa mixture. Place a lid on the pot and allow masa to steam until light and fluffy, about 25 minutes.

Spoon the masa mixture evenly across the peppers, just enough so that when rolled, the peppers will just barely meet. Using the foil, lift the edge and roll the peppers and masa up into a tight cylinder, twisting the ends of the foil to create an even tighter log. Immediately place in refrigerator to cool.

FOR THE ROULADE

Slice 6 large rounds of the roulade and remove the foil and plastic wrap. Lightly flour each side of the roulades.

Heat olive oil in a sauté pan over medium heat. Add the roulades and cook until slightly browned on each side and hot in the center, 3–5 minutes.

FOR THE MANGO

Combine all ingredients in a mixing bowl.

FOR THE CREAMED CORN

In a blender, combine corn and milk, process until smooth, then strain through a fine-mesh sieve.

Melt 2 tablespoons of butter in a sauté pan over medium heat. Add corn mixture and cook until creamy, 3–5 minutes. Add remaining 2 tablespoons of butter and season with salt and pepper.

AT SERVICE

Place a couple spoonfuls of tomatillo sauce just right of center on each plate. Place roulade on top of each spoonful. In the center of each plate, distribute the creamed corn. Place the salmon on top of the creamed corn and garnish with the mango mixture and cilantro sprigs.

Chef's Tip: *Mangos have one large, flat seed in the center, so stand the fruit on a cutting board with the thinnest side of the fruit facing you. Place the knife about ¼ inch from center, and cut straight down through the fruit. Turn the mango around and repeat, resulting in two "cheeks" and a center portion that is mainly the seed. For each cheek, cut a checkerboard pattern into the flesh, being careful not to slice the skin. Using a large spoon, scoop the chunks off the skin.*

Pacific Red Rockfish and Crispy Shrimp Tempura

Braised Daikon, Dashi-Soy Emulsion, Stir-Fried Pea Tendrils

SERVES 6

During the cold-water months in San Diego, most catches from sporting boats are from the ocean floor. Although rockfish are not super exciting to catch, this bottom dweller is one of my favorites to eat.

Suggested Wine Pairing: Puligny-Montrachet

For the dashi-soy emulsion

2 tablespoons light olive oil
1 Spanish onion, peeled and thinly sliced
5 scallions, roughly chopped
1 tablespoon chopped garlic
1 tablespoon chopped ginger
1 tablespoon cumin/coriander spice blend
    (page 283)
1 cup dashi broth (page 284)
1 cup tsuyu sauce
1 bunch cilantro stems
1 large daikon radish, peeled and medium diced
4 tablespoons cold butter

For the stir-fried pea tendrils

2 tablespoons light olive oil
12 cups tender pea vines or pea tendrils
    (reserve 1 cup for garnish)
1 tablespoon garlic, finely chopped
1 tablespoon ginger, finely chopped
Salt and pepper, to taste

For the mushrooms

2 tablespoons butter
4 cups hon shimeji mushrooms
Salt and pepper, to taste

For the local rockfish

6 (5-ounce) portions Pacific red rockfish
Salt and pepper, to taste
6 tablespoons light olive oil, divided
Togarashi, for seasoning

For the tempura shrimp

½ cup all-purpose flour
½ cup cornstarch
½ tablespoon baking powder
¼ teaspoon salt
¾ cup soda water
1 tablespoon vodka
1 tablespoon finely chopped chives
12 medium shrimp, peeled and deveined
    (leave tail on for presentation)

For the garnish

4 watermelon radishes, thinly sliced

FOR THE DASHI-SOY EMULSION

Heat olive oil in a saucepot over medium-high heat. Add onion, scallions, garlic, ginger, and cumin/coriander, and sauté until fragrant and soft, 2–3 minutes.

Add dashi broth, tsuyu, and cilantro, and simmer over low heat for 30 minutes. Strain the mixture through a fine-mesh sieve.

Place mixture back into the pot, add the daikon radish and simmer on medium-low heat until tender, about 1 hour.

Using a slotted spoon, remove the daikon to a bowl and reserve. Using an immersion blender, add in the cold butter a little at a time and whisk mixture until smooth.

Remove from heat.

Just before plating, rewarm sauce over low heat.

FOR THE STIR-FRIED PEA TENDRILS

Heat olive oil in a large sauté pan. Add pea tendrils, garlic, and ginger. Cook, tossing often, until wilted. Season with salt and pepper.

FOR THE MUSHROOMS

Melt butter in a large sauté pan over medium-heat. Add mushrooms, cook until softened, and season with salt and pepper.

FOR THE LOCAL ROCKFISH

Preheat oven to 350°F.

Season the rockfish on both sides with salt and pepper.

Heat olive oil in a large sauté pan over high heat. Add 3 pieces of rockfish to the pan and reduce heat to medium high. Sear rockfish until lightly golden brown, 2–3 minutes. Flip rockfish over and season with togarashi. (This will be the presentation side).

Remove rockfish to a large baking dish. Add 3 tablespoons of oil to the sauté pan and repeat searing process for the remaining 3 pieces of rockfish. Place remaining rockfish in a baking dish and bake in oven until cooked through.

FOR THE TEMPURA SHRIMP

In a large mixing bowl, combine flour, cornstarch, baking powder, and salt. Add the water, vodka, and chives, and whisk just until incorporated.

Heat a deep fryer to 350°F.

Dip each shrimp into the tempura batter and drop carefully into hot oil. Deep fry shrimp until golden brown and puffy. Turn if necessary for even color.

AT SERVICE

Add stir-fried pea tendrils to the middle of each bowl. Add daikon radish and mushrooms around the pea tendrils. Place 1 piece of rockfish on top of pea tendrils. Add 2 shrimp on top of rockfish. Add dashi-soy emulsion. Garnish with fresh pea tendrils and radishes.

Chef's Tip: *When going into the fish market, look for rockfish fillets that are extremely white and a little bit translucent.*

Summer Vegetable Pavé and Porcini Mushroom Gnocchi

Quinoa-Couscous Cake, Heirloom Tomato Sauce, Eggplant Sauté

SERVES 6

At Market we like to get creative with our vegetarian plates. We are always working with what's in season and get inspired by what we find. This roasted vegetable component is made into a meal when paired with creamy gnocchi.

Suggested Wine Pairing: Pommard

For the gnocchi

2 large russet potatoes, cleaned
1 egg, beaten
1 tablespoon grated Parmigiana Reggiano, more for garnish
½ cup all-purpose flour, more for dusting
½ teaspoon salt

For the mushroom cream

4 tablespoons butter
½ cup onion, small diced
½ cup leeks, small diced
4 cloves garlic, finely chopped
1 cup chopped porcini mushrooms (substitute any mushroom varietal)
1 teaspoon salt
1 tablespoon all-purpose flour
3 cups heavy cream
1 cup vegetable stock (page 288)
1 bay leaf
1 sprig thyme
2 teaspoons truffle oil
2 tablespoons sherry

For the quinoa/couscous cakes

1 cup cooked quinoa (cooked according to labeled instructions)
1 cup cooked couscous (cooked according to labeled instructions)
1 tablespoon finely chopped chives
1 egg
2 teaspoons cornstarch
½ teaspoon salt
½ cup light olive oil

For the spicy heirloom tomato sauce

4 tablespoons light olive oil
½ white onion, sliced
2 red bell peppers, cored, seeded, and roughly chopped
½ cup fresh fennel bulb, roughly chopped
8 cloves garlic, peeled and roughly chopped
½ teaspoon chile pepper flakes
1 sprig thyme
1 bay leaf
Pinch of dry oregano
½ teaspoon salt
1 cup chopped red heirloom tomatoes
1 tablespoon red wine vinegar

For the vegetable pavé

3 whole red bell peppers
3 tablespoons light olive oil, plus more for coating
Salt and pepper, to taste
1 eggplant, peeled and medium diced
4 cups arugula, loosely packed
House vinaigrette, for drizzling (page 285)
6 whole artichokes (may substitute jarred artichoke hearts)

For the sautéed gai lan

3 bunches gai lan (Chinese broccoli)
2 tablespoons light olive oil
½ teaspoon finely chopped garlic and toss

For the roasted hazelnuts

½ cup raw hazelnuts

For the garnish

Grated Parmigiana Reggiano
Fines herbes (page 285)
1 cup goat cheese
2 cups arugula

FOR THE GNOCCHI

Preheat oven to 375°F.

Place potatoes on a baking sheet and cook until done, 30–45 minutes.

Scoop out the inside of the potato and process through a food mill or ricer according to labeled instructions.

Place processed potatoes on parchment paper, forming a mound, and cool to room temperature.

Place the potato mound onto a floured surface. Drizzle egg over the potatoes followed by the Parmigiana Reggiano, flour, and salt. Knead to incorporate, forming a dough. Cover dough with plastic wrap and allow to rest for 5–10 minutes.

Break dough into 3 equal pieces. Roll one piece of dough at a time onto a floured surface into long tubes about ¾ inch in diameter. Cut the tubes of dough into pieces about 1 inch long. Using your fingertip, press against a piece of the dough and roll it slightly to form an indentation.

Prepare an ice bath by nesting a medium bowl in a larger bowl that's partially filled with ice and water.

Bring a large pot of water to a boil.

Drop in the gnocchi. When they float to the top, scoop them out with a slotted spoon and place into prepared ice bath. Immediately remove gnocchi with a slotted spoon to a plate lined with paper towels.

FOR THE MUSHROOM CREAM

Melt butter in a large saucepot over medium heat. Add onions, leeks, garlic, mushrooms, and salt. Sauté until onions are translucent and mushrooms are wilted, about 10 minutes.

Add flour, stirring frequently to incorporate, 1–2 minutes.

Add cream, stock, bay leaf, and thyme. Bring to a boil, whisking vigorously and incorporating flour into the cream (removing any lumps).

Add the truffle oil and sherry, reduce heat to low, and simmer for 5–10 minutes, stirring frequently and making sure not to burn the bottom (mixture should be the consistency of a heavy cream and coat the back of a spoon).

FOR THE QUINOA/COUSCOUS CAKES

In a large mixing bowl, combine quinoa, couscous, and chives.

In a separate mixing bowl, whisk the egg, cornstarch, and salt together. Pour mixture into the quinoa mixture and incorporate.

Form 6 cakes by gently pressing mixture into ring molds with the back of a spoon. If forming cake patties by hand, place mixture onto a floured work surface using a small amount of flour to keep them from sticking.

Heat the olive oil in a large nonstick sauté pan over medium-high heat. Add the cakes in small batches and cook until crispy and golden brown, about 1 minute per side.

FOR THE SPICY HEIRLOOM TOMATO SAUCE

Heat olive oil in a large sauté pan over medium heat. Add onion, peppers, fennel, garlic, pepper flakes, thyme, bay leaf, oregano, and salt.

Cook covered, stirring occasionally until soft, about 20 minutes.

Add tomatoes and vinegar, uncover, and leave on medium heat to simmer until thickened, about 30 minutes.

Remove thyme and bay leaf. Add mixture to a blender, and process until smooth.

FOR THE VEGETABLE PAVÉ

Preheat oven to 450°F.

Coat peppers with olive oil and season with salt and pepper. Arrange peppers on a baking sheet and roast in oven until completely wrinkled and charred, turning them twice during roasting, 30–40 minutes.

Place peppers in a mixing bowl, cover with plastic wrap, and allow to rest for 5 minutes.

Peel peppers and remove stems and seeds. Cut peppers into ½-inch pieces.

Heat 3 tablespoons of olive oil in a sauté pan over medium heat. Add eggplant, season with salt, and cook until soft, 5–10 minutes.

Add arugula to a mixing bowl, drizzle with vinaigrette, and lightly toss.

Slice ¾–1 inch off the top of the artichokes. Pull off any smaller leaves toward the base and on the stem. Cut excess stem, leaving up to an inch on the artichoke. Rinse the artichokes in running cold water.

Add the artichokes to a large pot, leaving about 2 inches of water at the bottom. Cover, bring to a boil, then reduce heat to medium low. Cook artichokes until the outer leaves can easily be pulled off, 25–45 minutes.

Remove leaves and choke, and dice the hearts. Store leaves in a covered container in the refrigerator to enjoy later.

FOR THE SAUTÉED GAI LAN

Trim about 1 inch from the bottom of the gai lan stalks.

Heat olive oil in a large sauté pan over medium-high heat.

Add the gai lan and cook until the thickest part of the stalks are fork tender, 5–10 minutes.

Add garlic, toss thoroughly, and remove from heat.

FOR THE ROASTED HAZELNUTS

Preheat oven to 350°F.

Place hazelnuts on a baking sheet and roast in oven until lightly darkened and skins are blistered, 10–15 minutes. Remove nuts from oven and wrap them in a kitchen towel until cool. Rub nuts in towel to remove loose skins. Remove nuts to a cutting board and roughly chop.

AT SERVICE

Combine the gnocchi with the warm mushroom sauce. Spoon gnocchi into 6 small ovenproof serving bowls. Garnish with Parmigiana Reggiano and fines herbes. Place bowls onto 6 large ovenproof dinner plates. Place the gai lan onto each plate and garnish with hazelnuts. Working in a ring mold or forming a tower by hand, place cake patties onto each plate followed by eggplant, peppers, and artichokes. Garnish each pavé with two tablespoons of the spicy heirloom tomato sauce. Using the back of a spoon, spread more sauce onto each plate. Place plates in the oven and warm in oven for about 10 minutes. Remove from oven and top pavé with goat cheese and arugula.

Chef's Tip: *Removing roasted peppers from the oven, placing them in a bowl covered with plastic wrap, and allowing them to rest for 5 minutes steams them, making it easier to peel the outer skin.*

Grilled Skirt Steak and Crispy Rice Cake

Japanese Eggplant, Sugar Snap Peas, Petite Potatoes

SERVES 6

Skirt steak is super flavorful. I created a special chile vinaigrette for this dish by adding different ingredients until I thought I got it just right. It makes a great marinade and sauce for grilled meats.

Suggested Wine Pairing: Napa Valley Cabernet Sauvignon

For the chile vinaigrette

2 cups light olive oil
¼ cup chopped garlic
¼ cup chopped ginger
1 cup small diced Spanish onion
1 cup small diced red bell pepper
⅓ cup tomato paste
⅓ cup tsuyu sauce
1 teaspoon salt
3 tablespoons soy sauce
1 teaspoons fish sauce
½ cup white distilled vinegar
2 tablespoons hot sauce
3 tablespoons green hot sauce
2 tablespoons hoisin sauce

For the steaks

6 (6-ounce) flank steaks
Salt and pepper, to taste

For the crispy rice cake

5 cups cooked sushi rice
2 tablespoons seasoned rice wine vinegar
½ cup chopped green onion
6 tablespoons light olive oil, plus more for frying

For the vegetables

36 assorted cherry heirloom tomatoes
4 tablespoons light olive oil, more for drizzling
Salt and pepper, to taste
36 assorted petite summer potatoes, cut into rounds
60 snap peas, cleaned
3 Japanese eggplant, peeled and cut into ½-inch thick discs

For the garnish

1 large bunch cilantro sprigs

FOR THE CHILE VINAIGRETTE

In a small saucepot add oil, garlic, ginger, onion, peppers, and tomato paste. Cook until soft, about 5 minutes.

Add remaining ingredients, and set aside. Just before service, warm over low heat and immersion blend.

FOR THE STEAKS

Combine steaks in a large mixing bowl with enough chile vinaigrette to generously and evenly coat.

Arrange steaks on a large baking sheet, cover with plastic wrap, and refrigerate for 24 hours.

Heat an outdoor grill to high heat. Remove steaks from marinade and season with salt and pepper. Cook to desired doneness; thinly slice.

FOR THE CRISPY RICE CAKE

In a large mixing bowl, combine rice with remaining ingredients, except the oil. Form the rice into six 3-inch ring molds, and place onto a large baking sheet lined with parchment paper coated with nonstick cooking spray. Cover with plastic wrap and refrigerate overnight.

When ready, carefully remove rice cakes from ring molds.

Heat olive oil in a large nonstick pan over high heat. Add the rice cakes and brown one side, flip and brown the other side. Remove cakes onto a plate lined with paper towels.

FOR THE VEGETABLES

Bring a large pot of salted water to a boil. Add the tomatoes and blanch for 15 seconds. Using a slotted spoon, immediately remove tomatoes to a bowl of ice and water. Repeat method by adding tomatoes back to the same pot of boiling water for an additional 15 seconds and removing again to a bowl of ice and water.

Remove tomatoes to a plate lined with paper towels. Peel, core, and finely dice.

Combine tomatoes in a mixing bowl with a drizzle of olive oil, and season with salt and pepper.

Heat a large nonstick sauté pan over high heat and cook tomatoes until caramelized, about 15 seconds. Remove and reserve.

Add potatoes to a saucepot and cover with cold salted water. Heat saucepot over medium low and cook potatoes until soft. Strain in a colander.

Heat 4 tablespoons of olive oil in a large sauté pan over high heat. Add peas and potatoes, and cook until lightly caramelized. Season with salt and pepper.

Arrange eggplant discs on a large baking sheet, and season with salt and pepper.

Prepare a grill over high heat, and cook eggplant for 2 minutes on each side.

AT SERVICE

Divide evenly and arrange sliced steak on each plate. Generously ladle warm vinaigrette over the steak. Place one rice cake next to each steak. Top the rice cake with grilled eggplant, potatoes, peas, and tomatoes. Garnish with cilantro sprigs.

Chef's Tip: *Although very flavorful, skirt steak can be a little tough in texture. Marinate it for 24 hours and slice it cross-grain to maximize its potential for optimum tenderness.*

Chef's Tip: *The steaks for this recipe can be prepared the night before, and the rice cake can be made up to one day ahead.*

Roasted Lamb Loin Chops and Minted Apricot Preserves

Aged White Cheddar Potatoes, Whipped Fennel, Gai Lan, Balsamic-Lamb Jus

SERVES 6

This is a seasonal twist on lamb with apple-mint jelly. Although apple-mint jelly is viewed by most as outdated and old school, there's still something to be said for the pairing of sweet with the flavor of grilled lamb. Here I've used first harvest apricots to make preserves as an ode to an old classic.

Suggested Wine Pairing: Dry Creek Valley Zinfandel

For the lamb loin and marinade

½ cup light olive oil
4 cloves garlic
1 tablespoon rosemary
¼ cup balsamic vinegar
1 tablespoon toasted ground fennel (page 287)
1 tablespoon toasted ground coriander (page 287)
Salt and pepper, to taste
18 lamb loin chops (trimmed of all silver skin and excess fat)

For the balsamic-lamb jus

1 pound lamb bones
5 tablespoons light olive oil, more for coating lamb bones
1 cup chopped Spanish onions
½ cup chopped carrots
½ cup chopped celery
¼ cup tomato paste
1 (750-mililiter) bottle red wine
1 gallon brown veal stock (page 282)
1 herb sachet (page 285), with 1 sprig rosemary added
¼ cup balsamic vinegar

For the minted apricot preserves

4 cups fresh apricots, diced
2 tablespoons lemon juice
3 cups granulated sugar
3 tablespoons chopped mint

For the aged white cheddar potatoes

4 large russet potatoes, peeled
Salt, to taste

For the béchamel

4 tablespoons butter
2 tablespoons white onion, finely diced
6 tablespoons flour
16 ounces cold milk
1 small bay leaf
Salt and pepper, to taste
1 cup panko bread crumbs
1 tablespoon light olive oil
1 tablespoon smoked paprika
½ teaspoon garlic powder
½ teaspoon onion powder
Salt and pepper, to taste
1 cup shredded white cheddar cheese
¼ cup finely chopped chives

For the whipped fennel

4 tablespoons butter
1 cup sliced Spanish onions
1 tablespoon minced garlic
2 bulbs fennel, sliced
1 teaspoon salt, more to taste
1 cup vegetable stock (page 288)
1 cup heavy cream

For the roasted gai lan

2 bunches gai lan (Chinese broccoli)
2 tablespoons light olive oil
½ teaspoon finely chopped garlic and toss

FOR THE LAMB LOIN AND MARINADE

Combine the first seven ingredients in a blender, and process until smooth.

Add lamb chops to a large mixing bowl. Cover with marinade and plastic wrap and marinate in refrigerator for 4–6 hours.

Remove lamb from refrigerator and allow to rest at room temperature for 1 hour before cooking.

Heat an outdoor grill to high heat.

Remove lamb chops from marinade and season with salt and pepper on each side.

Grill lamb chops for 3–4 minutes per side (or to desired doneness).

FOR THE BALSAMIC-LAMB JUS

Rinse bones well under cold running water, pat dry, and coat with oil. Place bones on a large baking sheet, and cook for 1 hour, turning occasionally, until evenly browned and caramelized.

Heat remaining 5 tablespoons of olive oil in a saucepot over high heat. Add onions, carrots, and celery, and cook until slightly brown.

Add tomato paste and cook until slightly caramelized, 4–5 minutes.

Add red wine and simmer over medium heat until liquid reduces by half its volume.

Add lamb bones, brown veal stock, and herb sachet. Simmer over medium-low heat until liquid is a sauce consistency, 1-2 hours.

Add vinegar and continue to reduce to a sauce consistency.

FOR THE MINTED APRICOT PRESERVES

Combine all ingredients in a large saucepot, and bring to boil over medium-high heat. Cook, stirring occasionally, until the sugar dissolves. Once mixture reaches a full boil, continue to boil for 15 minutes or until thick and bubbly. Stir frequently to prevent preserves from sticking to the sides of the pot. Remove from heat and reserve at room temperature.

Just before serving, add the chopped mint to the preserves.

FOR THE AGED WHITE CHEDDAR POTATOES

Slice each potato lengthwise into ½-inch thick slices. Using a 2-inch ring mold, cut 2-inch rounds out of the slices of potato (you will need 18 rounds total).

Add potato rounds to a medium pot and cover with cold water to 3 inches above potatoes. Add a small amount of salt and bring to a low simmer over medium heat, then reduce the heat slightly to bring water down to a very low simmer. Simmer at this setting for about 15 minutes or until potatoes are very soft but not falling apart. Check every 5 minutes for doneness with a paring knife (knife should insert easily). Do not overcook (potatoes are overcooked when they start to fall apart).

FOR THE BÉCHAMEL

Melt butter in a small saucepot over medium heat. Add onions and, stirring constantly, cook for about 2 minutes or until onions are soft and translucent.

Add flour and stir constantly for a roux (after a few minutes, the roux will turn from a yellowish color to a white color. This should take approximately 3–4 minutes). Once the roux has reached this white color, add the milk, and whisk until fully incorporated.

Add bay leaf and increase heat to medium high. Stirring constantly, bring the sauce to a boil.

Reduce heat to low and cook for 10–15 minutes, stirring often to avoid burning.

Remove béchamel from heat and discard bay leaf.

In a large ovenproof sauté pan, arrange the cooked potato rounds in a single layer, covering the bottom of the pan. Pour the béchamel over the potatoes. Reserve until just before serving.

Preheat oven to 325°F.

In a small mixing bowl, combine bread crumbs and olive oil. Arrange on a baking sheet lined with parchment paper. Brown in oven until golden brown, about 5 minutes. Remove from oven and pour the bread crumbs back into the mixing bowl.

Add paprika and garlic and onion powders, and season with salt and pepper.

Increase oven temperature to 400°F.

Place the sauté pan of potatoes and béchamel in the oven and cook until béchamel is hot throughout and slightly simmering.

Remove from oven and sprinkle with cheddar cheese. Return to oven just until cheese melts. Remove quickly. Do not leave in the oven for too long (this will cause the cheese to become greasy and break down).

Remove from oven and sprinkle with bread crumbs and chives.

FOR THE WHIPPED FENNEL

Melt butter in a saucepot over medium heat. Add onions, garlic, fennel, and 1 teaspoon of salt, and stir to incorporate. Cover saucepot and, stirring frequently, cook onions until translucent, about 5 minutes.

Add stock and increase heat to high. Cook vegetables, covered, until soft, 10–15 minutes.

Remove cover and continue to cook until all the liquid has evaporated.

Add cream and bring mixture back to a boil. Add to a blender, process until aerated, and season with salt.

FOR THE ROASTED GAI LAN

Trim about 1 inch from the bottom of the gai lan stalks.

Heat olive oil in a large sauté pan over medium-high heat. Add the gai lan and cook until the thickest part of the stalks are fork tender, 5–10 minutes. Add garlic, toss thoroughly, and remove from heat.

AT SERVICE

Place one dollop of whipped fennel to the left side of each plate. Using the back of the spoon, pull it to the right, across the plate. Working down the plate, spoon 3 white cheddar potatoes onto each plate at the edges of the whipped fennel, but separated enough to allow room for the chops (make sure to scoop some of the béchamel up with each potato). Sprinkle the bread crumbs on top of each cheddar potato. Distribute the roasted gai lan onto the plate. Place 3 lamb chops onto each plate with the bones resting off center on each potato. Drizzle with balsamic–lamb jus. Add apricot preserves to each chop.

Chef's Tip: *You will know the balsamic-lamb jus is ready when it reaches a thick consistency with good body.*

Grilled Prime Beef Tenderloin and Smoked Paprika-Chile Butter

Roasted Jalapeño Mashed Potatoes, Sweet Corn Sauté, Cherry Tomatoes

SERVES 6

This is a great dish to serve family and friends for a summer barbeque. Flavorful in-season cherry tomatoes are a nice contrast with grilled prime beef tenderloin. The tang of the corn soothes the prick of heat from the jalapeño mashed potatoes, adding another dimension that brings this whole dish together.

Suggested Wine Pairing: Aussie Shiraz

For the steak

6 (6-ounce) prime beef tenderloin steaks
Salt and pepper, to taste
Smoked paprika–chile butter (recipe below)

For the jalapeño mashed potatoes

6 whole jalapeños
2 tablespoons light olive oil, divided
Salt and pepper, to taste
2 whole garlic bulbs
Salt and pepper, to taste
1 cup heavy cream
4 tablespoons butter, room temperature
3 medium russet potatoes, peeled and roughly chopped
¼ cup room temperature crème fraîche

For the corn sauté

3 tablespoons light olive oil
½ cup red peppers, seeded and diced
½ cup pasilla peppers, seeded and diced
4 cups corn
2 teaspoons lime juice
2 tablespoons chopped cilantro
Salt and pepper to taste

For the tomatoes

6 cups assorted cherry tomatoes, halved
¼ cup house vinaigrette (page 285)
Salt and pepper to taste

For the smoked paprika–chile butter

1 cup butter, softened
1 tablespoon smoked paprika
1 tablespoon chile powder
1 tablespoon ground cumin
1 tablespoon ground coriander
1 teaspoon onion powder
1 teaspoon garlic powder
1 teaspoon salt

For the garnish

1 cup crumbled Cotija cheese

FOR THE STEAK

Season steaks liberally with salt and pepper.

Prepare a grill or cast-iron skillet over high heat. Cook steaks until caramelized, about 5 minutes on each side (depending on thickness and desired doneness). Remove steaks from grill and allow to rest.

Baste each steak with a small amount of smoked paprika–chile butter and allow to rest for 5 minutes.

Slice steaks into ½-inch slices across the grain.

FOR THE JALAPEÑO MASHED POTATOES

Preheat oven to 400°F.

In a small mixing bowl, toss jalapeños with 1 tablespoon olive oil, and season with salt and pepper.

Arrange jalapeños on a small sheet pan and roast until skins are blistered. Place back in the mixing bowl, cover tightly with plastic wrap, and allow to steam for 5 minutes. Remove the skin and seeds and discard stems.

Remove outer skins of garlic bulbs, keeping cloves intact. Cut ¼–½-inch off the top of bulbs. Place on a piece of aluminum foil, drizzle with 1 tablespoon of olive oil, and sprinkle with salt and pepper. Close foil tightly, forming a pouch. Roast cloves in oven until soft, about 30 minutes. Cool to room temperature. Using your hand, squeeze the bulb from the bottom, pushing the cloves out onto a cutting board. Roughly chop them.

In a small saucepot, combine cream, butter, garlic, and jalapeños. Using your hands, squeeze the roasted garlic (bulbs from the bottom), pushing the cloves out and into the pot; Bring to a simmer over medium-high heat, then pour into a blender and process until smooth.

In a medium saucepot pot over high heat, boil the potatoes in salted water. Reduce to a strong simmer until tender, about 15 minutes. Drain the potatoes and return them to the pot.

Add the jalapeño garlic cream and crème fraîche to the potatoes. Mash until fully incorporated and season with salt. Reserve covered.

FOR THE CORN SAUTÉ

Heat olive oil in a large sauté pan over high heat. Add peppers and sauté for about 30 seconds. Add corn and continue to cook for 1 minute. Add lime juice and cilantro. Remove from heat and season with salt and pepper.

FOR THE TOMATOES

In a mixing bowl, toss tomatoes with vinaigrette and season with salt and pepper.

FOR THE SMOKED PAPRIKA–CHILE BUTTER

In a mixing bowl, combine all ingredients, and whisk until thoroughly incorporated.

AT SERVICE

In a small pot, melt the remaining smoked paprika–chile butter over low heat. On each plate, spoon a large mound of jalapeño-mashed potatoes just left of center. Using the back of the spoon, press into the potatoes and pull to the right about 4 inches. Spoon corn sauté into the trough of the potatoes and a little beyond. Shingle the slices of 1 steak over the corn sauté. Drizzle melted butter over the steaks and in a circle around the dish. Place the tomatoes over the top of the steaks. Garnish wuth Cotija cheese.

Chef's Tip: *Flavorful varieties of cherry tomatoes include Sweet 100, Supersweet 100, SunSugar, and Sugar Snack.*

Ginger-Lavender Ice Cream Profiteroles
with Blueberry Compote

SERVES 8-10

This is a very simple dessert that is familiar in its components, but a little different in the flavor combinations. Lavender, when used mildly, adds a beautiful floral note that blends perfectly with blueberries. To give it a comfort element, I serve the blueberries warm to contrast with the cool ice cream and spice of the ginger. The crackled shortbread crust on top of the profiteroles adds more texture and a buttery vanilla finish.

Suggested Wine Pairing: VT Gewurztraminer

For the ginger lavender ice cream

½ cup rough chopped ginger
1½ cups water
1½ cups milk
1½ cups heavy cream
½ cup plus 3 tablespoons granulated sugar
Pinch kosher salt
2 teaspoons dried lavender (culinary grade)
8 egg yolks

For the shortbread topping

3 sticks plus 2 tablespoons butter (room temperature)
¾ cup vanilla sugar, plus extra for rolling
½ teaspoon kosher salt
1 egg
1 teaspoon vanilla paste
3 cups bread flour

For the pâte à choux

1 cup water
1 tablespoon granulated sugar
3 ounces butter
¼ teaspoon kosher salt
1 cup all-purpose flour
4 eggs

For the warm blueberry compote

2 pints blueberries, washed
¼ cup granulated sugar
1 teaspoon grated lemon zest
2 teaspoons lemon juice

For the garnish

Powdered sugar, for dusting
Tiny orange segments
Edible flowers

FOR THE GINGER LAVENDER ICE CREAM

Prepare an ice bath by nesting a medium bowl in a larger bowl that's partially filled with ice and water.

In a small saucepot, combine ginger and water and bring to a boil. Continue to boil for 1 minute, then strain, discarding the water.

In a medium saucepot, combine milk, cream, sugar, and salt. Bring just to a boiling point, then reduce heat to scald. Remove from heat, and add ginger/water mixture, then let sit covered for 1 hour.

Add lavender and scald again.

In a large mixing bowl, whisk egg yolks. Gradually add some of the ginger lavender-infused cream mixture while continually whisking.

Scrape the yolk mixture into a pan with remaining cream mixture and cook on low heat while stirring with a wooden spoon until mixture slightly thickens and coats the back of the spoon.

Quickly remove from heat and strain ice cream base through a fine-mesh sieve into chilled ice bath bowl. Stir gently until fully chilled.

Transfer to refrigerator to rest overnight. Freeze the ice cream base in ice-cream maker according to the labeled instructions.

FOR THE SHORTBREAD TOPPING

In an electric mixer with paddle attachment in place, cream the butter, sugar, and salt on medium speed for 5 minutes, scraping down sides twice.

Add the egg and vanilla, and blend for 10 seconds. Scrape sides down again and blend another 10 seconds until well incorporated.

Add 1 cup of the flour and blend on low speed until just incorporated. Scrape sides down and add second cup of flour, continuing steps until all the flour is incorporated and the dough is smooth. Flatten between plastic wrap and chill for at least 1 hour.

Work dough by compressing a few times on work surface to soften. Divide the dough in half and place half on sugar-dusted flat work surface. Sprinkle sugar on top and roll to 1/16-inch thick. Cut out with a 2-inch circle cutter and place dough circles in freezer, covered. You will need at least 30 and should have extra dough remaining.

FOR THE PÂTE À CHOUX

Preheat oven to 400°F.

Combine water, sugar, butter, and salt in a saucepot, and bring to a boil.

Add flour all at once to mixture and cook for 1 minute, stirring with a wooden spoon continuously over medium heat.

Remove from heat and cool for 30 seconds in electric mixer with paddle attachment on medium speed.

Add eggs, 1 at a time, on medium-low speed, scraping down sides of bowl after each addition. When all the eggs are incorporated, scrape one more time and blend on medium speed for 1 minute.

On a baking sheet lined with parchment paper, drop batter with a teaspoon into a 2-inch diameter and 1-inch-high round ball 2 inches apart from each other.

Top with frozen shortbread and gently press down into pâte à choux.

Bake for 15 minutes, then turn oven down to 325°F. Vent oven door 1/4 inch and continue to bake another 10 minutes. Remove and cool to room temperature. Store in airtight container for 1 day.

FOR THE WARM BLUEBERRY COMPOTE

Toss all ingredients together in a sauté pan and cook over medium heat, stirring a few times until juices start to release from fruit and mixture is at a boil, about 5 minutes. Remove and cool to room temperature in pan.

AT SERVICE

Cut profiteroles (3 per serving) in half and place a small scoop of ginger lavender ice cream inside each one, dusting with powdered sugar if desired. Warm blueberry compote in a sauté pan and spoon 2 tablespoons in bottom of each room temperature bowl or plate. Place prepared profiteroles on top and garnish with orange segments and flowers if desired.

Chef's Tip: *Be creative with fruit compote flavors and ice creams since the flavor of the profiteroles themselves is neutral.*

Chef's Tip: *Since you will have extra shortbread dough, roll it out ¼-inch thick in sugar, and cut out and bake at 350°F for 15 minutes for more cookies.*

Black Forest Cake

Cherry Cocoa Nib Ice Cream, Balsamic Chocolate Sauce

SERVES 9

Black Forest cake is one of those pastries that I associate with my early days in culinary school. It wasn't until many years later that I found a new respect for the classic chocolate, cherry, and brandy combination that I thought was left behind at school. This version doesn't stray too far from the original in terms of flavors and textures, but more in presentation. Whipped cream is replaced with a soft chocolate mousse, and ice cream flavored with Kirschwasser, cherries, and cocoa nibs is added.

Suggested Wine Pairing: Vintage Port

For the chocolate cake

1 egg
1 egg yolk
½ cup buttermilk
½ teaspoon vanilla extract
½ cup brewed coffee, warm
2 tablespoons melted butter
1 cup granulated sugar
⅔ cup plus 2 tablespoons all-purpose flour
⅓ cup cocoa powder
1 teaspoon baking soda
½ teaspoon baking powder
⅛ teaspoon kosher salt

For the cherries

2 tablespoons granulated sugar
1 tablespoon port wine
1 teaspoon balsamic vinegar
2 cups fresh bing cherries, pitted

For the chocolate mousse

1 cup heavy cream, whipped very soft
¾ cup chopped dark chocolate (64 percent cocoa)
1 egg
3 egg yolks
¼ cup granulated sugar
2 tablespoons water

For the balsamic chocolate sauce

2 tablespoons butter
1 tablespoon light corn syrup
1 tablespoon reserved cherry liquid
2 tablespoons water
2 tablespoons granulated sugar
2 tablespoons cocoa powder
Pinch kosher salt
2 tablespoons bittersweet chocolate (70 percent)
1½ teaspoons balsamic vinegar

For the cocoa nib Florentine

2 tablespoons plus 1 teaspoon butter
¼ cup granulated sugar
1 tablespoon honey
1 tablespoon heavy cream
Kosher salt, to taste
2 teaspoons bread flour
2 tablespoons cocoa nibs

For the cherry cocoa nib ice cream

2 tablespoons cocoa nibs
½ cup prepared cherries, chopped
1½ cups heavy cream
1¼ cup milk
½ cup plus 3 tablespoons granulated sugar
1 vanilla bean, scraped
Pinch kosher salt
8 egg yolks
3 tablespoons kirschwasser

At service

2 tablespoons granulated sugar

2 tablespoons water

2 tablespoons kirschwasser

4 tablespoons chocolate (70 percent bittersweet chocolate)

FOR THE CHOCOLATE CAKE

Preheat oven to 350°F.

Line two 9 × 9-inch pans with parchment paper lightly greased with nonstick cooking spray.

In a mixing bowl, whisk egg, egg yolk, buttermilk, and vanilla until smooth. Add the coffee in a stream followed by the melted butter.

In a large mixing bowl, sift the sugar, flour, cocoa powder, baking soda, baking powder, and salt. Mix well and add all of the liquid mixture at once, stirring until just combined.

Divide the batter into the prepared pans and spread even and level.

Bake until cakes spring back when gently touched with fingertips in the center, 15–20 minutes.

Cool to room temperature.

FOR THE CHERRIES

Combine sugar, wine, and vinegar in a medium sauté pan, and bring to a boil.

Add cherries all at once and cook, tossing every 20 seconds to coat cherries, for 4 minutes until some of the juice has released from the cherries. Cool to room temperature and transfer to refrigerator.

FOR THE CHOCOLATE MOUSSE

In a large mixing bowl, whip cream until soft peaks form, then set aside.

Melt chocolate over a double boiler and keep slightly warm.

In a large mixing bowl, whip egg and egg yolks on high speed to full volume, about 5 minutes.

Combine sugar and water in small saucepot. Cook until mixture reaches 240°F on a candy thermometer.

Turn egg mixture down to a medium-low speed, and add sugar in a slow steady stream down the side of the bowl. Turn mixer speed to high and continue to whip until mixture is room temperature. Turn mixer off. Add chocolate and gently fold together. Fold in cream gently.

FOR THE BALSAMIC CHOCOLATE SAUCE

Combine butter, corn syrup, cherry liquid, water, sugar, cocoa powder, and salt together in a small stainless steel saucepot over medium heat. When mixture comes to a boil, whisk continuously for 2 minutes while still at a boil.

Remove from heat and add chopped chocolate. Whisk until chocolate has melted and is smooth.

Whisk in balsamic vinegar and cool to room temperature.

FOR THE COCOA NIB FLORENTINE

Preheat oven to 350°F.

In a small stainless steel saucepan, combine butter, sugar, honey, cream, and salt. Bring to a boil and continue to cook until mixture reads 236°F on a candy thermometer.

Using a wooden spoon, mix in flour, cocoa nibs, and salt.

Spoon Florentine batter in 1-teaspoon amounts, 4 inches away from each other on a flat baking sheet lined with either a nonstick baking mat or aluminum foil coated with nonstick cooking spray.

Bake until golden brown, 10–12 minutes. Let cool before removing from pan.

Store in airtight container for up to 2 days.

FOR THE CHERRY COCOA NIB ICE CREAM

Preheat oven to 325°F.

Prepare an ice bath by nesting a medium bowl in a larger bowl that's partially filled with ice and water.

Place cocoa nibs on a small baking sheet, and toast in oven until fragrant, about 5 minutes. Cool to room temperature.

In a small mixing bowl, combine the cocoa nibs with cherries and place in freezer.

In a medium saucepot, combine cream, milk, sugar, vanilla bean (seeds and pod), and salt in a medium saucepan. Bring just to a boiling point, then reduce heat to scald. Cover and let steep 30 minutes. Bring back to a scald.

In a large mixing bowl, whisk egg yolks and gradually add some of the cream mixture while continually whisking. Scrape the yolk mixture into pan with remaining cream mixture and cook on low heat, stirring with a wooden spoon until mixture slightly thickens and coats the back of the spoon.

Quickly remove from heat and strain ice cream base through a fine-mesh sieve into a chilled ice bath bowl. Stir gently until fully chilled.

When chilled stir in kirschwasser, cover with plastic wrap, and transfer to refrigerator.

Freeze the ice cream base in an ice-cream maker according to labeled instructions. Fold in cherry cocoa nib mixture.

AT SERVICE

In a small saucepot, bring sugar and water to a boil. Let cool to room temperature, and add kirschwasser.

Invert cake pans and remove paper from cakes. Brush kirschwasser syrup evenly on both cakes.

Melt chocolate over a double boiler and spread evenly on the tops of both cakes. Place in refrigerator to set for 5 minutes.

Spread ¾ of the chocolate mousse on top of one cake and cover with cherries. Spread remaining mousse on top and invert second cake on top.

Place in freezer for 2 hours to set.

Remove parchment paper and cut into 3 × 3-inch squares. Serve with balsamic chocolate sauce, chocolate cherry ice cream, and cocoa nib Florentine.

Chef's Tip: *At Market we spray a mixture of melted chocolate and cocoa butter with an airless spray gun to achieve the effect shown in the photo. You could also cover the cake in chocolate curls for a more traditional look, or leave it so you can see the layers.*

Chilled Melon Soup

Frozen Yogurt, Summer Fruits, Blackberry Tuile

SERVES 8-10

Here is a very refreshing summer dessert that is light and, by default, gluten free. Since this dessert is driven solely by fresh summer fruits picked at the peak of their ripeness, there are myriad combinations to try. I like to serve this dessert on a warm summer afternoon as a follow-up to a light lunch in the shade. It's quick and easy to put together, leaving you time to enjoy your company.

Suggested Wine Pairing: LH Riesling

For the chilled melon soup

1 medium ripe honeydew or cantaloupe melon,
    about 5 cups diced
3 tablespoon granulated sugar
½ vanilla bean, scraped (seeds only)
3 tablespoons elderflower syrup
6–8 medium mint leaves
2 teaspoons melon flavored liqueur
Tiny pinch kosher salt

For the frozen yogurt

2 cups plus ¾ cup plain yogurt
½ cup granulated sugar
2 tablespoons corn syrup
1 tablespoon fresh lemon juice
Tiny pinch kosher salt

For the blackberry tuile

1 pint blackberries
1 tablespoon granulated sugar

For the garnish

3 cups of your favorite summer fruits
Handful of your favorite micro herbs

FOR THE CHILLED MELON SOUP

In a large mixing bowl, combine melon with sugar and chill in the refrigerator for 1 hour.

Transfer to a blender, combine with remaining ingredients, and puree until very smooth.

Strain through a fine-mesh sieve and let rest in refrigerator for 2 hours to allow air bubbles to settle. Skim any remaining foam from the top.

FOR THE FROZEN YOGURT

Combine all ingredients in a blender. Puree until smooth and sugar is dissolved. Freeze in ice-cream machine according to labeled instructions.

FOR THE BLACKBERRY TUILE

Preheat oven to 180°F. Combine the blackberries and sugar in a blender, and process on low speed being careful not to puree the seeds, then strain through a fine-mesh sieve.

Evenly and thinly spread the blackberry puree on a baking sheet lined with a nonstick baking mat and place in oven. After 2 hours, test to see if the tuile is done by peeling a small piece and letting it cool to room temp. When tuile is crisp, remove pan from oven and tear into small pieces (bend them while warm if desired).

Store in an airtight container until ready to use.

AT SERVICE

Pour ½ cup of soup into the center of each pre-chilled bowl. Garnish with summer fruits and top with scoop of frozen yogurt. Top with blackberry tuile and complementary micro herbs.

Chef's Tip: *Try using different heirloom melons that are in season during the summer months. Remember this dessert is only as good as the fruits it showcases.*

Crème Fraîche Panna Cotta

Concord Grape Sorbet, Brioche Croutons, Peanut Butter Powder

SERVES 6

I like to think of this as a grown-up version of a PB&J with some milk on the side. It has all the flavors of the classic, but the textures have been adapted to a more refined and refreshing plated dessert. It's a unique way to highlight fresh concord grapes when they are in season during summer, and is one of my favorite flavors to work into a sorbet. The brioche croutons replace the bread and lend a satisfying buttery crunch. Salted peanut butter is presented two ways, as a sauce and a powder that melts into its original form when it hits your tongue. The panna cotta is there like a cold glass of milk but has a slightly sweeter finish with the addition of crème fraîche and vanilla bean. Overall this is a fairly simple, fun dish that will satisfy the kid in you, or the kids in your life.

Suggested Wine Pairing: LH Zinfandel

For the crème fraîche panna cotta

Light, unflavored oil, for coating ramekins
1 cup heavy cream
¼ cup granulated sugar
½ vanilla bean, scraped
½ cup plus 2 tablespoons cold milk
1½ teaspoon powdered gelatin
¼ cup plus 1 tablespoon crème fraîche
Tiny pinch kosher salt

For the concord grape sorbet

⅓ cup granulated sugar
⅓ cup water
2 tablespoons Petit Syrah wine
3 cups concord grapes, cleaned and stemmed
2 teaspoons lemon juice
Tiny pinch kosher salt

For the brioche croutons

4 (¾-inch-thick) slices brioche
2 tablespoons butter, melted
1 tablespoon vanilla sugar
Tiny pinch kosher salt

For the peanut butter powder

½ cup creamy natural peanut butter
2 tablespoons powdered sugar
¼ teaspoon kosher salt

½ cup plus 2 tablespoons tapioca maltodextrin

For the peanut butter sauce

2 teaspoons granulated sugar
1 tablespoon water
2 tablespoons salted peanut butter
Pinch kosher salt

FOR THE CRÈME FRAÎCHE PANNA COTTA

Lightly grease six 4-ounce ramekins with oil. Wipe out any excess with a paper towel and chill in the refrigerator.

In a stainless steel saucepot, combine cream, sugar, and scraped vanilla bean (with pod) and bring just to a boiling point, then reduce heat to scald. Cover and let steep 10 minutes.

In a small mixing bowl, combine milk and gelatin. Stir to combine. Let bloom at least 5 minutes at room temperature. Gently stir into warm cream and vanilla mixture until gelatin is fully melted and combined.

Stir in crème fraîche and salt. Strain through a fine-mesh sieve and chill in refrigerator, stirring gently every 5 minutes until mixture thickens slightly.

Pour 3 ounces into each prepared ramekin and chill, covered, for at least 4 hours (or up to 3 days) to set.

FOR THE CONCORD GRAPE SORBET

In a small saucepot, combine sugar and water, and bring to a boil. Remove from heat and cool. Place all remaining ingredients in a mixer and pulse until grapes are broken up. Let mixture sit for 1 hour to overnight in refrigerator.

Return to a blender, and puree until almost smooth (trying not to break up seeds). Strain through a fine-mesh sieve and freeze in ice-cream machine according to labeled instructions.

FOR THE BRIOCHE CROUTONS

Heat oven to 350°F.

Remove the crust from brioche and cut into 1 × 1-inch cubes.

Combine in a bowl with butter, sugar, and salt, and lightly toss. Arrange on a baking sheet and toast in oven until evenly golden brown, tossing every 5 minutes, for 15 minutes total.

FOR THE PEANUT BUTTER POWDER

In a food processor, process all ingredients to a powder-like consistency. Store in an airtight container at room temperature.

FOR THE PEANUT BUTTER SAUCE

In a small saucepot, combine sugar and water and bring to a boil.

Remove from heat and whisk in peanut butter and salt. Cool to room temperature.

AT SERVICE

Unmold panna cotta by dipping the ramekins into hot water for 20 seconds. Hold on an angle and gently pull pudding away from side. Carefully invert onto plates to release. Spread a little peanut butter sauce next to the panna cotta with powder to follow. Scoop some of the sorbet on top of the powder and garnish with the croutons.

Chef's Tip: *Tapioca maltodextrin is a lightweight bulking agent derived from tapioca starch that has no perceptible flavor. When mixed with fat, it has the ability to absorb it, transforming the fat into a powderlike substance. It can be purchased easily from online sources.*

ESSENTIALS

Base Aioli

MAKES 2 CUPS

4 cloves garlic, peeled and finely minced
½ teaspoon salt
4 egg yolks (preferably pasteurized)
3 tablespoons lemon juice
2½ teaspoons lemon zest
½ teaspoon black pepper
⅛ teaspoon cayenne pepper
Salt, to taste
2 cups light olive oil

Add all ingredients except olive oil to a bowl or food processor, and whisk or process thoroughly. Add a slow stream of olive oil until thickened. If aioli gets too thick, add a little water.

Basil Agave Nectar

MAKES 2 CUPS

2 cups basil, blanched
¼ cup light agave nectar

Prepare an ice bath by nesting a medium bowl in a larger bowl that's partially filled with ice and water.

Submerge basil in boiling water for 3 minutes. Using a slotted spoon, remove basil and place in bowl of ice and water.

Remove basil to a cheesecloth and squeeze out excess moisture. Roughly chop.

In blender, combine basil with agave nectar and process until smooth. Chill in prepared ice bath.

Basil-Infused Vodka

MAKES 2 CUPS

2 cups high-quality vodka
1 cup loosely packed basil leaves, rinsed and dried

Combine all ingredients in a jar. Cover tightly and gently shake a few times. Store in a cool, dark place.

Shake the jar once a day for 1–4 days or until desired infusion level is reached (do not go longer than 4 days, as flavor will be too overpowering).

Strain through a fine-mesh sieve or coffee filter into a bottle.

Store covered in the refrigerator.

BBQ Spice Mix

MAKES ½ CUP

1 teaspoon coriander
1 teaspoon cumin
½ teaspoon cayenne
¼ teaspoon dry oregano
¼ teaspoon garlic powder
½ teaspoon fennel seed
¼ teaspoon onion power
1 teaspoon chile powder
½ teaspoon paprika
½ teaspoon smoked paprika
¼ teaspoon dry mustard
¼ teaspoon salt
½ teaspoon brown sugar
¼ teaspoon black pepper

Grind all ingredients in a coffee grinder until very fine.

Brown Chicken Stock

MAKES 1 GALLON

5 pounds chicken bones and trimmings
Light olive oil, for coating chicken
16 cups water
3 Spanish onions, roughly chopped
4 carrots, roughly chopped
6 celery sticks, chopped
1 teaspoon peppercorns
2 bay leaves
½ bunch parsley stems
2 sprigs thyme

Preheat oven to 375°F.

Rinse bones well under cold running water. Pat dry and coat with oil.

Place bones on a baking sheet and bake for 1 hour, turning occasionally.

Once evenly browned and caramelized, place bones in a large stockpot. Add water and bring to a boil, then reduce heat to low and simmer bones for 4 hours.

Add onions, carrots, and celery to the same baking dish, and roast in oven for 1 hour.

Add roasted vegetables to the stockpot with chicken bones. Add peppercorns, bay leaves, parsley, and thyme. Strain the entire contents of the pot through a colander and discard the solids.

Place the stock in the refrigerator. When completely chilled, remove the surface fat.

Use stock immediately or pack in containers and freeze for up to 3 months.

Chef's Tip: *If available, add 1 pound of chicken feet. This adds extra gelatin to the stock, giving it good body.*

Brown Veal Stock

MAKES 1 GALLON

10 pounds veal bones
Light olive oil, for coating veal bones
8 quarts water
1 cup chopped onions
½ cup chopped carrots
½ cup chopped celery
¼ cup tomato paste
1 herb sachet (page 285)
1 teaspoon salt

Preheat oven to 375°F.

Rinse bones well under cold running water. Pat dry and coat with oil.

Place bones on a large baking sheet and cook for 1 hour, turning occasionally.

Once evenly browned and caramelized, place bones in a large stockpot. Add water and bring to a boil, then reduce heat to low and simmer bones for 4 hours.

Add onions, carrots, and celery to the same baking dish, and roast vegetables for ½ hour.

Remove vegetables from the oven and add tomato paste. Place vegetables back in oven and roast until caramelized, about 30 more minutes.

For the final 2 hours, add roasted vegetables to the stockpot with veal bones. Add herb sachet and salt.

Strain the entire contents of the pot through a colander and discard the solids.

Place the stock in the refrigerator. When completely chilled, remove the surface fat.

Use stock immediately or pack in containers and freeze for up to 3 months.

Chef's Tip: *For the veal stock, add 2 pigs feet. This adds extra gelatin to the stock, giving it good body.*

Candied Kumquats

12 kumquats
1 cup granulated sugar
1 cup water

Cut kumquats in quarters and remove any seeds. In a small saucepot, combine sugar and water, and bring to a rolling boil.

Turn heat down to a low boil and add kumquats. When it returns to a low boil, continue to cook for 3 minutes.

Remove from heat and let kumquats cool (in syrup) to room temperature, then chill in refrigerator.

Kumquat Syrup

Syrup from Candied Kumquats recipe (refer to recipe)

Chicken Stock

MAKES 1 GALLON

5 pounds chicken bones and trimmings
16 cups water
3 Spanish onions, roughly chopped
4 carrots, roughly chopped
6 celery sticks, chopped
1 teaspoon peppercorns
2 bay leaves
½ bunch parsley stems
2 sprigs thyme

Place all ingredients in a large saucepot and bring to a boil. Reduce heat to medium low and simmer stock uncovered for 4 hours.

Strain the entire contents of the pot through a colander and discard the solids.

Place the stock in the refrigerator, and when completely chilled, remove the surface fat.

Use stock immediately or pack in containers and freeze for up to 3 months.

Chicken Velouté

MAKES 2 QUARTS

4 ounces butter
4 ounces flour
2½ quarts chicken stock (see recipe)
½ teaspoon salt
¼ teaspoon pepper

Melt the butter in a small saucepot over medium-low heat. Add flour, and stir until 2 shades lighter, about 2 minutes.

Add chicken stock and simmer on low heat for 30 minutes. Season with salt and pepper.

Strain through a fine-mesh sieve.

Cumin/Coriander Spice Blend

1 cup whole coriander
½ cup whole cumin
1 tablespoon whole fennel seed

Preheat oven to 350°F.

Place coriander, cumin, and fennel on a baking sheet and spread it out with your hands. Toast spices until two shades darker and very fragrant, approximately 10 minutes.

Remove spices from oven and allow to cool.

In small batches, place spices in a spice or coffee grinder and process until fine.

Store in an airtight container in your pantry for up to a month, although spices are always better when used fresh the same day.

Curried Spice Blend

2 tablespoons curry powder
2 teaspoons garlic powder
1 teaspoon paprika
½ teaspoon cayenne pepper
½ teaspoon salt

In a bowl, combine spices. Store unused portion in an airtight container.

Dashi Broth

MAKES 4½ CUPS

4½ cups water
⅓ ounce dashi kombu
1 ounce dried bonita flakes

Combine water and kombu in a saucepan over medium heat. Just before the water boils, take out the konbu, add the bonita flakes, and turn off the heat. Leave the stock until the bonita flakes sink to the bottom of the pan and then strain.

Demi-Glace

5 tablespoons light olive oil
8 ounces chopped onions
4 ounces chopped carrots
4 ounces chopped celery
2 ounces tomato paste
1 (750-mililiter) bottle red wine
1 gallon brown veal stock (page 282)
1 herb sachet (page 285)

Heat olive oil in a saucepot over high heat. Add onions, carrots, and celery, and cook until veggies turn slightly brown.

Add the tomato paste and cook until slightly caramelized, 4–5 minutes.

Add red wine and, over medium heat, reduce liquid by half its volume.

Add brown veal stock and herb sachet, and simmer over medium-low heat until liquid is reduced and slightly thickened, 1–2 hours.

Chef's Tip: *Demi-glace can be frozen and used for any meat-related sauce.*

Fines Herbes

1 packed cup fresh chopped parsley
½ cup fresh chopped chives
¼ cup fresh chopped tarragon
¼ cup fresh chopped chervil
2 tablespoons fresh chopped thyme

Combine all ingredients in a small mixing bowl.

Fish Stock

MAKES 1 GALLON

10 pounds fish bones
5 quarts water
½ cup chopped Spanish onions
½ cup chopped leeks
½ cup chopped celery
4 ounces sliced cremini mushrooms
Herb sachet (page 285)
1 teaspoon salt

Combine all ingredients in a stockpot over medium-low heat, and simmer for one hour, skimming off the fat from the top. Strain mixture through a fine-mesh sieve.

Herb Sachet

10 parsley stems
3 sprigs thyme
1 teaspoon peppercorn
1 bay leaf

Cut a double layer of cheesecloth into a 5 × 5-inch square.

Add all ingredients to the center of the cloth and tie the top tight with butcher twine to form a small package.

House Vinaigrette

4 cups light olive oil
1 cup red wine vinegar
2 tablespoons finely minced shallots
1 tablespoons Dijon mustard
1 teaspoon salt
½ teaspoon pepper
¼ cup water

Combine all ingredients in a mixing bowl, and whisk until incorporated.

Lemon Vinaigrette

1 cup lemon juice
1 cup light olive oil
½ small diced red onion
2 tablespoons finely chopped chives
2 tablespoons finely chopped parsley
Salt and pepper, to taste

In a mixing bowl, combine all ingredients, and whisk until incorporated. Refrigerate for up to 1 week.

Mayonnaise

MAKES 2 CUPS

2 pasteurized egg yolks
¼ cup white wine vinegar
1 tablespoon Dijon mustard
Salt, to taste
1½ cups light olive oil

In a mixing bowl, combine egg yolks, vinegar, mustard, and salt. Whisk until blended and bright yellow, about 30 seconds.

Gradually add the olive oil, 1 tablespoon at a time, whisking constantly until the mixture resembles mayonnaise.

Gradually add the remaining olive oil in a very slow thin stream, whisking constantly.

Mushroom Duxelle

4 cups cremini mushrooms, finely chopped
¼ teaspoon salt

In a sauté pan over medium-low heat, add mushrooms and salt. Stirring constantly, cook mushrooms until all the moisture is removed. Mushrooms should be very dry, loose, and not stuck together.

Mushroom Stock

MAKES 8 CUPS

2 tablespoons light olive oil
1 Spanish onion, peeled and thinly sliced
6 garlic cloves, peeled and finely chopped
2 leeks, finely chopped
4 cups cremini mushrooms (stems and trimmings)
1 teaspoon salt
½ teaspoon peppercorns
6 parsley stems
2 sprigs thyme
2 bay leaves
10 cups cold water

Heat olive oil in a saucepot over medium heat. Add onions, garlic, leeks, mushrooms, and salt. Cover and cook for 10–15 minutes.

Add remaining ingredients and cover with cold water. Bring to a boil, reduce heat to low, and simmer, uncovered, for 1 hour.

Strain stock through a fine-mesh sieve

Mustard Vinaigrette

1 cup lemon vinaigrette (page 285)
2 tablespoons grain mustard
2 tablespoons Dijon mustard

In a mixing bowl, combine lemon vinaigrette with mustards, and whisk until incorporated. Refrigerate for up to 1 week.

Orgeat Syrup

2 cups raw almonds, sliced or chopped
1½ cups granulated sugar
1¼ cup water
1 teaspoon orange flower water
1 ounce vodka

Preheat oven to 400°F.

Toast almonds for 4 minutes, tossing halfway through.

Cool almonds and finely chop in a food processor or blender.

In a saucepan, cook sugar and water until water begins to boil and sugar dissolves. Add almonds and simmer on low for a few minutes. When it starts to boil again, remove from heat. Cover and let it sit, off the heat, for about 6 hours.

Strain through 3 layers of cheesecloth, squeezing cheesecloth well to get out all liquid.

Add flower water and vodka. Stir, and this is ready to use right away.

Simple Syrup

MAKES 2 CUPS

2 cups water
2 cups granulated sugar

Combine sugar and water in a small saucepot. Stir over medium heat until sugar dissolves. Remove from heat and cool to room temperature for 1 hour. Cover and refrigerate.

Sweet Chile Glaze

MAKES 3 CUPS

1 tablespoon light olive oil
1 tablespoon chopped garlic
1 tablespoon chopped ginger
1 tablespoon scallions
½ cup orange juice, strained through a fine-mesh
    sieve
1 (25-ounce) bottle sweet chile sauce, strained
    through a fine-mesh sieve
2 tablespoons white soy sauce

In a small sauté pan, simmer garlic, ginger, and scallions until fragrant.

Add orange juice and reduce liquid to a sauce consistency.

Add sweet chile sauce, remove from heat, and cool to room temperature.

Stir in soy sauce.

Sweet and Sour Mix

3 cups water
3 cups sugar
2 cups fresh lemon juice
2 cups fresh lime juice

Make a simple syrup by combining sugar and water in a small saucepot. Stir over medium heat until sugar dissolves. Remove from heat and cool to room temperature for 1 hour. Cover and refrigerate.

In a large pitcher, combine simple syrup and lemon and lime juices and stir well.

Chill until cold. (Can be stored, covered, in the refrigerator for 1 week.)

Toasted Ground Coriander

1 teaspoon coriander seeds

Add coriander to a small frying pan and sauté over medium heat. Move frying pan back and forth over the heating element to promote even toasting. Toast the coriander seeds until they are one or two shades darker, about 2 minutes. When the seeds have cooled, grind them in a coffee grinder.

Toasted Ground Fennel

1 teaspoon whole fennel seeds

Add fennel seeds to a small frying pan and sauté over medium heat. Move frying pan back and forth over the heating element to promote even toasting. Toast the fennel seeds until they are one or two shades darker, about 2 minutes. When the seeds have cooled, grind them in a coffee grinder.

Tomato Water

4 pounds vine ripened golden heirloom tomatoes
    (approximately 10 medium tomatoes)
1½ tablespoons salt
2 teaspoons Old Bay Seasoning
2 teaspoons ground celery seed
1 tablespoon chile flakes
¼ cup lemon juice
Salt, to taste (optional)

Roughly chop tomatoes into large pieces, and add to a large mixing bowl.

Add salt, Old Bay Seasoning, celery seed, and chile flakes. Working in batches, add tomatoes to a food processor, pulsing until just broken down (do not overprocess) and place back into large mixing bowl.

Line a large bowl with an 18 × 18-inch piece of cheesecloth. Pour tomato mixture into the cheesecloth. Using butcher twine, tie the ends of the cheesecloth together to form a semi-loose sack. Tie the sack and suspend it over a bowl so the tomato juices (aka water) can flow into the catch bowl (do not squeeze the cheesecloth because this will cloud the tomato water). Allow sack to hang refrigerated overnight or a minimum of 8 hours (but not longer than 48 hours).

Discard cheesecloth and tomato pulp. Add lemon juice and adjust seasoning with salt.

Vegetable Stock

MAKES 1 GALLON

16 cups water
3 Spanish onions, roughly chopped
4 carrots, roughly chopped
6 celery sticks, chopped
1 teaspoon whole peppercorns
2 bay leaves
½ bunch parsley stems
2 sprigs thyme

Place all ingredients in a large saucepot. Bring to a boil, reduce heat to medium low, and simmer uncovered for 4 hours.

Strain the entire contents of the pot through a colander and discard the solids.

Place the stock in the refrigerator, and, when completely chilled, remove the surface fat.

Use stock immediately or pack in containers and freeze for up to 3 months.

Velvet Falernum

MAKES ONE BOTTLE

5 ounces rum
3 tablespoons minced ginger
Zest of 4 limes
15 whole cloves
1 star anise
1 cup simple syrup (page 286)
⅛ teaspoon almond extract
3½ tablespoons lime juice
1 tablespoon lemon juice

Combine rum, ginger, lime zest, cloves, and anise in a jar or bottle and let steep for 24 hours.

Strain contents through a cheesecloth or a coffee filter, making sure to squeeze and ring out all liquid.

Add simple syrup, almond extract, and lime and lemon juices. Shake until everything is thoroughly mixed and has turned a greenish-yellow color.

INDEX

Carl Schroeder, Executive Chef/Owner

Carl Schroeder grew up in La Jolla, CA and has San Diego in his soul. After completing his business degree he attended the esteemed Culinary Institute of America in Hyde Park, NY. Upon graduating in 1996 he worked at a number of notable restaurants across the USA. He learned in top kitchens from legendary chefs including Michael Mina at Aqua (San Francisco, CA), and Bradley Ogden at Lark Creek Inn (Larkspur, CA).

In 2002, Schroeder returned to his native San Diego when he rejoined Ogden as Executive Chef opening Arterra Restaurant in Del Mar, CA to rave reviews. Here he won numerous awards including: Best Hotel Chef Series—James Beard Foundation; California Chef of the Year 2004—California Travel Industry Association.

Schroeder ventured out on his own in 2006 to open Market Restaurant + Bar in Del Mar, CA as Chef/Owner. At Market he's three times been a James Beard Foundation Semi-Finalist for Best Chef Pacific (2009, 2011 & 2013). Also, he was honored to receive 29/30 points for food from Zagat Guide 2011/2012. Building on his successes at Market, in May 2010 Schroeder turned his new passion for casual dining into his second venture: Banker's Hill Bar & Restaurant in downtown San Diego. He later opened a second Banker's Hill location in the San Diego International Airport.

He has consulted for restaurants worldwide, and has been featured in *Bon Appétit, Gourmet, Art Culinaire*, the *New York Times*, the *Los Angeles Times*, the *San Diego Union Tribune*, *San Diego Magazine, Riviera*, and many other publications.

James Foran, Pastry Chef

A native of New York, James Foran has always been drawn to the culinary arts. Graduating with a degree in pastry arts from Johnson and Wales University, he dove headfirst into a demanding yet hard-to-pass-up opportunity with the great Jean-Georges Vongerichten at The Drake Hotel. Building essential French pastry techniques and a strong work ethic over his period with Vongerichten, Foran moved on to work in San Francisco advancing as executive pastry chef at such highly acclaimed establishments as Vertigo Restaurant, One Market, and The Mandarin Oriental Hotel.

While visiting San Diego, Foran came to realize how much of his work is truly inspired by having access to locally farmed produce, and soon after left the desert to be back in California. The move to SoCal formed the beginning of a lifelong culinary bond and mutual respect with Chef Carl Shroeder as pastry chef of Arterra Restaurant and now Market Restaurant since it opened in 2006. "Carl and I have always been a source of inspiration for each other. It's very important that our menus reflect seasonality, creativity, and a balance from the first course to the last." As well as creating and collaborating with Carl at Market, James is also a full-time pastry arts instructor/coordinator at Grossmont College in San Diego.

Maria Desiderata Montana, Author/Photographer

Maria Desiderata Montana is the publisher of the award-winning food blog San Diego Food Finds (sandiegofoodfinds.com). She is also a nationally published and award-winning author, food and wine journalist, and photographer. She learned to cook and appreciate European cuisine from her parents, who were born and raised in Calabria, Italy. Maria is the author of the *Food Lovers' Guide to San Diego* (Globe Pequot Press), *San Diego Chef's Table: Extraordinary Recipes From America's Finest City* (Lyons Press), *San Diego Italian Food: A Culinary History of Little Italy and Beyond*, and *The Inn at Rancho Santa Fe Cookbook*. She is extensively published in several newspapers and magazines, where she has written a variety of food and entertainment stories as well as her own monthly recipe column. Maria guest appears on local radio and TV to share her knowledge of food and cooking, and regularly assists celebrity and high profile chefs with cookbook projects. Maria lives in San Diego with her husband, John, and their two children, Lucia and Frank.